READING ARCHITECTURE WITH FREUD AND LACAN

Reading Architecture with Freud and Lacan: Shadowing the Public Realm methodically outlines key concepts in psychoanalytic discourse by reading them against key modern and post-modern architects. It begins with what is, arguably, the central concept for each discipline by putting the unconscious in a dialectic relation to space. Each subsequent chapter begins with a detail in architectural discourse, a kind of provocation that anchors each excursion into the thought of Freud and Lacan. The text is cyclical, episodic, and cloudlike rather than expository; the intention is not simply to explain the concept of the unconscious but, to different degrees, perform it in the text. The book offers powerful critiques of current planning practice, which has no tools to address our attachment to places. It concludes with powerful critiques of our incapacity to change the environmentally damaging ways we live our lives, which is an effect of our incapacity to recognise the presence of the death drive in our nature. The text is an extended thesis – spanning the chapters – that the field of the Other is the common grammar that organises subjects into civilisations, which has consequences for how we treat the public realm in architecture, politics, and the city. The field of the Other is a slightly different slice through the urban social world. It shadows – but does not correspond exactly to – more familiar categories like private/public, inside/outside, figure/ground, or piazza/boulevard.

Reading Architecture with Freud and Lacan will be an essential resource to anyone interested in how the environment we build is a reflection of our desire. Psychoanalysis is one of the great humanist discourses of the 20th century and this book will be a valuable reference to the humanist in architects, planners, and social scientists, whether they are students, professionals, or amateurs. It will appeal to historians of the 20th century, and to psychoanalysts and architects who are interested in how their respective discourses interdigitate with each other and with other discourses.

Lorens Holm teaches Architecture at the University of Dundee, where he runs a design research unit called *rooms+cities*. His published work focuses on reconciling Lacanian thought on subjectivity with contemporary architectural/urban practice. He recently organised the international conference *Architecture & Collective Life*.

'Lorens Holm's highly informative primer on the relation between architecture and psychoanalysis will be much welcomed. The two disciplines have recently entered a productive dialogue and in this respect *Reading Architecture with Freud and Lacan* in its rigour and cogency is a major contribution to both'.

Nadir Lahiji, *author of* Architecture in the
Age of Pornography: Reading Alain Badiou

'It is with a sense of urgency, but also a lightness of touch, that Holm draws on his intimate knowledge of Lacan's work to address architecture in this time of climate crisis. Aiming to "reboot" architecture's ethical potential, Holm takes us through some of the most challenging theoretical twists of psychoanalysis. Erudite and witty, "wreck[ing] havoc with linear arguments, clear categories, and objective forms of research", Holm dedicates his precise – and kind – intelligence to flagging our urgent need for Lacan's understanding of the unconscious as a space of inter-subjectivity. Holm argues that via Lacan we can change our culture – as one that values individuality above all else – "all fantasies of the ego" – and instead grasp architecture's capacity for articulating the relation between individual and collective. This is Holm's best book on architecture and Lacan yet, and makes for some gripping, yet vital reading'.

Jane Rendell, *author of* The Architecture of Psychoanalysis,
Professor of Critical Spatial Practice, The Bartlett School of Architecture, UCL

READING ARCHITECTURE WITH FREUD AND LACAN

Shadowing the public realm

Lorens Holm

Routledge
Taylor & Francis Group

LONDON AND NEW YORK

Cover image: Lorens Holm

First published 2023
by Routledge
4 Park Square, Milton Park, Abingdon, Oxon OX14 4RN

and by Routledge
605 Third Avenue, New York, NY 10158

Routledge is an imprint of the Taylor & Francis Group, an informa business

British Library Cataloguing-in-Publication Data
A catalogue record for this book is available from the British Library

Library of Congress Cataloging-in-Publication Data
Names: Holm, Lorens, author.
Title: Reading architecture with Freud and Lacan: shadowing the public realm / Lorens Holm.
Description: Abingdon, Oxon: Routledge, 2023. |
Includes bibliographical references and index. |
Identifiers: LCCN 2022005964 (print) |
LCCN 2022005965 (ebook) | ISBN 9780367077983 (hardback) |
ISBN 9780367077990 (paperback) | ISBN 9780429022845 (ebook)
Subjects: LCSH: Psychoanalysis and architecture.
Classification: LCC NA2543.P85 H65 2023 (print) |
LCC NA2543.P85 (ebook) | DDC 720.19--dc23/eng/20220715
LC record available at https://lccn.loc.gov/2022005964
LC ebook record available at https://lccn.loc.gov/2022005965

ISBN: 978-0-367-07798-3 (hbk)
ISBN: 978-0-367-07799-0 (pbk)
ISBN: 978-0-429-02284-5 (ebk)

DOI: 10.4324/9780429022845

Typeset in Bembo
by KnowledgeWorks Global Ltd.

Mark Cousins, Director of General Studies and Head of the Graduate Program in Histories and Theories at the Architectural Association School of Architecture, whose PhD students – I was one – have formed an expanding core of critical enquiry for years, in the area of psychoanalysis philosophy history and politics, in schools in London, in the UK and around the world. His thinking and his approach to problems remain the driver behind my own thought. This text is dedicated to his memory, with love, respect, and humility.

CONTENTS

Acknowledgements		*viii*
Preface on entitlement		*ix*

1 Introduction to psychoanalysis [the unconscious]   1

2 Reading Giedion reading history through Lacan
  [symbolic, imaginary, and real space]   19

3 Brunelleschi and the visual field [desire and space]   44

4 Rossi and the field of the Other [planning or the unconscious]   60

5 Frampton and Scott Brown/Venturi [the social institution
  of the city or the death drive]   81

6 To conclude with climate change [discourse and
  the ethics of psychoanalysis]   107

Postscript: Subjective theory and practice [rooms+cities]	*128*
Bibliography	*137*
Figure credits	*147*
Figure notes	*149*
Index	*155*

ACKNOWLEDGEMENTS

In a free-associational order …

My close colleagues in IPSA, the Institute for Psychoanalytic Studies in Architecture, including:

Francesco Proto, Tim Martin, John Shannon Hendrix, Andrew Payne, Angie Voela, Donald Kunze, Stamatis Zografos, Wouter van Acker, Berrin Terim, Nadir Lahiji, who generously read this manuscript, and Cameron McEwan my longstanding teaching and thinking partner in all things relating to architecture and the categories by which the intellect organises it, who generously read this manuscript.

The *Architecture's Unconscious* network at University of Newcastle, including Adam Sharr, Kati Blom, Andrew Ballantyne, and Emma Cheatle, whose thinking informed the inception of this project.

Jane Rendell always a supporter and contributor and whose *The Architecture of Psychoanalysis* has achieved something unique in contemporary English academe – to be so sensibly English and so speculative at one and the same time.

The community of scholars and researchers that formed around *Architecture and the Unconscious* (2016), including David Green and Lesley Caldwell, London analysts whose discussion at the launch of *Architecture and the Unconscious* – unbeknown to them – have informed this book.

My fourth-year Humanities students at the University of Dundee who have been on the receiving end of my interpretative approach to architecture in lectures and seminars.

The fifth-year architecture students in my rooms+cities design research unit who have taken up the challenge.

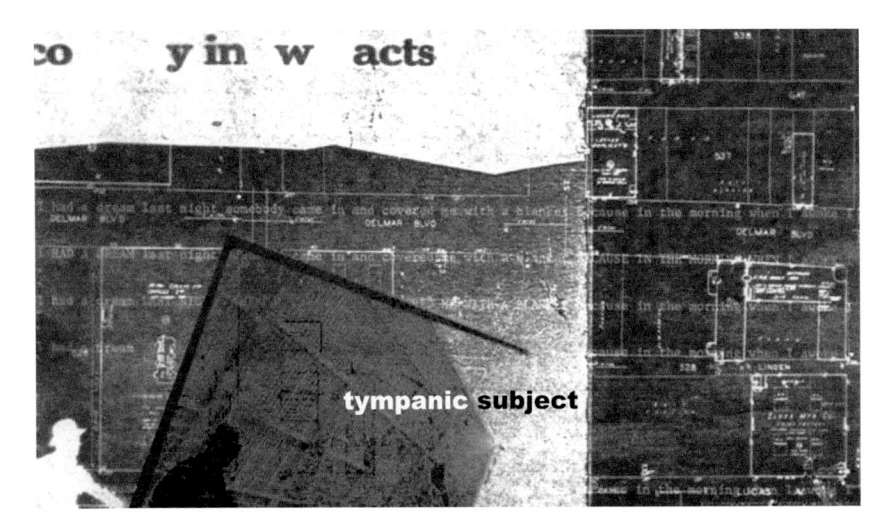

FIGURE 0.1 The possibility of a tympanic subject.

PREFACE ON ENTITLEMENT

In 2010, Routledge published my book *Brunelleschi Lacan Le Corbusier: Architecture Space and the Construction of Subjectivity*. In this book, I used psychoanalytic theory to interpret two key moments in the history of architecture: the formalisation of modern space by the invention of perspective and Le Corbusier's traumatic encounter with that *arché* object of modern architecture, the Parthenon. I say *modern* space, *modern* architecture. That book was nothing if not a reflection upon modernism. Psychoanalysis is the paradigm of modern discourse. Psychoanalysis kicked off when Sigmund Freud, the young neurologist, formalised the unconscious at the turn of the century and placed it in the centre of the new discourse of psychoanalysis. Jacques Lacan was arguably Freud's closest reader, whose systematic interpretations of Freud's text lifted it out of 19th-century biologism and put it in the context of post war structural theory. By the 1950s, Sigfried Giedion and other historians of modern architecture simply assume that their readers will understand their references to the unconscious and other psychoanalytic concepts without the need for elaboration.

The book thus identified what I argued to be the canonic space and object of modernism and put them in dialogue, with Lacan as their interlocutor. By arguing that Lacan uses perspective as the template for the key psychoanalytic structures of desire and identity, I cast the long shadow of modernism over the renaissance. Perspective was not modern when it was invented by Brunelleschi in the early decades of the 15th century, but it became modern by the time psychoanalysis invented the modern subject in the early part of the 20th. By relating Le Corbusier's obsession with the Parthenon to the death drive, I cast an equally long shadow over the future of modernism as it grapples with the global problems of today. This text will return to these theoretical points first discussed in *Brunelleschi Lacan Le Corbusier*, but it will put them in a broader psychoanalytic context and in the broader context of modern architecture. In the manner of the psychical material in the subject's past, this book will return to these points by re-working them.

How to begin an essay on Lacan for architects titled *Reading Architecture with Freud and Lacan* …. And why? Two disciplines in dialogue, but the title is marked by asymmetries. For one, it puts architecture as the discipline *vis-a-vis* Freud and Lacan and not architecture *vis-a-vis* psychoanalysis. Freud and Lacan are subjects, and Architecture is the terrain they inhabit. For another, I am writing it, and I am an architect. It is an outsider's view of psychoanalysis and an insider's view of architecture. From one we see forest; from the other trees. Positioning is already an architectural act. By putting Freud and Lacan alongside me in the field of architecture that we inhabit by a process of close reading, we read architecture from the position of psychoanalysis (Freud Lacan) from the position of architecture (*moi*). If a discourse is a flow of thought between two disciplines, a flow of thought that pirouettes and eddies around its objects, where we place ourselves will direct this flow differently. The text will treat psychoanalytic concepts fluidly and perhaps not always in close conformity to the canon. It will use them to reason through the architectural world, making sense of it, in a way that never loses sight of the position of the reader in his own reading.

If the title implies a series of asymmetries, we can make mischief with it. The implication of the title is that architects need to be propped by other thinkers to do their reading. Eisenman and Tschumi drew on Derrida. I am suggesting you draw on Freud and Lacan. As if architecture were not already a form of thought. As if thinkers were not indebted to the art of structure for the structure of their thought. As a paid-up member of the *architecture and psychoanalysis* study club, it is my opinion that not enough study has gone into the fact that thought is structured and hence always already informed by architecture. Kant said, 'Human reason is by nature architectonic'.[1] Imagine, instead of an architect writing a book on architecture for architects from the position of Freud and Lacan, which conjures the image of Lacan guest lecturing the RIBA on clinical diagnosis for clients and architects, *Reading Psychoanalysis with Mies van der Rohe and Le Corbusier*, written for analysts by an analyst. Imagine Mies lecturing the Tavistock Institute on the spatial implications of the analytic setting (a place of safety, patient on couch staring at ceiling, analyst staring out window, all Cartesian coordinates of the modernist grid); or on God in the details. Imagine the 'detail' between the ego and the id (the ego is a kind of principle of reflective cladding on the id *plan libre*). Or maybe we get Venturi to do the lecture on shopping therapy. I have always thought that Le Corbusier was rather like Freud, enamoured of the plasticities of the new age, the precision in their poetics. I have always thought that Lacan was rather like Mies. Lacan is the Mies of psychoanalysis the way Hitchcock is the Mies of film. Hardline formalists in their chosen fields. Modernists with a close attention to detail.

We build rooms and cities to construct the human world that we live well in. The room is the locus of our subjectivity, the places to which we attach our desire and organise our drives; the city is the intensely networked assemblage of rooms – the infrastructures and tectonics, the planning frameworks and politics, the social relations and lines of sight, that organise rooms. The city lost its walls a long time ago and is now becoming planetary. The subject is the inhabitant of this constructed world. The polymathic planner Patrick Geddes argued that the city was our greatest cultural artefact. The Marxist philosopher Henri Lefebvre declared that access to the city was a basic human right – the right to the city – because the city is both the site of capitalist production and the field in which we produce our subjectivity in resistance to capitalist production.

By drawing on Freud and Lacan, we are extending this thesis. The psychoanalytic subject is above all the subject of the unconscious. The principal condition of the psychoanalytic subject – at least in the thought of Freud and Lacan – is that it is unconscious. Lacan calls the human subject a speaking being, someone whose salient characteristics are that it directs its speech to others and that its speech is driven by its unconscious. You cannot objectify the unconscious, turn it into an object of conscious reflection, you can only subjectify it, which means, in different ways, perform it in the presence of others. The aim of psychoanalytic practice is to punctuate and mobilise the unconscious of the subject so that it can realise its desire. It has to use the devious means of analysis because it can only do it if the subject is distracted. We construct our subjectivity with others by architectural, digital, and other means. We do it by many means – principally by speech in language, but in the field of rooms and cities, we do it specifically by spatial means so that we can accommodate our bodies and maintain its capacity for life.

… *Shadowing the public realm* – remember the hand that inhabits the margins of Aldo Rossi's *veduta*. The public realm is shadowed by something that is not public but is common to all subjects. Attention to the unconscious leads to an intersubjective world that shadows the sectarian world of public life. This world is joined up and collective to all subjects because we all contribute to it. The unconscious is our commons. Signifiers do not point to themselves, they point to other signifiers. We trace our signifier chains along the most circuitous and bifurcating paths and they join up with the signifiers of others; signifiers in all their forms, including words, images, objects, gestures, and actions. One way we follow these chains – familiar to casual readers of psychoanalysis – is by the therapeutic practice of free association. The unconscious has a precise syntactic formulation. Freud described the dream as an other scene, and Lacan, following Freud, as a double inscription. The city signifiers that constitute unconscious life are always inscribed in at least two contexts. They are always also elsewhere than where we think them.

To put this *elsewhere* into the architectural discourse on the city is an act of resistance to power. If this essay aims to think subjectivity *architecturally* – how architecture's history of engagement with rooms and cities can be used to understand the human subject's sense of itself – it aims also to think architecture *subjectively*. There are fundamental theoretical problems of architecture, about the univocality of position, about what is inside and what is outside. Or what a place is: how we are attached as individuals or communities to places. In an age when place-making is synonymous with spectacle and money-making, the term *place* could use a reboot that lifts it out of the language of greed made respectable by market-driven, government policy bodies, planning authorities seeking to justify squanderous consent, public-private partnerships, and the like, and puts it back into relation to the subject who dwells. The text will conclude by looking at the theoretical basis for architecture's allegiance to collective life and architecture's ethical role with respect to climate change. The capacity for architecture to articulate the relation between individual and collective, the one to the many, shadows the public realm of politics. We invoke the psychoanalytic theory of the death drive to understand our complicity as individuals in environmental damage and Lacan's theory of discourse to sketch architecture's capacity for an ethical response to this complicity.

Architects do not always construct the city, but architecture is the discipline in which the city is most comprehensively theorised such that Aldo Rossi could write a comprehensive book on cities called *The Architecture of the City*. Theory informs practice by putting it in the context of the thought of others. The presence of others is critical. There is no solipsistic theory. When Lacan theorises the subject so that he can analyse his patients, he draws on the thought of Freud, Hegel, Descartes, the Sophists. When Rossi theorises the city so that he can build, he draws on the thought of Boullée, Loos, Levis-Strauss, and Halbwachs. They draw on the whole history of western intellectual culture as well as practices that are never written but evidenced in tradition, artifacts, and daily practice. We theorise the subject in the city so that we can better understand how we construct our subjectivities. Theory is thus already an ethical position, because it puts the practice of the individual in relation to the thought of many others, the one in relation to the many.

The focus of the text is Lacan, but Lacan was a close reader of Freud and Freud has crept back into the text. This text is dogmatic and episodic. It returns multiple times to key concepts like space, desire, the unconscious, the Other, and the death drive. Each time it reworks them anew. You will find a path, but it is not a linear path along which we move without looking back.

The book aims to be two things. It is a primer for architects who want to know about Lacan and it is a polemic about how psychoanalytic thinking can inflect architectural discourse on cities. Lacan said of the discourse of the university that there is always an agenda concealed beneath the seemingly neutral surface of knowledge. In this book, I hope I have gone some way towards making it explicit.

Note

1 Immanuel Kant, *Critique of Pure Reason (Kritik Der Reinen Vernunft, Riga, 1781)*, trans. Norman Kemp Smith (London: Macmillan, 1929), p. 429. Cf. also p. 653. 'By architectonic I understand the art of constructing systems. [S]ystematic unity is what first raises ordinary knowledge to the rank of science, …'.

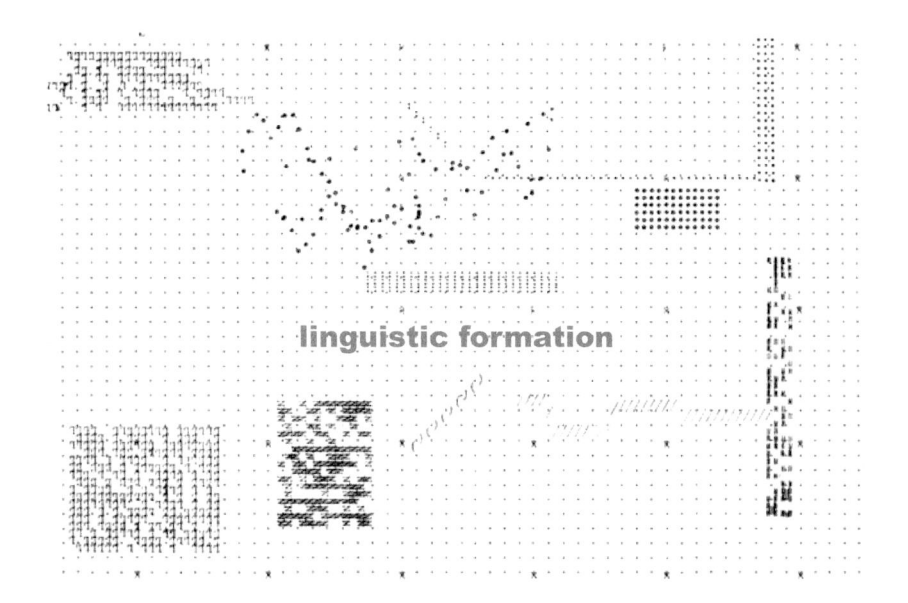

FIGURE 1.1 The possibility of a linguistic formation.

1

INTRODUCTION TO PSYCHOANALYSIS [THE UNCONSCIOUS]

> The meaning of a dream is an unconscious wish.
>
> (Freud, *The Interpretation of Dreams* (1900))

> The three books that one might call canonical with regard to the uncon-scious – *The Interpretation of Dreams* [1900], *The Psychopathology of Everyday Life* [1901], and *Jokes and their Relation to the Unconscious* [1905] – are simply a web of examples whose development is inscribed in the formulas of connexion and substitution; ….
>
> (Lacan, 'The Agency of the Letter in the Unconscious' (1957) in *Ecrits* p. 170)

DOI: 10.4324/9780429022845-1

Jacques Lacan (1901–1981) was a psychoanalyst and theorist of psychoanalysis, and it is the objective of *Reading Architecture with Freud and Lacan* to bring the two disciplines, psychoanalysis and architecture, together in the same text. The obvious place to begin is at their respective centres: the unconscious and space. The unconscious is the central concept of psychoanalysis, at least any psychoanalysis that proceeds from Freud. The preoccupation with the concept of the unconscious distinguishes psychoanalysis from related material sciences like psychology or neuroscience, and from psychological self-help regimes.

The greater part of this introduction will focus on the unconscious in the thought of Freud and Lacan. It will explain the central position of the unconscious in psychoanalysis and indicate how it might be instrumental in our thinking about architecture. A more detailed look at its implementation for architecture will await subsequent chapters.

This introduction will be followed by a chapter on space in modernism, which begins with Sigfried Giedion's three space conceptions. Each chapter will begin with an architect and an architectural idea and use it as a provocation to discuss Freud and Lacan. Because Giedion recognises that space is a conceptual or symbolic entity, not a material one, Giedion provides a way into one of the keystones in Lacan's thought, the three registers of subjective experience, of which the most central is the symbolic. Giedion will be followed by a chapter on unconscious desire in the visual field, which begins with Brunelleschi's demonstration of perspective as a form of authoritative viewing. Thereafter chapters on Rossi and the field of the Other, Scott Bown/Venturi, and the drives. The final chapter sketches the ethical position for architecture with respect to climate change.

Jacques Lacan was a major figure in French intellectual life for much of the 20th century. His teachings and writings explore the significance of Freud's discovery of the unconscious within the theory and practice of psychoanalysis, as well as in philosophy, art, literature, and the social sciences. The discipline of psychoanalysis, as a theory and practice, coincides with the modern movement in art and architecture. Lacan's achievement was to reboot Freudian psychoanalysis for 20th-century structuralism. Lacan remains a leading figure in post-modern thought and reference in the humanities and arts, including politics, law, philosophy, literature, and criticism.

The unconscious

Lacan was Freud's closest reader and he argued that nothing that Freud wrote makes sense without the concept of the unconscious. The unconscious may not exist, but if it doesn't, neither does psychoanalysis.[1] Freud referred to the unconscious as his Copernican discovery: Copernicus' astronomy recentred the solar system around the sun, displacing the earth from that privileged position.[2] Lacan refers to 'the self's radical eccentricity with respect to itself'. We think our world revolves around consciousness – our awareness of ourselves in the world – until Freud demonstrated that it revolves around something else that will always elude our scrutiny. Freud was nothing if not a close observer of Victorian life and mores. He demonstrated the central position of the unconscious through a series of closely argued papers incorporating patient observation with cultural history – principally literature, philosophy, and myth. The unconscious has a history in 19th-century romantic fiction and a history that goes back, under a number of names to antiquity.[3] In the history of western thought, there has always been an unknown core, a blank spot, which is instrumental in our lives. It was Freud who understood its importance and made it the central figure in the psychoanalytic understanding of the human subject.

Freud argued that dreams are the 'royal road to a knowledge of the unconscious activities of the mind', and that 'a dream is the fulfilment of an unconscious wish'.[4] The path from wish to action is labyrinthine. The dream expresses a wish, but it is not the sort of wish that can be enunciated so directly by the *I want* of consciousness. Instead, it is enunciated in the dream whose fragmentary images the subject remembers upon waking. These remembered fragments become the object of free association in the analytic setting. Lacan translates Freud's *wish* as *desire* and distinguishes *desire* from *want*. I may want the red shoes, not the blue ones, but what I desire is to find a new object once I have got the red ones. I go on desiring as if the object of desire were a placeholder for a series of objects. I go on desiring until I die, and then my children go on desiring for me.

In *The Interpretation of Dreams*, Freud distinguishes the latent from the manifest content of the dream. The manifest content includes fragments that the subject remembers upon waking and which may have an internal coherence, but never seem to have significance for the dreamer. This content is produced by unconscious processes Freud calls dream work, chief among them being condensation and displacement. Condensation is when many images congregate to create one semantically dense image, as in the linguistic trope of metaphor. Displacement is when one image replaces another, as in metonymy. The latent content or unconscious wish is arrived at by the process of free association, which seeks to reorganise these condensed and displaced images into a pattern of desire that makes sense to the subject. The architectural theorist John Hendrix develops the significance for architecture of the dream work in his book *Architecture and Psychoanalysis*.[5]

Lacan focuses on the unconscious as the key platform for the subject's interaction with others, but the unconscious is only ever sensed as a horizon, albeit an internal one. It is always with you, but you never arrive at it. We are driven by we know not what, to we know not where. In this respect psychoanalysis is unlike other disciplines. Freud's 'discovery' placed an absent object – and Lacan, a blank spot – at the centre of this new and emerging praxis, whereas most disciplines are built upon positive knowledge. Exploring the unconscious takes the form of retrospection and remembering and working through, but it is never 'found', it is always deferred or displaced; it is known only through its barely recognised effects. In analysis the patient is encouraged to explore their forgotten childhood when the primary features of their subjectivity were developed: the patterns, paths, and landmarks of their relationships with their significant others, principally parents, and their responses to encounters, situations, habits, clichés, and the like.

The unconscious is a symbolic entity, a presupposition necessary to explain the subject's speech and actions. It has the necessity and certainty of a natural object, but without relinquishing its status as a wager, a speculation, in the way that space is the central speculative entity of architecture. (*You will not find space in architecture, only the surfaces that shape it, but without it, there can be no question of human occupation.*) Without the unconscious, there is no Freudian psyche, no psyche as it is understood in modern thought of the subject. You will not find it anywhere, but only its symptoms. The unconscious is, to borrow a phrase from the political theorist Hannah Arendt, the human condition; and the forms of appearance that architecture opens up to the unconscious is the architectural condition of humans.[6]

It was Lacan, reading the structural linguist Roman Jakobson, who made the link between condensation and metaphor, and displacement and metonymy. In Lacan's reboot of Freud, the unconscious loses the 19th-century metaphors of body processes that it retained in Freud's text, and assimilates to linguistic phenomena. The unconscious is primarily an effect of speech. He refers to the unconscious as *the discourse of the Other* and *the field of the Other. The unconscious is structured like a language.*[7] The unconscious is an immersive phenomenon. We are in it because we are surrounded by speakers, the way we are in space because we are surrounded by objects. In our Rossi chapter, we shall link this linguistic field of the unconscious to the field of the city.

Lacan's close attention to speech is a theorisation of analytic practice. In an analysis, all that is admitted as evidence is what the subject says. It is not the remembered elements of the dream that constitutes the road to the unconscious, but the subject's account of them, how the subject recalls them and what s/he associates with them. The analyst listens to how the patient punctuates his/her account, the pauses, hesitations, and interjections, the confident passages, the flat bits, and the like. I borrow the word *punctuation* from the Lacanian analyst, Bruce Fink.[8] The unconscious remains inaccessible to the subject because all that are known of it are its signifiers, the significance of which the subject is largely unaware, whether these be the words by which s/he describes the dream images, or the slips of the tongue, mistakes, and the like that punctuate them. Lacan insists that the aim of analysis is not to explain the dream but to make sense of it. *Sense* is used in the sense of sensing, in the sense of understanding, and in the sense of direction or orientation. To be made aware of your desire is to know where it is taking you. A good analyst will never give you advice. That's for self-help guides, horoscopes, friends, or councillors. Analysis is not a DIY manual for the self, which having read, you can move on from. You never reach the end of free association, as you never stop desiring. Analysis puts into play the subject's signifiers so that the subject can reposition him/herself within them and they can be instrumentalised in new ways. It is like refinding your bearings in the city after having been lost. Likewise, this book will not explain architecture to you, but it may lead to new orientations within it. The unconscious may be unknown, but it is as externalised and inter-subjective as the language of which it is a function. Lacan insisted that the unconscious was not in you. It is more an ambient environment. To the extent that it can be said to be anywhere, it is between you and others. It is like architecture, at least an architecture that can be formalised as a system of signs so that it can communicate.[9]

The analytic setting

As a young neurologist in Vienna, Freud developed the radical new practice of psychoanalysis as a cure for psychopathologies based on a particular form of dialogue between patient and doctor, the so-called *talking cure*. Of central importance to this dialogue is the 'analytic setting'. It is a particular form of dialogue in which the patient speaks to a silent analyst. The patient associates freely, and the analyst meets this free association with what Freud called 'free-floating attention'. More likely than not, s/he is not paying attention to the patient's words and listening instead to the way they are enunciated by the patient's tone of voice, punctuations, hesitations, and slips. Analysis works best when the patient knows as little about the analyst as possible. The analyst remains a blank screen so that the patient's assumptions about their relationship can be examined as a transference from the patient's past and current relationships. Freud's papers on technique describe the analytic setting and explain its importance for psychoanalysis.[10]

The analytic setting has particular spatial and temporal characteristics. It is a space that the analysand constructs over time with the analyst. The setting represents a protected position, a position of safety, in the life of the subject, where the analysand's unconscious desire can emerge without scrutiny and ridicule (the ridicule of others and self-ridicule). It is where the psychoanalytic functions of projection and transference happen (both spatial concepts). The objects you ask for are not unconscious, but the desire that drives these object choices is. Unconscious desire is like the pattern and direction of your object choices. The analytic setting is thus the chamber of anticapitalism. Desire is always articulated with respect to an other, in this case, the analyst, and it needs a space in which it can happen. What I desire is the recognition of my desire by my significant others. Although the analyst is sitting in a chair looking out the window and the patient is lying on a couch staring at the ceiling (*Miesian coordinates*), their respective gazes are coordinated. They are both *not* looking at the patient's unconscious.

The concept of the analytic setting is one of the most remarkable inventions in psychoanalytic thought. The most important is the aforementioned spatial scenario defined by two subjects, the one staring at the ceiling talking, the other staring out the window *not*-listening. It is easy to see how this syntactic space could be diagrammed as two subject positions (two viewing positions) with different orientations and different framed screens. The problem of subjectivity is precisely the architecture of their correspondence. Lacan proposes one version of this space with his diagram of the vision field. The setting is also an affective space, which can be defined architecturally as one in a transformation series with other safe spaces like the nursery, the prison cell, the tent once the fly is zipped up, and the corner of the rabbit hutch. Its progenitor might have been the adoring gaze of the mother within which the infant basked, but this has long ago melted away. The analytic setting is also a financial and legal entity, an agreement between analyst and patient guaranteed by payment of the fee, and protected by client confidentiality. It is recognised in British courts. The analytic setting is also just a room, the analyst's consulting room with a picture on the wall that strikes the new analysand as intrusive. It is defined by four walls a door and a window, their respective material qualities, its position on a corridor, in a building, on a boulevard, in a city, in a network of highways and national borders, international treaties, trade deals, and extradition rights. It is probably first understood within a typology of enclosure and connection.[11]

Each analytic setting is a condensation (Freud) of these four rooms. The relations of analyst and patient impinge upon this space, as do their respective relations to significant others, including their neighbours, the policeman, the local butcher, the teacher. This space can be shattered by the loss of trust between analyst and analysand. The analysis reaches its end when the analysand is able to leave the consulting room and carry this safe place with him/her in his/her encounters with other others. In each of these rooms, we see a different iteration of inside and outside, and a different correspondence between room and subject.

Any encounter with an other brings with it the possibility of the analytic setting. You probably glimpse it when you come away from a conversation feeling that you taught yourself something about yourself, even if you don't know precisely what. Even that site of grotesque spectacle, the Big Brother house, has the potential to be an analytic setting, except that the imaginary order keeps shattering it. In the analytic setting, vision is met by a blank screen (the ceiling, the window); it is blank to allow for the emergence of something that neither patient nor analyst knew before. In Big Brother, the inhabitants are always trying to learn something about themselves. But instead of knowledge, they are misled by their self-image, to simply restate incessantly what they already know about themselves because it has already been fully visualised.[12]

Freud's texts

Sigmund Freud (1856–1939) trained as a doctor and neurologist; he regarded psychoanalysis as a science and its practice as a cure for a certain form of unhappiness. His first significant psychoanalytic text is *The Interpretation of Dreams*, published in 1905, although Derrida, in his deconstruction of Freud's thought, focuses on the earlier *Project for a Scientific Psychology*, an unfinished and unpublished text; the *Project*, or *Entwurf* (draft) is a transitional text and Freud is caught between the science of neurology and language of interpretation. He struggles to develop a neurological model comprised of neurological pathways for what will later be understood by Lacan as the discursive lines of linguistic phenomena. In *The Interpretation* ..., he first proposes the existence of the unconscious. 'A dream is the fulfillment of an unconscious wish' cements the relation between the unconscious and desire. Freud was a prodigious writer. *The Standard Edition of the Complete Psychological Works of Sigmund Freud* runs to 24 volumes.[13] In addition to 8 case histories, it includes 22 books and 16 papers in a publishing career that extended from 1886 to the year of his death in 1939. They were translated from German under the general editorship of the British analyst James Strachey in collaboration with Freud's daughter Anna Freud, assisted by Angela Richards, Alix Strachey, and Alan Tyson. The Hogarth Press was founded by Leonard and Virginia Woolf of the Bloomsbury group. There have been many paperback reprints by Penguin and Norton.[14] The most important dictionary for Freudian concepts is the Jean Laplanche and Jean-Bertrand Pontalis *The Language of Psycho-Analysis* (1973). This work references Freud's work and the work of his contemporaries and students, including references to Lacanian concepts and interpretations.

Lacan's texts

Jacques Lacan (1901–81) regarded himself as a student of Freud (*you are Lacanians, I am a Freudian*).[15] Lacan's text is a paradigm of close reading of texts. You will find that most of our explications of Lacan will refer back to Freud. He explores Freud the way he might explore a dream. He regarded psychoanalysis as *the science of the letter* or the science of speech. He drew upon the structural anthropology of Claude Levi-Strauss and the semiology of Ferdinand de Saussure. He relieved psychoanalysis of a shadow ontology of biological substances and containers, replacing them with linguistic processes. Instead of the flow of libido, a kind of liquid love that is either a substance like the ether that is not found by science or else simply a hydraulic metaphor, Lacan substitutes the real flow of speech. My love does not pour from me to you on my kisses (*that's metaphor*), but my signifiers do, be they kisses, or declarations of *death do us part*.

Lacan was a key figure in French post-war intellectual discourse, which clustered around the intersection of Hegel, Marx, phenomenology, and structuralism, and took the form of public lectures, university seminars, and publications. This discourse included the post-war thinkers who continue to dominate debates today in the arts and social sciences, including structural anthropologist Claude Lévi-Strauss, the linguist Roman Jakobson, the sociologist Michel Foucault, the Hegelian Alexandre Kojève, the Marxist Louis Althusser, the phenomenologist Maurice Merleau-Ponty who was a close friend, the librarian, surrealist, and pornographer Georges Bataille, Roger Caillois and the College of Sociology,[16] and André Breton, Salvador Dali, and the surrealists. Reading Lacan is an education in the liberal arts and sciences, and it behooves his readers to trace his copious references to Classical and Enlightenment thinkers. Lacan's text references Aristotle, Plato and Socrates, Saint Augustine, Descartes, Kant, and Hegel. He references Renaissance and Surrealist paintings. Lacan and Lacanian studies has a large online presence: there is an online dictionary of Lacanian psychoanalysis and web journals. There are also excellent lectures online.[17] Key followers include the philosophers Slavoj Žižek and Alain Badiou, many of whose texts situate Lacan within popular culture, contemporary politics, and Marxism[18]

Lacan's writings comprise 35 papers, collected and published as *Écrits* (1966) and 27 book-length *Seminars*, running from 1953 to 1980, most of which are close readings of key Freudian concepts in the light of his own practice. A selection of nine papers was first published in English as *Écrits: a selection* (1977) translated by Alan Sheridan. The full volume was published as *Écrits: the first complete edition in English* (2006), translated by Bruce Fink. Probably the most referenced paper in *Ecrits* is the 'The Mirror Stage as formative of the function of the *I* as revealed in psychoanalytic experience' (1937/1949). It has been influential on the Western understanding of visual culture and identity. The *Seminars* are the edited transcripts of Lacan's fortnightly seminars, held throughout the academic year, over a 27-year teaching career beginning with *The Seminar Book 1: Freud's Papers on Technique 1953–54* (1988) ending in *The Seminar Book XXVII: Dissolution* (*Ornicar?* 1980). Each year comprises extended investigations of a single theme. At least half have been published as books or in the journal *Ornicar?*. Seven have been translated into English and published by Norton. A number of others have been translated from the unedited typescripts by Cormac Gallagher and published privately.[19]

Lacan insisted that we are fundamentally speaking beings, *parle êtres*. Although the *Seminars* were public lectures, they were delivered from notes, in a conversational style marked by extemporaneous digressions and sliced through by asides, jokes, double entendre, neologisms, obscure references, and off-the-cuff responses to the audience. I am not alone in finding that reading the *Seminars* is helped if you punctuate them with the timing and cadence of a speaker. The *Seminars* were compiled from Lacan's notes, the notes of his audience, and some tape recordings and edited by Jacques-Alain Miller, Lacan's son-in-law and executor. The only one on which he collaborated with Miller was the eleventh seminar from academic year 1963–64, which is the most widely read in English, probably because it is the most expository. *The Four Fundamental Concepts of Psychoanalysis* (1978) will be – along with several of the *Écrits* – our key texts. The best English reference is Dylan Evans, *An Introductory Dictionary of Lacanian Psychoanalysis* (1996), which is an index to most of Lacan's texts, introducing most Lacanian concepts in clear and concise ways.

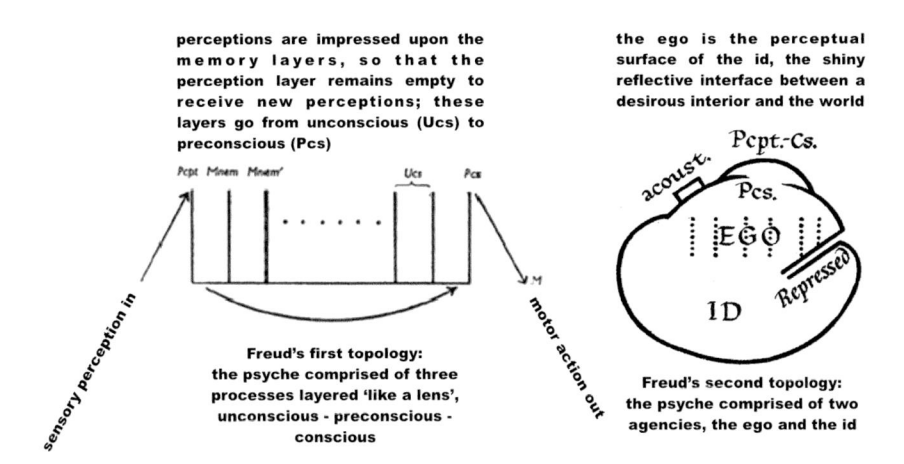

perceptions are impressed upon the memory layers, so that the perception layer remains empty to receive new perceptions; these layers go from unconscious (Ucs) to preconscious (Pcs)

Freud's first topology: the psyche comprised of three processes layered 'like a lens', unconscious - preconscious - conscious

the ego is the perceptual surface of the id, the shiny reflective interface between a desirous interior and the world

Freud's second topology: the psyche comprised of two agencies, the ego and the id

FIGURE 1.2 Two drawings of the self: Freud's first and second topographies.[20]

From the topographies of the psyche to the subject of the unconscious

In psychoanalysis, the subject has an articulated form. For Lacan, the subject has the form ego–unconscious. He derives this formula by crossing Freud's two topographies. Freud had developed two different ways of thinking the organisation of the psyche. According to the *first topography*, proposed in 1915, the psyche is a lamination of conscious, preconscious, and unconscious processes. In *The Interpretation of Dreams,* he published a diagram that organises the psychical apparatus as a series of layers extending from sense perception to motor response (both conscious), through a series of memory layers that include unconscious and preconscious layers.[21] In 1923, he proposed a *second topography*, according to which the psyche is comprised of three agencies, the Ego, the Id, and the Superego. In 'The Ego and the Id' (1923), he publishes an organ diagram in which a blob-like id is encased in the reflective outer surface of the ego. The id is the agency of unconscious desire, the ego is the conscious agency that engages with the world and mediates between the id and reality, an engagement that Lacan will liken to reflection.[22]

Lacan's formula replaces consciousness with ego or *moi* and puts it in relation to the unconscious. He puts an agency in relation to a process. In Lacan's topography, the psyche is comprised of an ego in an unconscious field, as opposed to two processes or two agencies in dialogue. Like a fish swimming in water or a human body in space, except that it is the human psyche, appearing to itself as an ego figure within the field of its signifiers that it never fully understands. If there is a model running in the background, it is the Cartesian *Cogito*, which gazes out at the external world of light and geometry from a single point of consciousness. We, too, shall find this geometric precision beguiling. Ego and unconscious are absolutely different, and we shall see in the Giedion chapter that the ego is a function of what Lacan calls the imaginary order and the unconscious is a function of the symbolic. He distinguishes subject from ego: the *I* is the signifier of the ego and the unconscious, and not simply of the ego. In 'The mirror stage', he explains the formation of the ego as the precipitate that emerges from the infant's encounter with a mirror. The ego is effectively the subject's self-image and it is the agency of self-deception or *meconnaissance*, or misrecognition. In the film *Taxi Driver* (1976), Robert De Niro stands in front of a mirror pretending to be a tough guy hero when everyone else sees a scrawny loser. The ego is the image I have of the self I think I am. It is not the image that others have of me.[23]

Lacan's subject, ego-unconscious, maps neatly onto a number of binaries like façade-plan, cover-book, advertising image-desire, surface of appearance-depth of thought, but this is already the ego's view of itself, for the way I communicate with others is largely unconscious. It goes on all the time. It is a continuum. It is frictionless. The ego erects the walls and polices the border crossings that tend to isolate us into discrete individuals. My ego focuses on the me here now, separate from you there then, and refuses to acknowledge that my identity and desire are distributed across the entire field of others with whom I am in concourse.[24]

Lacan introduces the term *subject* into psychoanalytic discourse from its use in the social sciences, philosophy, and the law; it is not present in Freud's text. A subject is not the same as a person or a self. A subject is a position in a signifying system or symbolic matrix; a person has an imaginary inner essence. A subject is a position in the symbolic matrix the way subject and object are positions in a grammar or the eye point is a position in projective geometry. The concept of subject position is important in this book. For Foucault, the subject occupies a position in the matrix of knowledge that defines an episteme. In the film *The Cook the Thief His Wife and Her Lover* (1989), each person is defined by a position in a matrix comprising cooks, thieves, wives, lovers, and their relationships. The subject of the king is someone bound by the kingly rules of genuflexion and allegiance, the promise of knighthoods, 'your majesty's, and the like. A subject of psychoanalysis, a subject of the unconscious, a subject of speech, a subject of the king. The architect Mario Gandelsonas argued that we can talk about a subject of architecture only when architecture is organised as a syntactic system, such as it was Eisenman's project to develop with his House projects in the glory days of *Oppositions* and the IAUS.[25] In order to have a spatial subject, a subject of space, space will need to be conceived as a syntax and the subject a position within it. We argue, in our Brunelleschi chapter, that this is what Brunelleschi did when he demonstrated his invention of perspective to the citizens of Florence. In that chapter, we put the Lacanian concept of unconscious desire in relation to the representation of space.

It should be clear that in psychoanalysis, the subjective is not so simply what most people equate with the personal. In Lacan, the subjective may be personal, but it is not private. For which, in *Seminar 7: The Ethics of Psychoanalysis*, he mints the neologism *extimate* (= external + intimate, a gloss also on the eccentricity of the subject, the subject is eccentric to itself). Lacan insists that all subjectivity is inter-subjectivity. The *who you really are* (identity) or the *what you really want* (desire) is not conveyed to others and hence activated in the human world except to the extent that it is externalised through language and other social codes that situate the subject in its matrix. The dream image has to be put into words in order to trace its latent significance as the fulfilment of a wish. To say that your desire is subjective is not to remove it from scrutiny but to insert it into the language and idioms of design and the matrix of object choices that shape you. In *Seminar 2: The Ego in Freud's Theory and in the Technique of Psychoanalysis*, Lacan argues that 'the subject is a subject only by virtue of his subjection in the field of the Other'.[26] There may be a drive that is internal, a life force or pulsion that emerges from within, but at the point where this drive gets expressed, it is already shaped by the symbolic environment that Lacan calls the field of the Other. This symbolic environment solicits your desire by putting it in a linguistic form. Lacan capitalises it – the capital O Other – to distinguish it from the small other, which are all the people and objects, significant or otherwise, you encounter.

Lacan's subject is fundamentally split. This position has a genealogy in western thought. It is related to Marx's argument that capitalism alienates man from his own labour. In Lacan's text, man is alienated from his own desire. It is always masked by the I *want* … of the ego. The subject is made aware of its desire only as something strange in its fleeting encounters with its own slips of the tongue, jokes, mistakes, bungled actions, dream images, and the like. Marx and Lacan derive their positions from Hegel, who argued that Spirit is split and inhabited by absence. For Lacan, the subject is split in all sorts of ways. It is ego and unconscious. Imaginary and Symbolic. Inner and outer worlds. The subject is an other to others and to itself. It is other to itself because it is constituted in the field of the Other.[27]

The unconscious and the city

Both Freud and Lacan use the city as an analogue to the unconscious. Lacan quipped, before an audience in Baltimore, that 'the best image to sum up the unconscious is Baltimore in the early morning'. He was probably parodying Freud, who, in the beginning of *Civilisation and its Discontents*, compared the unconscious to Rome. They were making quite different points about the unconscious. Lacan was referring to empty streets where the only thing going on were traffic lights (*lights on nobody home*). For Lacan, the unconscious is a form of externalised cybernetics, a language beyond our control. Freud invokes an image of the Eternal City in which you only have to shift positions to see each building in all its historical conditions. He is making the point that the unconscious is the inexhaustible reserve that makes memory possible; 'everything is preserved' and nothing that is forgotten is ever lost to the subject.

Both the city and language are external to us. If one of the main aims of Lacan's text is to articulate what we might call a linguistic unconscious, Lacan is offering the tantalising possibility of an urban unconscious. He is alluding to the material aspect of the unconscious and to its Otherness. It is carried on the sibilance of others. The unconscious is about the word, your words and the words of others, and what words do when they are left alone and without the constant interference of our attention: when you slip your tongue and you disown it (*I didn't mean that!*) and your analyst responds with silence.[28]

The unconscious seems to have three conditions: it is beyond access by the subject, it is purposive, and in Lacan's reading of Freud, which focuses on speech and language, externalised. It has an other property too. The unconscious is marked by the uncanny. The unconscious is formed by repression – an aspect of the unconscious we have not yet treated – and when unconscious material returns to the subject in the medium of language, cities, and other social codes, it feels strange to the subject. It is the terrain of haunted houses. It is accompanied by anxiety. The outlaw banished from the city walls always threatens to return. Peter Eisenman quotes Freud's analogy to Rome in his introduction to Aldo Rossi's *The Architecture of the City*, where it reflects a lingering anxiety about the relation between modernism, memory, and the historic city.

Architecture and psychoanalysis are already entwined

The detour into Freud's and Lacan's treatment of the unconscious and the city indicates that the discourses of architecture and psychoanalysis are already entwined. The overarching argument of this text is that the subject of the unconscious is fundamentally spatial in ways that extend beyond the fact that individuals are located in space. If the subject is spatial, it does not seem to know it. Freud said, 'psyche is extended, knows nothing of it'.[29] At the end of this text, we will have to look at what is at stake in this not knowing. The overarching aim of this argument is to trace the consequences for architecture and subjectivity, of the fact that psychoanalysis repudiates the division between the inner world of the subject and the outer world of his/her objects. If the Cartesian Cogito gazes outward, it is outward upon the field of the Other. And the field of the Other combines inner and outer worlds into a single significant world, the world symbolised for subjectivity.

Lacan's subject is embedded in the symbolic world that Lacan calls the field of the Other because although we know it intimately; it retains its capacity to alienate us even as it positions us. Psychoanalysis is committed for its intelligibility to spatial thinking and spatial relations of inside/outside, near/far, over/under, flow, motion, transition, translation, displacement, condensation, and the like, to articulate the apparatus of psyche and its relations to others. It is confirmed by the compelling spatiality of the diagrams with which psychoanalysis explicates these relations. If the task of this book is to bring psychoanalytic thinking to bear on architecture for architects, it is equally to bring architectural thinking to bear on psychoanalysis.

What psychoanalysis is and how to read this book

In my view, psychoanalysis is not a science because, although it is empirical, it is not causal. It explains a dream by understanding its significance for the subject, not by finding a causal trigger. In so far as it is opposed to science, it is because it attributes an agency to that significance that is similar in its efficacy to a cause. Psychoanalysis is a rigorously empirical evidence-based practice. It has no use for the myth of the inner and hidden. It is not concerned with your experience of space (*what it feels like, that's a form of phenomenology*) but with what you say about that experience, in other words, how your experience is structured by you, which is also what architecture does. In a field where it would be very easy for the ego of the analyst to collude with the subject, psychoanalytic practice is organised around maintaining the separation between them. Psychoanalysis – like philosophy and cultural critique – is amenable to architecture because it is a model for interpretation of our actions and the artefacts that issue from them. In this regard, psychoanalysis is party to a border skirmish, where science competes with other forms of agency to explain the human world. If biology discovers the cause for desire in a gene or chemical (*desire in general? a particular desire?*), it is questionable whether it will have explained it as human agency. This is the territory of psychoanalysis.[30]

Psychoanalytic concepts have precise readings, but they are not stable categories. If you are an architect, there is no point in learning what an ego is (*read the definition, acquire the concept, relate it to a façade*) without also realising that an ego wrote this introduction, and an ego is reading it, and neither ego would be doing either the writing or the reading if it did not also return to that ego a certain measure of confirmation. The ego makes an investment – writing and reading are not easy – and it expects a return. The ego sees itself reflected everywhere in the world. In this world, the unconscious is invisible, at best a shadow. The subject is immersed in a field – this field of the Other – that ramifies everything the ego does with a signification that it barely registers, let alone acknowledges. We participate in the torment that shadows us.

Psychoanalysis is an elaborate machine for making sense of the world. It always acknowledges the position of the sensor in his/her own arguments. Argument, or the discourse that is comprised incrementally of many arguments, is a flow of speech (*and where we place Lacan in it, will direct its flow differently*). If you are an architect hoping to learn about the ego and the unconscious, this learning is as much about adopting a fluid approach to thinking about projects – fluid because the concepts are continually shifting, nothing remains the same – as it is about acquiring concepts. And if you acquire these concepts in the hope of acquiring a certain form of slip-free certainty, you will be disappointed. If this book gives you anything, it will be less a glossary of useable concepts as it is a self-reflective way of arguing that wrecks havoc with linear arguments, clear categories, and objective forms of research.

We have seen Freud describe this fluidity as the dream work. Many ideas and images condense into one thicker, more opaque, and ambiguous image, a kind of montage; or one idea or image replaces another in a cinema loop. This book cannot, therefore, be as linear as one would expect from a primer. There is nowhere to start, no simple or originary first point or beginning. Except that, in fact, it started with the unconscious. Any start starts *in medias res*, halfway through a journey and must glance backwards and forwards to survey the field.

We are thereby forced by the nature of our subject matter – psychoanalytic thinking in/through/from architecture – to eschew what we call the commodification of intellectual culture, treating concepts and ways of thinking as if they were commodities that can be assumed for their exchange value, and then discarded again when we are done with them. Indeed, recently psychoanalysis has been in the forefront of resistance to neoliberal trends in public life and to the invasion of market values in academe and public health.

Afterward: what is a subject?

This text explores architecture from the position of the spatial subject. It treats this inhabitant for whom architecture is home as a subjective category. A subject is an other with whom I work out my subjectivity. By speaking to others, by laughing with them, writing to them (love letters, text messages, Snapchat, Twitter, extended treatises), by building buildings with them, by positioning myself spatially with my objects and my others, in all these ways, my own subjectivity appears to me and to others. Subjects are always under construction. There is a stability of identity, but it is the stability of continuity, like the flow of a river, or the incremental construction of a city. Subjectivity is a negotiation that never ends.

Subjects are different from other categories of individual that figure in built environment discourse. In planning policy documents, end users or consumers are treated as auditable units within a matrix of service delivery and amenity provision. They are discrete, and any lack in the individual is accidental and can be compensated. In psychoanalytic texts, the subject is an empty site for whom loss is constitutive because the unconscious is never here. Although policy documents have similar aims to psychoanalytic texts – the wellbeing of people – the language and orientation of these documents are foreign to subjectivity. They treat the individual as if it were fundamentally complete, and they treat the environment as if it were a service and the inhabitants of the environment as consumers of those services; features we will recognise in the last chapter as hallmarks of the discourse of the capitalist. The reality of our relation to the environment is entirely different, has everything to do with loss and the non-fulfilment of desire and very little to do with the satisfaction of needs.

The architectural subject may play many roles: designer, builder, occupier or user, owner, amateur of …. We don't know much about it yet, but at the least:

- It spaces/is spaced – the inhabitant exists in space and uses space to express/define/articulate/communicate its desire. It communicates spatially – where you put your chair, how you set your table, how you linger in your window, how you park your car ….
- It speaks/is spoken to –
- Its sees/is seen –

We will argue in the next chapter that another aspect of the spatiality of the subject is the relation it has to its own voice. Other forms of subject may not be so explicitly spatial or so explicitly marked by loss. The swimmer communicates its desire through fishy motion; it does not speak or see.

The spatial subject inhabits a room because it has a spatial practice, however minimal – setting the table is a spatial practice – whereas a ball on the floor, even though it is in space, does not. The subject uses architecture to construct itself within the elaborate codes of architecture. It has participated either directly or indirectly in the construction of those codes by participating in a spatial culture, by watching TV, by putting bread in the oven, by talking to others, etc. In this sense, it is involved in a recursive relationship with its environment.

How is the present reflection on human nature new? My primary sources are 20th-century structuralist public intellectuals who were themselves drawing on the history of reflection upon human nature going back to antiquity. What is new is the aim of weaving subject thinking through architecture and putting it alongside policy thinking on the environment. This is also one of the aims of Jane Rendell's recent *The Architecture of Psychoanalysis*, which put subject thinking in relation to the history of UK social housing.[31] It raises new problems: how to put a thoroughgoing subjective discourse in relation to evidence-based policy, which policy will never understand unless it learns to speak the language of the subject. It is not too much to claim that if the debate about the environment could be framed in terms of the subject, and architecture as the space with which we articulate our subjectivity, and not as the platform for consumer satisfaction, we might find less antisocial behaviour. We might find fewer people putting their money in the Cayman Islands where no one will know about it or fewer people voting for the UK to leave Europe because the aesthetic of separateness, uniqueness, and independence – all fantasies of the ego – is simply less attractive.[32]

We have a responsibility to ourselves to humanise our world, to humanise our institutions, to humanise ourselves. We ask, how, fundamentally, do you change the world? This text is committed to the proposition that we change the world most profoundly by changing the way we talk about it. Policy documents legitimise a form of words: currently, our institutions and positions of power are occupied by the market-led language of individuality and choice. It is a monoculture in the ecology of ideas. The talking cure, upon which this reflection on the architectural subject is based, puts great faith in the proposition that the best way to solve a problem is to talk about it with others because it is by talking to others that we form and reform what we are. The talking cure addresses an other form of individual that recognises the fundamentally and radically social nature of desire. This is part and parcel with binding ourselves into collective social formations. We will conclude this text by looking at climate change from the position of the subject who articulates its subjectivity by articulating its environment.

I use architecture, the way I use language, to construct myself.

Notes

1 Lacan, 'The Instance of the Letter in the Unconscious or Reason since Freud (1957)', in *Ecrits: The First Complete Edition in English*. Translated by Bruce Fink, Heloise Fink and Russell Grigg (New York: W. W. Norton, 2006), p. 435.

2 Freud, 'A Difficulty in the Path of Psychoanalysis (1917)', in *Standard Edition of the Complete Psychological Works of Sigmund Freud*, translated into English and edited by J. Strachey (London: The Hogarth Press and the Institute of Psycho-Analysis, 1956–74), volume XVII. Lacan refers to Freud's 'Copernican revolution' in several texts.

3 See, John Shannon Hendrix, *Unconscious Thought in Philosophy and Psychoanalysis* (Palgrave Macmillan, 2015), with chapters on Plotinus, the Peripatetics, Averroes, Robert Grosseteste, the 18th and 19th centuries including Kant, Shelling, Hegel, Hartmann and Theodor Lipps, and finally, Freud and Lacan.

4 Sigmund Freud, *The Interpretation of Dreams, The Standard Edition*, translated by J. Strachey (New York: Avon Books, 1965 [1900]) pp. 647 and 121, respectively.

5 John Shannon Hendrix, *Architecture and Psychoanalysis: Peter Eisenman and Jacques Lacan* (New York: Peter Lang, 2006).

6 According to Arendt, the appearance of the self is the human condition, and the space of appearance is the condition of an architecture that responds to it, for which see Hannah Arendt, *The Human Condition* (Chicago: University of Chicago Press, 1958).

7 Jacques Lacan, *The Four Fundamental Concepts of Psychoanalysis* (New York: Norton, 1981) pp. 149, 203.

8 Bruce Fink, *A Clinical Introduction to Lacanian Psychoanalysis: Theory and Technique* (Cambridge, MA: Harvard University Press, 1997), pp. 14–15.

9 The unconscious is a conceptual fact about the world, not a material one; a consequence of this status is that it has undergone review and revision throughout its history. For a good short history of the unconscious, see the Introduction in John Shannon Hendrix and Lorens Holm, eds., *Architecture and the Unconscious* (Abingdon: Routledge, 2016). In this paragraph: About being lost, see Freud's account of being lost in Orvieto, an Italian hill town familiar to him, in his paper 'The Uncanny' (1919). About never reaching the end of free association and hence never reaching the end of desire, see Freud's account of the 'navel' of the dream, which is the arbitrary point where dream interpretation stops (due to exhaustion, boredom, and time) in *The Interpretation of Dreams* (1900).

10 See Freud's 'Papers on Technique' in *The Standard Edition of the Complete Psychological Works of Sigmund Freud* (London: The Hogarth Press and the Institute of Psycho-Analysis, 1956–74). See also Jacques Lacan, *The Seminar of Jacques Lacan, Book I: Freud's Papers on Technique 1953–1954* (Cambridge University Press, 1988) translated by John Forrester.

11 The photographer Shellburne Thurber has exhibited photographs of analytic interiors, for which see http://www.shellburnethurber.com/analytic-interiors. There are a number of papers about the analytic setting. See Mignon Nixon, 'On the Couch', *October* 113 (Summer 2005), pp. 39–76.

12 *Big Brother* was a TV series that ran yearly from 2000 to 2018. It was the pioneer of the reality TV show in which contestants live together for several months under continual scrutiny of surveillance cameras. See https://en.wikipedia.org/wiki/Big_Brother_ (British_TV_series). It is probably the best demonstration of the effects on the subject of the imaginary order, about which, see Chapter 2.

13 *The Standard Edition of the Complete Psychological Works of Sigmund Freud*, translated into English and edited by J. Strachey (London: The Hogarth Press and the Institute of Psycho-Analysis, 1956–74). Henceforth, *The Standard Edition*.

14 The Strachey translation was republished as *The Pelican Freud Library* in 11 paperback volumes (Penguin, 1970–80). Penguin has recently begun publishing a new series with new translations.

15 Said to his students, cf. Lacan, 'Overture to the 1st International Encounter of the Freudian Field' in *Hurly-Burly* issue 6 September 2011, p. 12.

16 See, for instance, Denis Hollier, ed., *The College of Sociology (1937–39)* trans. Betsy Wing, *History and Theory of Literature* (Minneapolis, MN: University of Minnesota Press, 1988).

17 Websites that publish material on and by Lacan include 'Lacan Dot Com' at http://www.lacan.com/ and 'Lacanian Ink' at http://www.lacan.com/lacink/archive.html. See also the Lacan wiki, NO SUBJECT, which is based on the Evans dictionary, at http://nosubject.com/index.php?title=Main_Page. NO SUBJECT also includes downloadable PDF versions of the unpublished Seminars and – amazingly – read aloud versions of some of the unpublished Seminars in their entirety by members of the Lacan in Ireland group. The lectures of the London Society of the New Lacanian School, NLS, are published on YouTube. Finally, the Institute for Psychoanalytic Studies in Architecture, IPSA, a new group which emerged out of the conference *Architecture & Collective Life* (Dundee, 2019) of which I am a member, is building an online presence of scholarly presentations on subjects that lie at the intersection of architecture and Lacanian thought, for which see http://art3idea.psu.edu/ipsa/index.html.

18 Lacan was a controversial figure within the psychoanalytic community and remains controversial within psychoanalysis, the social sciences, and humanities. It has partly to do with his uncompromising rejection of ego psychology as the road to falsification of the self. It also had to do with his unconventional practice that included the variable length psychoanalytic session, which led to his expulsion in 1953 from the International Psychoanalytic Association (IPA) and in 1963 to his resignation from the Société Française de Psychoanalyse (SFP) and consequent founding of his new school, the École Freudienne de Paris (EFP), and the subsequent struggles for institutional recognition.

19 There are other texts that were not published in *Écrits* like 'Television: a challenge to the psychoanalytic establishment' (*October 40*, 1987), 'Kant with Sade' (*October 51*, 1989), 'Desire and the interpretation of desire in Hamlet' (*Yale French Studies 55/56*, 1977), 'Of Structure as the Inmixing of an Otherness Prerequisite to Any Subject Whatever' in *The Structuralist Controversy: The Languages of Criticism and the Sciences of Man*, edited by Richard Macksey and Eugenio Donato, 186–95 (text) - 200 (discussion) (Baltimore and London: The Johns Hopkins University Press, 1970/1972). The Cormac Gallagher editions of the Seminars are available in PDF format at 'Jacques Lacan in Ireland' at http://www.lacaninireland.com/web/ and sold as bound hard copies at specialist psychoanalytic bookshops like Karnac Books, London.

20 For a discussion of these diagrams, see Sigmund Freud, *The Interpretation of Dreams (1900)* (London: George Allen & Unwin, 1971), the chapter on 'Regression' pp. 533–49, and Sigmund Freud, 'The Ego and The Id (1923)', in *Sigmund Freud: On Metapsychology*, edited by A. Richards and J. Strachey (London: Penguin, 1991), pp. 339–408, in particular Section II 'the ego and the id' pp. 357–6. See also Jacques Lacan, 'On a Question Prior to any Possible Treatment of Psychosis (1958)', in *Écrits* (New York: Norton, 2006), pp. 445–488 and in particular the section 'III With Freud' pp. 457ff.

21 Cf. Freud, *The Interpretation of Dreams*, pp. 537, 538, 541, where he develops the diagram in three stages. He says about the layers that they may be spatial (like compound lenses) or temporal; what is important is that they form a sequence. Freud seems to be vacillating between body metaphors and speech metaphors.

22 For which see Freud, 'The Unconscious' (1915), pp. 167–222, and 'The Ego and The Id' (1923), pp. 339–408, in *Sigmund Freud: On Metapsychology*, edited by A. Richards and J. Strachey (London: Penguin, 1991).

23 The difference between ego and subject marks a difference in schools of psychoanalytic thought. The ego psychology based in America is about strengthening the ego. Freudian and Lacanian psychoanalyses are about finding a route past the ego to the unconscious.

24 I borrow *concourse* from my Loeb translation of Vitruvius; see the chapter on Scott Brown/Venturi.

25 Mario Gandelsonas, 'From Structure to Subject: The Formation of an Architectural Language' in *Oppositions 17* (1978), pp. 6–29. Eisenman, Gandalsonas, Agrest, Ockman, *et al.* founded the Institute for Architecture and Urban Studies (IAUS) in New York City and its journal *Oppositions* in the late 1960s. *Oppositions* was the first publication site for a number of seminal post-modern thinkers including Rem Koolhaas, Anthony Vidler, and Peter Eisenman.

26 Dylan Evans, *An Introductory Dictionary of Lacanian Psychoanalysis* (London: Routledge, 1996), p. 196.

27 Mark C. Taylor, ed., *Deconstruction in Context: Literature and Philosophy* (Chicago: University of Chicago Press, 1986). This great collection includes extracts from Hegel, Kojève, Kant, Saussure, Husserl, Sartre, Merleau-Ponty. Cf. in particular Hegel, 'Preface and Introduction' to *Phenomenology of Spirit*, pp. 67–97. And Kojève, 'In the Place of an Introduction' in *Introduction to the Reading of Hegel*, pp. 98–120.

28 In his paper 'Seminar on "The Purloined Letter"' (1955), a reading of Poe, Lacan maps the unconscious onto language and calls it *the field of the Other* in *Ecrits* (New York: Norton, 2006) pp. 6-48.

29 Sigmund Freud, 'Findings, Ideas, Problems', *The Standard Edition*, volume 23, pp. 299–300.

30 The analytic setting is a linguistic laboratory. Psychoanalysis has an uneasy relation to the sciences because the relations it builds are linguistic, not cause-and-effect. Psychoanalysis is a form of ground up theory that emerged out of countless hours of patient observation. It poses a problem for science: a rigorously empirical discipline dedicated to bringing new facts into the world that does not follow the scientific method.

31 Jane Rendell, *The Architecture of Psychoanalysis: Spaces of Transition* (London: I.B. Tauris, 2017).

32 The UK left the EU in January 2020 following a referendum in 2016. Much of this text was written during a pro-leave campaign that was marked by bad faith claims and divisiveness.

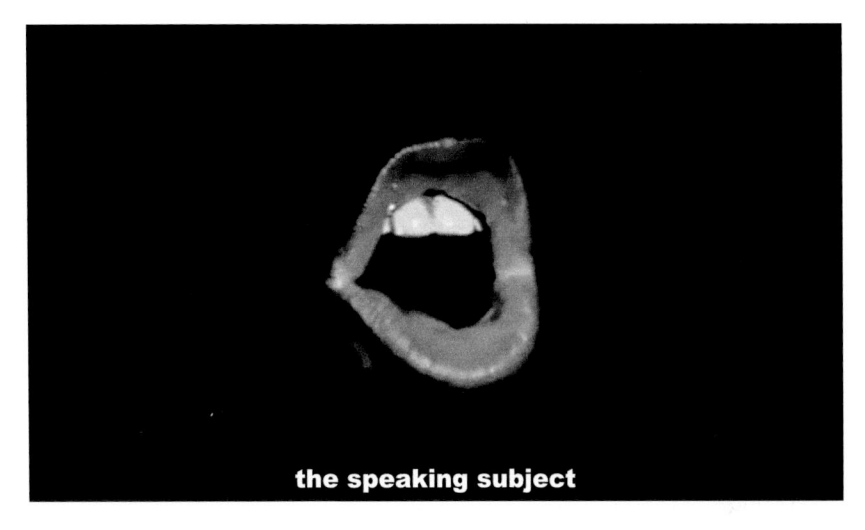

FIGURE 2.1 The speaking subject is a single-sided surface.

2

READING GIEDION READING HISTORY THROUGH LACAN [SYMBOLIC, IMAGINARY, AND REAL SPACE]

Giedion

Architectural space conception

At the end of *The Eternal Present: the beginnings of architecture*, the historian Siegfried Giedion delineates the history of architecture into three periods, which are uniquely determined by three types of space (pp. 495ff.): the Archaic, the Classical, and the Modern. *The Eternal Present* is a history of the architectural culture of the 'earliest high civilisations' (p. 2). Sumer and Egypt – along with Greece – constitute the first, Archaic, space. This is a Modernist's history of space, whose purpose is to explain Modernism by showing what came before it.[1]

DOI: 10.4324/9780429022845-2

He calls these types of space 'architectural space conceptions'.

a. Space: as if space were the condition of architecture, closer to the heart of architecture than materials, style, utility, or politics.
b. Architectural: the space that architecture makes, as opposed to the random space of the wilderness (Vitruvius); the anticipatory space of the white page (Alvar Aalto); the *de facto* space of caves, the abstract space of mathematics; the emptiness of outer space; all of which, in different ways, precede architecture.
c. Conception: for Giedion, space is a conceptual category. If space is a concept, it is subjective (*a concept is always a concept for someone*). It is a way of ordering ourselves in the world. Giedion does not ask what space itself is, space independent of the conceptual labour of the human subject.[2]

The three spaces

1. **Archaic space of Sumer, Egypt, Greece**
    'The first architectonic space conception is an architecture of volumes in space'. He quotes Le Corbusier. 'Structural objects – volumes – were placed in limitless space' (p. 521). These volumes have no significant interior. 'Neither the Greeks nor the Egyptians ever developed interior space with the same intensity they expended on relating their architecture to the cosmos' (p. 521). 'The first architectural space conception was concerned with the emanating power of volumes, their relations with one another, and their interactions' (p. 522). 'Both Sumer and Egypt could construct interior space when the need arose, even vaulted space, but they had no interest in it' (p. 523). Giedion describes an 'aversion to interior space - great hypostyle, Karnak: … whose 134 colossal papyrus columns fill the void of the hall so that no interior space can develop. This was strengthened by offsetting the column centers in alternate rows' (p. 509). Again, the Archaic was concerned with 'volumes in space: the cosmic unity between pyramid, sky, and the limitless desert' (p. 505). We note that Giedion's colleague Bruno Zevi writes of the Parthenon that we '… admire its human scale, … deplore its negation of space'. He then disqualifies it from the canon: 'The Parthenon is a non-architectural work, but it is still a masterpiece of art; …' Norburg-Schultz makes similar claims.[3]
2. **Classical space of Rome**
    Carved out (vaulted) interior space, for example the Pantheon. 'Interior space, and with it the whole vaulting problem, became the highest aim of architecture' (p. 521). The second conception involved 'the symbolic relating of interior space to the cosmos, …' (p. 523). An engraving of a renaissance nave like Brunelleschi's San Lorenzo, Florence, or a renaissance street like Bramante's via Giulia, Rome, both paradigms of perspective space, should make it clear that the overriding concern of the Classic is the interior.
3. **Modern space**
    A dynamic interaction of interior and exterior, exemplified by 20th-century western architecture: an obvious allusion to the fluid dynamics of

3 forms of City

Objects on a plain [Mycenae]

Continuous interior [Nolli's Rome]

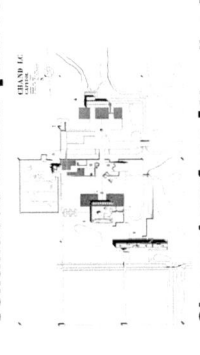

Charged surface [Chandigarh]

3 forms of Building

Archaic space [outside space - the blue of the sky, the shadow of the sun]

Classic space [inside space - the masonry interior, the wrap-around projected image]

Modern space [inside/outside space - the dynamic threshold]

FIGURE 2.2   Giedion's Modern history: three space conceptions correlated to three forms of city.

the free-plan and the tautness of the free façade: the thresholds in the living rooms of Villa Savoye and Villa Church at Ville d'Avray; the facade of Villa Stein at Garches. Slutzky and Rowe's transparency literal and phenomenal. Still life painting by Le Corbusier, Leger, Juan Gris. The grid and transparent intersecting planes of Mies.

In *Space Time and Architecture*, Giedion associates the Classic space conception with the invention of perspective and the Modern with cubism. He relates perspective to the rise of the individual subject and then relates it to urbanism. 'At the start of the fifteenth century, in Florence, this conception was translated into artistic terms through the discovery of perspective. Throughout the following five centuries perspective was to be one of the constitutive facts in the history of art, … With the invention of perspective the modern notion of individualism found its artistic counterpart'.[4]

Following Giedion, we can extend his classification of architecture to cities. The Archaic city would include the citadel cities of Greece, like the Acropolis or Mycenae, the preponderance of object buildings in apparently unregulated space on wide open craggy plateaux and coastal planes, no enclosure, sun and openness everywhere. The Classic city would be Nolli's Rome, which reads as a continuous plastic expanding and contracting interior, narrow streets opening out into piazza, but everything within walls. The paradigm Modern city would be the Chandigarh site plan in which spatial figures cross and interpenetrate each other and slide through buildings like liquid through sluice gates. Robert Slutzky used this metaphor for this stage of Le Corbusier's work.[5]

In *The Psychologizing of Modernity*, Mark Jarzombek situates Giedion within early to mid-20th century German art and architectural historiography, defined by the prevalence of psychology and speculative philosophy derived from Hegel. 'Hegel's distinction between the Oriental, the Roman, and the German worlds became the difference between the Greek world, the Roman world, and Modernism'.[6] Giedion's argument in *The Eternal Present* is simply an extension of an earlier theme in *Space Time and Architecture*, in which history runs the sequence Greek, Roman, Modern, but to see the roots of Modernism in Greece (Mies, Le Corbusier) and Rome (Colin Rowe) is simply to note what we already know. For our purposes, Giedion is conjoining the thinking of Freud on the Modern subject and Hegel on the historical development of Spirit and the thesis-antithesis-synthesis template that he imposes upon it.[7]

4. Prehistoric space

Giedion's neat classification immediately becomes problematic. He mentions a fourth space. Prehistoric space is a non-oriented space that appears in cave paintings where hands and buffalo are positioned with no regard to up. 'Vertical and horizontal had not yet achieved predominance. The eyes of primitive man … held all directions in equal esteem' (pp. 502–503) (*Space before it has imposed upon it, Le Corbusier's vertical axis of man, horizontal axis of vision).*[8] Introduced as an afterthought, Prehistoric space seems to open his argument up to all sorts of interpretations. It seems that for Giedion, a space conception is like a north arrow. What concepts do is orient subjects. We might call this the spatial function of concepts – and prehistoric space does not orient. If Archaic space is all outside, and all Classic space inside, and Modern space has the properties of both, then Prehistoric space seems to be neither inside nor outside. It would be easy to say that as part of a *history,* pre-historic space simply precedes the others, but as a *form* of space, it seems to be outside Giedion's tripartite system, threatening either the cogency of his system or the universality of space. His Prehistoric space has, moreover, an uneasy relation to a number of other outsides. The cosmos, which he poses as other to architecture and man, seems to be nothing if not also a form of outside. He also mentions outer space, the physical blackness of the universe.

We opened this chapter with Giedion's history because he insists upon the conceptual nature of space and the necessity for spatial subjects – theses that we intend to pursue – and because its flaws open it to other readings. It is a handy way to introduce Lacan's three orders of subjective experience: the symbolic, the imaginary, and the real. They will help to untangle the flaws in Giendion's argument. Lacan's tripartite system is one of his key analytic frameworks and one of the few that does not have a direct counterpart in Freud's thought.[9] Giedion's insistence that space is a conception, places it in Lacan's symbolic order. We are going to argue that space functions in quite different and precise ways, which we can relate to the symbolic, the imaginary, and the real. By reading Giedion with Lacan, we hope to trace the entailments of the spatial subject through architecture and psychoanalysis. It should be pointed out that Giedion does not reference Lacan. Indeed, Lacan was unavailable to Giedion. This is where the intellectual project parts company with the historical one.

Lacan

Lacan exhorts his students time and again that in order to understand the complexities of the Freudian subject, it is necessary to refer to the symbolic, imaginary, and real orders or registers of subjective experience.[10] For Lacan, it is axiomatic that the world comes to subjects as experience. It is not the world that we encounter but our experience of the world. Beginning in 1953 with the paper 'The function and field of speech and language in psychoanalysis', where these terms are introduced as nouns, reference to these orders are encountered throughout his text and his understanding of them evolved with his praxis. In a nutshell, the imaginary refers to perceptions and feelings; the symbolic to thought. With the imaginary and the symbolic, we have all that we see, hear, touch, and otherwise perceive, coupled with all the ways that we organise perception into significant experience and communicate it to others. If the symbolic and imaginary constitute what we know as reality – architectural or otherwise – what Lacan calls the real is something most people have never heard of. It is never the object of perception, it is never assimilated in our thought. In *The Four Fundamental Concepts of Psychoanalysis*, Lacan refers to 'the missed encounter with the real'. Unlike the symbolic and the imaginary, which are our creations, the real is really out there, we just always miss it. Although the real makes its proximity felt through a formless anxiety, it is what we always miss, when we encounter the world.[11]

Imaginary

Think of the imaginary register as relating to images, rather than its connotation in English, of fantasy and illusion. I experience the world as a continuous stream of sense perceptions, visual and otherwise, and there is an immediacy to it. It is the locus of the ego with its close attachment to reality. Only I have my images and feelings. Feelings are like inner perceptions and are private to each individual. In order to share them, I have to speak them or record them; which takes them out of the order of perception and materialises them in the order of representation.

The imaginary order is inaugurated by what Lacan calls the mirror stage, which is the moment the enfant first sees itself as an image. This self-image is the kernel of the ego; the imaginary order is the field of identity and the home of the ego that wants to see its discrete and well-formed image everywhere. Lacan emphasises its temporal and spatial dimensions. The paradox of the self-image is that it is always 'over there', an externalised aspect of the self that the self never fully assimilates. Thereafter we see ourselves reflected in others, whether they be our parents, friends, media personalities and sports figures, celebs or strangers, or advertisements. There is now that new individual, the influencer, who should be called 'reflector'. Soundbites have the compelling nature of images. Identity is a hall of mirrors.[12]

The imaginary order is not fantasy because it is constitutive of the world. Nor is it illusory, but it is misleading. It will lead you astray because the image is 'captivating'. We tend to respond to the image with either love or loathing, not reason. The lesson of Narcissus is that when you fall too much in love with an image, whether your own or the image of an other, you die a lonely death, if not literally, at least for others: you become the bore at parties. We are misled by our egos because who we think we are (the image we identify with) is never what others think we are. Lacan calls it *méconnaissance*: mis-knowledge of the self. We can think we are whoever we want when we stand in front of the mirror, but what matters is when we step out the door and greet what others think we are. Identification is fundamentally narcissistic, superficial, and aggressive. It is about seeing yourself in others and others in you. It is why we should regard identity politics with suspicion and why nationalism is such an easy position to assume and so quickly goes to xenophobic violence.[13]

Symbolic

If the imaginary order is intra-subjective – a relation of the subject to its image – the symbolic order is inter-subjective, a relation of one subject to another. *Symbol* is meant in its broadest sense to include all signs: words, images, diagrams, *maison domino*, events, gestures, masques, assassinations, memes, and emoji. Anything that conveys a message from one subject to another. The sign is comprised of signifier and signified, Lacan writes it 'S/s', signifier over signified. He develops this structure from the linguist Ferdinand Saussure. For Saussure, signifier and signified correspond to word and concept. Lacan pays particular attention to the signifier, the word; he lets the signified fend for itself. Signifiers are organised in open-ended interweaving chains. Imagine everything you do and say forming continuous streams of signifiers, looping off you in multiple directions. All subjects have a place in them. These chains constitute the kinship relations that bind one subject to another or attach subjects to places, in contrast to the aloneness of imaginary relations. We will develop these ideas when we return to the unconscious.[14]

The medium of the symbolic is language, language has to be interpreted in its broadest sense to include any code by which one subject communicates to an other. Lacan developed the idea of the symbolic from the structural anthropologist Claude Lévi-Strauss. In his *Introduction to the Work of Marcel Mauss*, Lévi-Strauss writes 'Any culture can be considered as a combination of symbolic systems headed by language, the matrimonial rules, the economic relations, art, science and religion. All the systems seek to express certain aspects of physical reality and social reality, ….' Mauss was interested in the function of gifts and exchange within these systems. In his *Dictionary of Lacanian Psychoanalysis*, Evans says 'the gift of speech is words'. The sociologist Emile Durkheim called these relations social facts (whence, Giedion's 'constitutive facts'). They are facts about the world, even if they are socially constructed, in the way that a building is a constructed fact about the world.[15]

Lacan calls the symbolic order *the field of the Other*, and paradoxically, it can lead to a sense of otherness. There is an intimacy that we have with our own images, you can never have my images, but symbols always come from others. Language pre-exists us, we are born into it, we learn it from our parents, it comes with rules for its correct use that we do not create but must abide by. Although language emerges from our mouth, it is validated as a message only when it is received by others. As architects, we know this well. We have to learn the rules and codes of practice; and our buildings have to conform to them before they are accepted into the canon. If imaginary relations are dyadic because they are a matter of the subject and its image, symbolic relations are triadic. They go through the field of the Other: me, an other subject, and language. Or me, my design project, and the discourse of architecture comprising its rules, grammar, elements, typologies, and histories.

Real

The real is what is excluded from the imaginary and symbolic orders. It is difficult to convey just how intractable the real is. It is radically unknowable. Lacan says, 'the real is impossible'. It is the order of what philosophy calls brute fact. It is the blue of the sky before the word *blue* organises our colour experience. It is the unmediated presence of things before they are organised by spatial relations. The real is the object of science although by the time it becomes science it is already registered in the subject as symbolic and imaginary. To objectify the real, to refer to the real *object* is already to impose the category of the object upon it. The real is the coming into form of the formless, at the terrible moment before it enters our human world as form. It's the mouth that erupts through the chest of the hapless crewmember in *Aliens*.[16] Horror movies play on the imminent catastrophe of the real, and typically, once our worst fear has erupted through the taught screen of reality, the sense of dread becomes laughter. The real marks the limit of the symbolic and imaginary. It shares an affinity in philosophy to Kant's *things-in-themselves* which are things such as they exist outside the individuating categories of space and time, although this is not a link Lacan makes. There is an affinity between the real and psychosis (Koolhaas argued that Le Corbusier was psychotic). In Lacan's text, psychosis is a disfunction of the symbolic order; what the psychotic subject cannot assimilate in the symbolic returns to it in the real, where its significance eludes it.[17]

The image is regarded with suspicion in Lacanian psychoanalysis. The attraction of the image depends not upon its accurate reflection of the world – this is the myth of realism – but upon the degree to which you see yourself reflected in it. It is fundamentally narcissistic. If the success of the image depends upon allure, success in the symbolic order depends upon the cogency of an argument or the coherence of a plan. In other words, the degree to which you are bound to it by its sense. We might expect the real to appear as non-sense in visual or linguistic registers; even the ugly image has an allure. Whilst the non-sensical image may presage the real, we would expect the real to escape both registers like a bump on the head at the moment of impact when it stuns its owner.

The Borromean knot

Lacan uses the Borromean knot to diagram the inter-dependence of the symbolic, imaginary, and real. It comprises three interconnected rings, no two of which are linked, but if one is removed, they all come undone. [Figure 2.5, centre] It is unlike most knots in that it is not a continuous thread that crosses its own bights.[18] Its use is an example of Lacan's increasing dependence upon topology to visualise subjects instead of Freud's body metaphors. Although the three orders can be separated analytically, they are inextricable in experience. Any experience has symbolic imaginary and real aspects, and Giedion's space concepts should be understood as three closely integrated aspects of any architectural space rather than as a sequence of discrete spaces. In Lacan's text, the three orders are not equivalent: the symbolic and imaginary prop each other and the real is understood as the outside or limit condition of the other two. The imaginary order is the stuff of my immediate sense experience, and the symbolic order provides the conceptual apparatus that I develop with others in order to frame that experience. The interpretation of dreams is a paradigm. The dream image is an imaginary phenomenon, but it is through interpretation in the presence of an other (in the analytic setting) that I develop its significance for me. Without interpretation, the dream image remains fleeting and unknown. From a Lacanian perspective, it is the mistake of phenomenology to attribute to perception an originary status. Perception is not self-evident without the conceptual apparatus that makes sense of it.[19]

Giedion with Lacan

Cosmos

Cosmos is introduced as the space that Archaic subjects inhabit, but in Giedion's text, it seems to function as the other to all three space conceptions. It is beyond the scope of this text to trace the discourse on cosmos, but we need to look at how it functions in Giedion's text. If we call architectural space subjective because it is the space built by subjects, the position of cosmos with respect to this space is to be always beyond it. Whatever the form of settlement, and whatever the world view of its inhabitant, there is always an existential predicament beyond it, be it *gods* or *fate* or *destiny* or *existence* or *universe* or *world-at-large*.

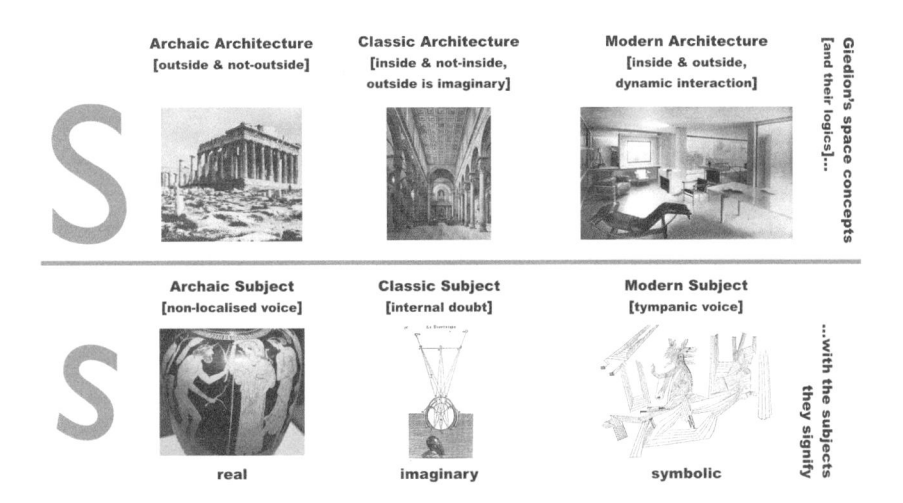

FIGURE 2.3 Giedion's Modern history: three space conceptions = three forms of building and the three forms of subject that they signify.

If we were Hegelians – and Giedion was – we might add *Spirit* to this stream of signifiers.

In the narrative arc of Giedion's history, we use architecture to position ourselves with respect to cosmos, and this is the basis for dividing history into spatial eras. For Archaic subjects, cosmos is everywhere, and they inhabit it directly whether they are inside or outside their temples. The Classical subject conceives the world as an image that screens itself from cosmos. The Modern subject, who knows both inside and outside, and can see them together, lives on the edge between an interior that screens it from cosmos and full exposure to it. The Modern subject treads a fine line.

We can map Giedion's narrative onto Lacan's symbolic imaginary and real. To do so, let us reprise Giedion's positions in terms of thresholds. According to Giedion, it was the art historian Alois Reigl who first noted that Greek temples had no windows. The window is one of the ways that architecture signifies the relation between inside and outside, which is one reason why windows tend to be embellished.[20] We might say that the Archaics had walls but no thresholds. Their walls carried little or none of the symbolic significance that we attribute to thresholds. Walls may have held the roof up, kept rain and beasts out, but not the gods. Architecture for the Archaic subject was ineffectual in that it failed to 'threshold' the subject from cosmos. The Archaic subject experienced cosmos directly as if it were real. Architecture remained open to cosmos because the wall was close to the real of unconceptualised matter. The sense of exposure associated with Archaic architecture may correspond to the contemporary condition of agoraphobia (think of the scenes of the rooftop of Villa Malaparte in the film *Le Mepris*, the camera panning the deep blue sea, the horizon, Odysseus and the Gods, the sun slicing through them).[21]

The threshold registers on the subject differently in each era. The classic subject experiences the threshold as if it were a screen upon which the cosmos is projected as an image. The cosmos is always pictured the other side of the threshold. We note the preponderance of illusionistic fresco painting in renaissance and baroque churches. Typically, fresco either extended the interior or opened it up to the sky. In the perspectival regime demonstrated to architecture by Brunelleschi (see Chapter 2), the perspective window or picture plane is always between the subject and its world. Think of Alberti's metaphor for perspective painting in *Della Pittura*: it is like opening up a window in a wall. Think also of Andrea Pozzo's illusionistic paintings that extend the choir and ceilings of Il Gesu; or Boullées' project for the Newton Cenotaph. This function of the threshold to screen the subject from cosmos is imaginary, for although masonry walls may hold up the roof, keep rain and beasts out, they cannot screen the subject from its destiny. This is paradoxical because we associate Classical architecture with a robust sense of space and of the robust enclosure that shapes it. If Cosmos is experienced directly for the Archaic subject – immediate, unmediated, heading in the direction of the real – it is imaginary for the Classic subject.[22]

In comparison to the estranging material austerity of the Archaic and the full-bodied image of the Classic, Modern space feels intellectual and denatured. Think how many people find it cold. Think of the almost invisible thresholds in Mies' montages for the Resor house project (*did he erase the lines after he drew them?*) or the virtual thresholds of the Barcelona Pavillion. We can understand Le Corbusier's Indian projects as an attempt to recover, using the plasticity of concrete, this lost robustness within a Modern space conception in which the threshold is symbolic. Lacan would say that this loss of the material body of architecture is the nature of signification. The signifier displaces the object. The gift of language comes with a price.

The Modern threshold offers the promise of exposure or enclosure, outside or inside, there or here, but it never fully delivers. The difference between inside and outside is signified for the subject, but inside and outside are not rooms or fixed categories. Their position depends upon the position of the subject. They are expressed architecturally by the floor plate that slides seamlessly beneath a thin threshold. The Modern threshold is related to Rowe's phenomenal transparency, spatial figuration without walls, or other material boundaries. It is why Alberti's metaphor of the window in the wall and Mies' montages for the Resor House project are immediately understandable as different spatial propositions.[23] The Modern subject always inhabits the threshold, always crossing it from inside to outside, always facing Cosmos and about to enter it. It is the fate of the Modern, never to arrive.

The Klein Square

What makes Giedion's history compelling is its seemingly simple binary logic, a term, and its opposite. And yet the problem dogging his history is that outside and inside are architectural positions, not types of space. Space can be outside or inside the house, but how can space itself be outside (Archaic) or inside (Classic) or a combination of the two (Modern), or neither (Prehistoric). Since space is everywhere, what would the outside of space be? The problems associated with the everywhereness of space are compounded by the other terms his argument has to exclude in order to preserve its sense. It has to exclude something as other to space; only at each stage of his argument that other seems to be different. The main other is cosmos; a secondary other is prehistoric space; there is also outer space (*where does that fit in the system, if it isn't either cosmic or pre- or non-historic?*) Lacan's three registers were proffered as a way to untangle these other outsides, but it is not yet clear how.

One way to untangle the binary terms of an argument is to map them onto the Klein Square.[24] [Figure 2.5, left] The Klein Square distinguishes the opposite of a term from its negation. We put the two terms that are meant to be opposites on the two upper corners of the square and on the corresponding lower corners, the negation of these terms. *Outside* (cosmos) is opposite to *Inside* (perspective). These are the basic terms or building blocks of Giedion's argument. And beneath

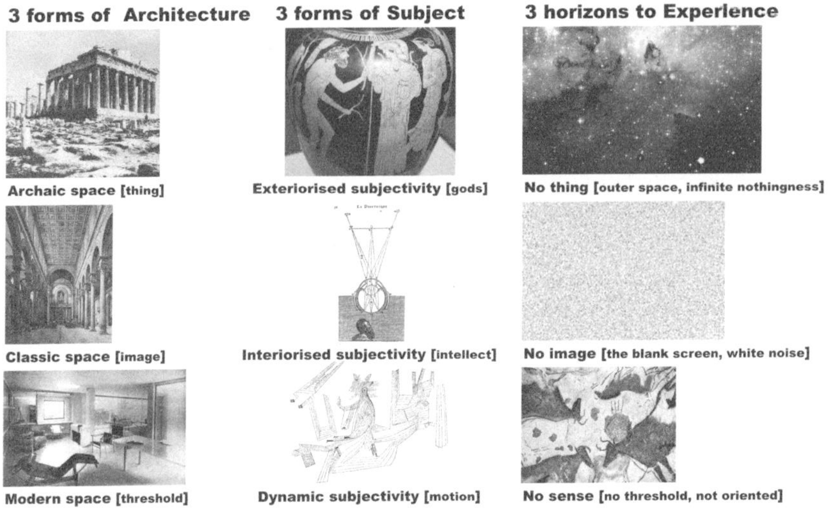

3 forms of Architecture   **3 forms of Subject**   **3 horizons to Experience**

Archaic space [thing]

Exteriorised subjectivity [gods]

No thing [outer space, infinite nothingness]

Classic space [image]

Interiorised subjectivity [intellect]

No image [the blank screen, white noise]

Modern space [threshold]

Dynamic subjectivity [motion]

No sense [no threshold, not oriented]

FIGURE 2.4 Giedion's Modern history: three space conceptions, three subjects, and three horizons to subjective experience.

them their negations: *not-outside* (outer space) and *not-inside* (the blank screen). Giedion's space conceptions appear as derivatives of these basic positions, appearing on the second outer square. It is best to think of the term and its negation as limit conditions rather than the components of Giedion's space conceptions. Thus Giedion associated cosmos with his Archaic space conception; we locate the Archaic space conception between a cosmos filled with the sun-blasted objects of man and the infinite emptiness of the universe. It may seem paradoxical to place Archaic space at the conjunction of *outside* and *not-outside*, but to say, as Giedion does, that the Archaic has no interest in the inside is not to say that they make no spatial distinctions, but only that what they distinguish from the outside is not an inside, but simply something that is not an outside. Many spatial conditions might constitute the negation of outside, other than inside, in this case, outer space. Giedion associated perspective with Classic space; we locate Classic space between an imaginary depth and the blank screen upon which it is projected. Again, what is not the imaginary inside of Classic space, is not outside, but the empty screen: think of static, white noise, or no reception. The empty screen is the only limit condition that Giedion does not mention, and we add it alongside outer space and pre-historic space in order to complete his argument. Modern dynamic space is a conjunction of the opposing terms *inside & outside*. Prehistoric space – below it, its counterpart – is a conjunction of their negations, *not-inside & not-outside*. It fails to orient subjects with respect to these two terms.

The symbolic, imaginary, and real appear as two axes in the Klein Square diagram of Giedion's space conceptions. The Modern and Prehistoric mark either ends of the symbolic axis because it runs from sense to non-sense, from the coherent message to babble. Although Giedion introduced Prehistoric space as if it were the limit to his whole history, we see that it is more properly the counterpart to Modern space in the way that Archaic and Classic are counterparts, on opposite sides of the Klein Square. Archaic and Classic conceptions form a horizontal axis that runs from real to imaginary. Over the course of Lacan's development, the allegiances between the symbolic, imaginary, and real shift. In his earlier work, the symbolic and imaginary are grouped together as defining lived experience and real is the limit condition to both. The proximity to this limit is experienced as anxiety in relation to a presence we never quite glimpse. In Lacan's later work, the imaginary and real are associated as being alike unassimilated to symbolic experience, the one is pre-symbolic, the other is beyond the symbolic. This is how they appear on the Klein Square. The symbolic is associated with absence – in structuralist accounts of meaning, meaning is always deferred – and the real is always full.[25]

Subjects

Giedion's text, like most Modernist texts, is permeated with references to psychoanalysis (he says space conceptions are a cultural unconscious), but he lacks a theory of the subject. Giedion recognises that there is a relation between space and subject. Giedion quotes a neurologist (V. von Weizsacker, 1943) who says that Modern neuroscience cannot explain the perception of space and time *outside* the subject without recourse to space and time *inside* the subject. 'This assertion that space and time also exist within us, that we are not merely immersed in them, and that there exists an interrelation between inner and outer agitation is the best explanation of Paul Klee's drawing, *Scene with running woman* (1925)' in which the motion of the woman texturises the woman and the space (like Duchamp's *Nude descending a staircase*); as if a dynamic inside interacted with a subjective outside. This is Giedion's picture of the Modern subject. What is significant for us is that he shifts his spatial distinction inside/outside architecture to another distinction, inside/outside the psyche.

Let us, as a wager, in response to Giedion, define an Archaic, a Classic, and a Modern subject; and again, on a wager, define them by drawing on Archaic, Classic, and Modern literature. Authors have the capacity to capture in fiction the truth of an age, and both Freud and Lacan drew on literature and the visual arts to explicate psychoanalytic concepts.[26] In the way that Giedion has done, fiction condenses a huge amount of varied empirical data into a single narrative. This is an indicative sample, not a comprehensive survey; the latter would entail an extended research project with a literary historian. We point the way with a representative selection comprising one 'classic' Archaic, Classic, and Modern author.

Archaic space and the Archaic subject

> But the subject was there to rediscover *where it was* – I anticipate – the
> real. ... I use, quite intentionally, the formula - *The gods belong to the field
> of the real.*
>
> *(Lacan)*

> Greek thought remained remote from the psychological probing and
> introspection which were to become the motive force of Christian
> preaching ... [27]
>
> *(Zevi)*

Even a cursory reading of the *Odyssey* reveals a striking fact about the Archaic
subject. They spoke to the gods, and the gods spoke to them. Hearing voices is a
condition of the chaotic life of psychotics, and yet we are loath to say that Archaic
Greek culture was a universal form of psychosis. We need to understand what
the intervention of the gods as a fact of daily life says about the Archaic subject
and its Archaic space. Odysseus traverses the *Odyssey*: a man totally exposed to
the gods, the shifting surface of the wine dark sea, a man in a story that begins
in *medias res* and seems to have no end. Let us take Odysseus at his word. Let us
also assume that because there are no gods now, there were none then. Let us,
therefore, assume that when Odysseus summons Athena, he is holding council
with himself. What we would style as internal council appears to Odysseus as
external dialogue. Odysseus' thought has the reality for him that we usually
attribute to the speech of others. Odysseus has a very different relation to his
own voice than we do.

The Classic and Modern subjects

If, for the Archaic subject, doubt is externalised, for the Classic subject, doubt
is internal and projected into the world. Lacan addresses Descartes frequently in
his text. Lacan says that with the invention of the *Cogito* or subject of cognition,
Descartes introduces the concept of the subject subject to philosophy. Descartes
begins *Meditations on First Philosophy* (1641) as a quest for certainty. He can doubt
the existence of everything except the consciousness that doubts. Only by strip-
ping from his thought all that he doubts is he able to construct – as a thought
experiment – an external world of logical certainty. Descartes' *Cogito* is a single
point of doubting consciousness from which he projects the outer world. In *The
Dioptrics*, which is Descartes' treatise on vision and optics, this *Cogito* first appears
as a sentient being totally encased in a black box from which the world is a projected array of triangulated light. This seeing subject appears as the humanist
paradigm in whose image he sees God. We are familiar with this trope from
Alberti's metaphor for perspective as a window in a wall.[28]

In Samuel Beckett's text, the Modern subject appears in the form of a
dynamic threshold. The novel, *The Unnameable* (1966), is comprised of a single

monologue spoken by an unnamed subject, punctuated by jump cuts. There is no conventional narrative continuity. The subject is on a perpetual journey in which he is never able to attach himself to a body, an identity, a mother, a history; he keeps returning to the figure of the tympanum, for whom speech is poised between silence and babble, being and nothingness, to define his nameless condition. His corporality is replaced by the dynamism of words. In the play *Not I* (1973), the subject of a continuous monologue is lit so that only her mouth is visible. It is spoken as a single urgent sentence whose continuity works against the unity of the subject. If it has an architectural figure, it would be a surface with a mouth in it, not a talking head, but a talking surface. Not a space, nor even a wall with a depth, but a surface from which speech flows in one direction only.[29]

The speaking subject lacks being

The 'subject's [lack of being]' is 'the heart of the analytic experience, as the very field in which the neurotic's passion is deployed'.

Being belongs to the symbolic order since it is 'that relation to the Other in which being finds its status'.[30]

In a radical interpretation of Descartes' *I think therefore I am* that should perhaps be *I think therefore I is*, the speaking subject – Lacan's *parle-être* – calls itself into being as a signifier in the signifier chain by naming itself in the presence of others. Lacan distinguishes being from dumb existence, dumb in the sense of pre-lingual or non-symbolic. Being is what the subject brings to the table by speaking to others. The critical feature of the symbolic order is that it comes with an absence and that absence is the defining feature of the subject. Behind this lack, is an ethics of deferrals and delays (remember Duchamp's *Delay in Glass*) that it would take a course in structural linguistics to unpack. The subject's meaning is never present in its words but is always deferred along the signifier chain. The subject's object of desire is always already lost; it will never have been whole. The subject finds its speech-bourn being, not in itself, but in the signifier chains that constitute the field of the Other. In *Seminar 7 The Ethics of Psychoanalysis*, Lacan mints the term extimacy [*extimité* = exterior + intimate] to indicate the dual location of the speaking subject. There is a symbolic lack that is both intimate to the speaker and in the field of the Other.[31]

The speaking subject also calls its objects into being. There is the real Parthenon that exists as a pile of stones. And there is the Parthenon such that Vitruvius could found a code of proportions, Freud could discover his own Oedipal Complex, Giedion could found a theory of space, and Le Corbusier could be tormented by its *ineffable space*. Nor is it a dumb Le Corbusier who was tormented. That's just a talking head. What torments is a symbolic and imaginary Parthenon, tormenting a symbolic and imaginary Le Corbusier; a Parthenon and a Le Corbusier called into being by speech and given its own temporality. This weave of signifier chains shadows the real world, giving it sense for subjects. This text should have made clear that architectural space is no more given in existence than are the subject and its objects. Language has to name it, put it into a discourse, call it into being. Neither architecture nor the subject need a subjective inside in order to exist as material things, but they desire one. How, in this architectural context, do we make sense of this locus. How can we use architectural thinking to explore the implicit spatiality, the location and orientation of the split subject, it's being, where speech comes from?

It is a question of what relation the subject has to its own voice. For most of us, it simply accompanies us. If pressed, we may say it comes from within. We may have had opinions about it. Most of us have, at times in our lives, liked our voice or wished it were more sonorous; actors get good at projecting it. But most of us do not regard our voice as something to which we have a relationship, let alone a precise one, let alone a spatial one, or that we use architecture to work out our relationship to it. It simply accompanies us. This is where our reading of Giedion through Lacan is leading. We use architecture to articulate the relations of the subject to itself because architecture is a more accessible and tangible medium than the defiles of the signifier; in a similar way, Vitruvius used the orders of the well-formed temple to work out the proportions of the Vitruvian man.

Odysseus raises the shocking possibility of an oracular voice in a world where the significance of the threshold goes unnoticed by architecture; Descartes, a voice that springs fully formed from an internal space of doubt. And Beckett's *Not I*, a tremulous, unstable voice, located in the threshold itself. Descartes' *Cogito* is probably the clearest formula for the subject for whom speech comes from within and for whom space has the imaginary character of a projection. Beckett's *Not I* is not grounded in any form of interior or exterior. The imaginary subject may be a container for meanings, but the symbolic subject is an articulator of difference. Words do many things, but we no longer regard them as containers that contain meanings. We construct the threshold and its horizon by speaking. We build it in architecture. This threshold may go unmarked in the megaron, it may be ornate and monumentalized in the Renaissance palazzo or 'phenomenal' in Le Corbusier and the Moderns.

The architectural model of the speaking subject

The later Lacan (the 1970s Lacan), who turned to topology to model the subject, made the extraordinary claim that the subject had the form of a Mobius strip and not a container. A Mobius strip is visually represented as a loop with a 180-degree twist in it. The loop forms a single sided surface. Because of the twist, if you drill a hole through its surface, you come out on the same side, 360° along the loop. It is beyond our scope to explore topology, but we can see the direction Lacan was heading. The subject is continuous with the field of signifiers – whether this field be language, social relations, or the city – and not a container within the field. There is no inside to the speaking subject except the real inside of blood and guts. Which is why the real often takes the form of an intractable materiality that threatens to reduce reality to a screen. Which, in the loopy manner of psycho-analytic thought returns us to the threshold as the internal surface of space. The speaking subject is always crossing a threshold and facing a horizon. This gives it an orientation, not a location. The subject is always going forward, heading out the psychical door, no matter which side of the architectural threshold it is on.

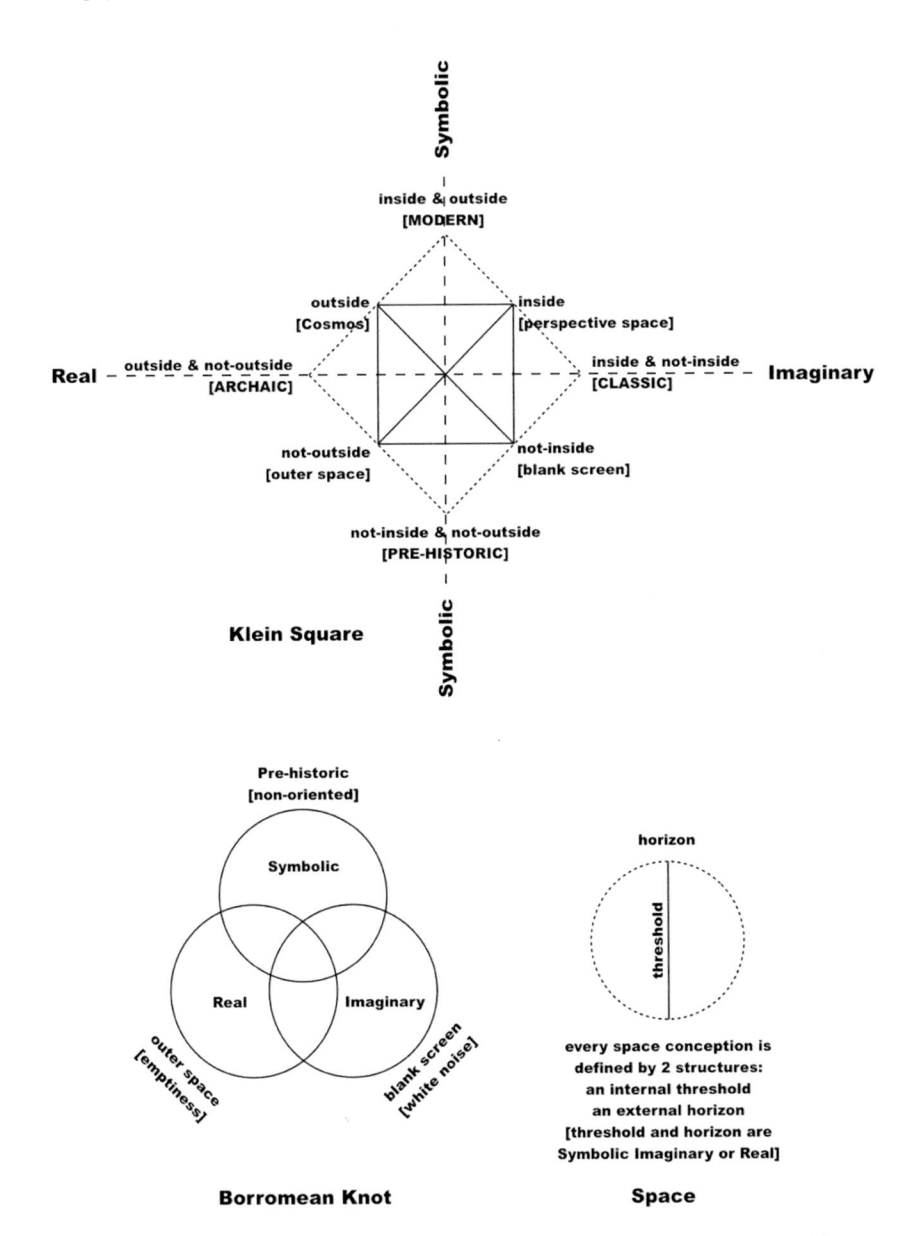

FIGURE 2.5 Diagramming Giedion's history: the subject appears as a series of binary oppositions, as a series of horizons, and as a spatial formation.

(In *The Interpretation of Dreams*, Freud gives his apparatus a direction.) There are not two sides to the threshold of the Modern subject, an inside and an outside that form stable containers, only one side, and the direction the subject is facing depends on where s/he is on the Mobius strip in relation to others. The subject never crosses the threshold because there is no other side to a Mobius strip, s/he only ever travels along it. If this subject has an architectural figure, it would be the *Not I* surface with a mouth in it, not a talking head, but a talking surface. Not a talking container, nor even a wall with a depth, but a surface from which speech flows in one direction only. This is our architectural contribution to modelling subjectivity.

Lacan's formula ego-consciousness is itself a dynamic spatial formation. We said it was a combination of Freud's first (conscious-unconscious) and second (ego-id) topographies. The ego is the agency of identity and repression. According to Freud, the unconscious is formed by repression; according to Lacan, the signifier slips under the bar of signification to become a signified. We shall return to the unconscious when we discuss Rossi's city of collective memory. Here we want to emphasize the spatial ramifications of ego-unconscious. In his paper 'The ego and the id' Freud describes the ego as the reflective outer surface (*now we know it to be a reflective Mobius*) of a psyche whose interior (the id) is the seething cauldron of unconscious desire. The ego is the psychical agency that is attentive to the outer world; the unconscious field of signifiers defines the inner world. The ego is associated with perception and images and the capacity of the subject to identify with objects in the world. We see ourselves reflected in the world. The unconscious is the reservoir of signifiers; those streams of signifiers that are not dammed/damned by the ego emerge into consciousness to form speech, that flow of words that never stops unless we are dead. These signifier chains are the agency of attachment and engagement that bind us to our Parthenons.

If Freud modelled the psyche as an organ-like container, Lacan modelled it as a surface. This is the key difference between them as far as architecture is concerned. Although the body is a container, a skin bag of blood and bones, the psyche is not a container. We associate the threshold with the ego and its agency. The unconscious wells up behind this ego surface, a pressure of signifiers, a narrative head, as it were, calibrated to a lifetime of pressure that begins with the formation of the ego. The ego dares not turn its head to see what catastrophe is looming of its own making. It only knows that behind it is the unconscious pressure that is the source of its speech, the surface from which – if it needs reminding – speech leaks out, slips out, slips of the tongue.

Giedion the Modern subject

Giedion's task in *The Eternal Present* is to understand the Modern by understanding the Archaic and Classic as projections of the Modern. We need to ask where Giedion, the Modern viewing subject, is in this history, and how it positions him. In *Space Time and Architecture*, Giedion says that the task of the historian is to make sense of the present by interpreting the past. The more embedded in the present you are (what Mies and Giedion called *Zeitgeist*), the more authoritative your history. The significance of facts is not stable; facts that are selected as significant are already the result of historic reconstruction. Each present has to work through the past for itself. The past is a projection of the present.[32] This essentially subjective account of the Modern raises questions about the relation of Modern space to Classic and Archaic space.

It is easy to see the Archaic, Classic, and Modern as three rooms in a temporal enfilade, each with their proper qualities (which is how Giedion writes about them – outside, inside, outside/inside = a double exposure), except that this does not account for the fact that one of them is marked. Giedion views the Archaic and the Classic from the position of the Modern. He is not viewing all three spaces from an other outside, which would produce an objective history, but which would beg the question of where he is, and which would again stumble on the problem of the inclusive everywhereness of space. With space, there cannot be a third-person outsider. To the extent that he is also viewing the Modern, it is a look back upon himself and his space that he could only see in the mirror. Giedion's Modern space, the space he is in and viewing at the same time, is not a third category but a form of reflection upon the Archaic and Classic, as if Giedion were viewing the two pasts together and seeing them in a rear view mirror. This double vision, this view of self and other, or view of self as other and view of other, is the formula for subjectivity that Lacan developed in his account of the visual field. It also points to the fact that there is a narcissistic element of any subjective system, which is in a dialectic relation to the signifying elements of the system.

We need to summarise and conclude this reading of Giedion's history with Lacan's subjective registers. His space conceptions survey the different ways that subjective space functions for subjects. We aligned the Archaic with the real, the Classic with the imaginary, and the Modern with the symbolic, with the proviso that only in Giedion's history, which delaminates them temporally and in the analytic setting which picks them apart analytically, could they be considered separately. Every encounter with the world registers on the symbolic, imaginary, and real of the subject.

By reading Giedion with Lacan, we have made a number of discoveries about space that need drawing together, even at risk of repeating ourselves. Giedion's space is a conceptual apparatus with a quite particular structure. It has two surfaces: a threshold and a limit condition. [Figure 2.5, right] We have seen that the threshold is imaginary, symbolic, and real, or else it simply does not exist. Giedion's three space conceptions, plus prehistoric space, mark these four positions on our Klein Square. To say that the threshold is real is tantamount to saying that it is present in the material form of a wall but that it does not organize space for subjects. The threshold is there, but it is not operational. We encounter a real threshold on the rare occasions when we stumble through an opening in a wall and find that it is without significance. The imaginary threshold operates as a screen upon which the outside is projected as an image. We encounter the imaginary threshold when we feel protected by the space we are in, and the world is kept at bay as an image, as when we stand at our hotel window and feel that the strange city we have just arrived at is a very faraway place. The symbolic threshold does what all signifying systems do: it articulates difference rather than creates meanings. It articulates the difference between inside and outside without creating discrete inside and outside spaces. The Modern subject inhabits the gap between them, and inside is whichever side of the threshold the subject is on because the subject carries it with it. The threshold orients in the sense that we are always crossing it in one direction or another. Prehistoric space does not have a threshold, operative or not, so does not orient in any register, which is probably why Giedion excludes it from his system.

To the threshold, which functions as an internal surface, internal because it is always crossed, we add the outer surface or limit condition that is never crossed, in visual terms, the horizon. The limit of the Archaic space of objects, whose real threshold does not function to separate us from our objects, is the realest of real spaces, the limitless emptiness of outer space. Outer space is as close as Giedion's thought gets to the real.[33] The limit condition of Classic space, whose threshold is imaginary is the blank screen, where vision and projection end. That this is a history written from the position of Modern space is confirmed by the fact that Prehistoric space – and not outer space – constitutes Giedion's horizon. The horizon of the Modern subject for whom space is defined by a symbolic threshold, the horizon of a history of space seen from a Modern point of view, of which the Modern is the final stage in a conceptual development, is a space which is not a conception at all. It is to Modern space what non-sense is to sense. These three limit conditions are different forms of non-orientation. They are the ways that the different spaces bump up against the real. We have found that even real space has a limit. This limit – which corresponds to its Borromean ring – is the expiration of sentience in outer space, for even the real is predicated on sentience. If this seems paradoxical, it is because the real is usually understood as the limit to the symbolic and imaginary and not itself defined by a limit.

Together threshold and horizon constitute the typological character of Giedion's space conceptions and link space to subjects to form a subjective architecture. Space and subject form a couple. Threshold and horizon are the constitutive elements of a subjective architecture. They have a material reality that manifests differently in different architectures, and they have the potential to be the basis for an analytic study for a new typology of architecture.

It is important to make clear what a space is and what it is not. These inner and outer surfaces are entirely conceptual. You will not find them as elements in a building. You will only find them in the sense that you understand how the elements of a building – its doors, walls, and windows – function for the subject. Space is not a fictional material like ether. Nor does it have a texture or tactility, as reported by architectural phenomenologists. Nor is it a nothing, like whatever is traversed by the geometry with which we lay out a plan. Or a polite fiction, according to which space is really just the walls that enclose it. As a conceptual fact, space has a power and an efficacy, if not a causality. Architectural space is a conceptual apparatus constructed by subjects using architecture in order to mediate their relation to reality. For Giedion, the development of architecture is understood as the succession of different ways of mediating that relation. Giedion posits a cosmos, never adequately defined but which signifies the enormity of an overarching reality whose only significant feature is that it is beyond the human world and that it is somehow witness to man's actions. It forces us to ask of ourselves, who we are and what we want. Giedion argued that each present reconstructs its past. Probably each present has its cosmos, the reality that holds us to account and from which space shields us. In our present, the cosmos is probably the existential condition of climate change.

Giedion's architectural history leads us to the extraordinary thesis that the subject is spatial and oriented and that its primary spatial characteristic is the relation of the subject to its own voice. It should be clear that subjectivity has little to do with feelings and everything to do with the precise relations between subjects and their voice and between subjects and others (what Lacan refers to as *innenwelt* and *umwelt*, the inner and outer world of the subject). To the best of my knowledge, this is an original contribution by architectural thinking to psychoanalytic discourse. Indeed most architects would probably find Lacan's formula for the subject, ego-unconscious, implicitly spatial. I regard it as an omission that Lacan does not apply architectural thinking to the subject. The history of architecture is the history of subjects using architecture to work out their spatial modalities. We shall take forward the question of the space of the subject in the next chapter on perspective, but in a different way, in relation to identity and desire.

The conditions for inhabitation of architecture and subjects are the same. The Archaic subject experiences it's voice as if it were outside, something it could encounter in the way that it might encounter an other subject. The Archaic subject is essentially a solid. The Classic subject is a container, a sounding chamber with an internalised sentience, and its voice comes from within. The Modern subject is a surface that articulates spatial difference without defining or enclosing space; its voice emerges from the difference between sides. These ways of characterising the subject suggest different formal properties and formal metaphors. The Archaic can be shaped but not hollowed. The Classic subject can be filled with qualities. The Modern subject can be folded, looped, bent, stretched, … whatever you can do with a surface.

The nothing that makes inhabitation possible

It has been the joint aims of this chapter to trace the consequences of treating space as a conceptual category by reading it against Lacan's three registers of subjective experience. It should be clear that architecture is one of the great conceptual systems, along with, e.g., the money, marriage, and language systems, such that buildings and cities have been codified in treatises, statutory instruments and guidance notes, renaissance paintings, and movies. To insist that space is conceptual is to call attention to the signifying aspects of architecture. We create meaning in the world by articulating difference. Architecture is positioned against junkspace, the space whose effect is to destroy difference and thereby to destroy meaning in the world: the difference between, e.g., inside and outside, private and public, city and countryside .... We will return to architecture's mandate in the conclusion. Here we want to make one final point about symbolic systems.

Every symbolic system constructs a subject and an object. That object is a conceptual object. We don't find them in the world, we construct them. They are moreover, inter-subjective. In the marriage system, it is a particular form of union. In the money system, it is value. In the Architecture system, it is space. For the Modern subject, space is the nothing that makes inhabitation possible. Without the conceptual category of space, we could not talk about what architecture does for subjects. Architecture would be inert material and the Parthenon would be just stones. Space is the precondition for inhabitation, without which inhabitation is simply location. Subjects had to create space so that it could inhabit architecture. The subjects inhabit space the way they inhabit themselves. When we inhabit architecture, we are in something of which we are conceptually part. Architecture constructs the subject of space, the spatial subject, if not an individual alone, then one of many, at least a western Europeanised one, because a concept is always the concept of someone and architecture is the tool and labour of humans. Space is a concept articulated through architecture *by* a subject *for* an other subject. It is an offer. An exchange. A generosity. A creation. Space is a concept that we impose upon the world by architectural means driven by desire.

Notes

1 Unless indicated otherwise, all page references in the text are to Sigfried Giedion, *The Eternal Present: The Beginnings of Architecture: A Contribution on Constancy and Change* (London: Oxford University Press, 1964).

2 Giedion's space *conception* has affinities to the philosopher and social theorist Michel Foucault's *episteme*. The episteme refers to the organization of knowledge, the conditions for its production, its uses, and the forms of its dissemination, that defines a historical period. In *The Order of Things*, Foucault distinguishes between the Classical and Modern episteme. In the former, knowledge is organised by the glittering resemblances between things 'analogies, sympathies, juxtapositions': things are the same or different. In the Modern episteme, the age of encyclopedias, knowledge is organized by a classificatory grid, a network of signs that positions man within it. These correspond roughly to Lacan's imaginary (resemblances, the same or different) and symbolic orders (network of signs). See Foucault, *The Order of Things: An Archaeology of the Human Sciences* (New York: Vintage, 1970). See also the short entry *episteme* in Craig Calhoun, *Dictionary of the Social Sciences* (OUP, 2002), p. 145.

3 Bruno Zevi, *Architecture as Space: How to Look at Architecture: 186 Photographs Drawings Plans* (New York: Horizon Press, 1957), pp. 76 and 78, respectively. See also Norburg-Schultz, *Meaning in Western Architecture*.

4 Sigfried Giedion, *Space Time and Architecture: The Growth of a New Tradition* (Cambridge, MA: Harvard University Press, 1967), quote pp. 30–31, urbanism pp. 41ff.

5 Robert Slutzky, 'Aqueous Humor', *Oppositions* 19/20 (1980), pp. 28–51.

6 Mark Jarzombek, *The Psychologizing of Modernity: Art, Architecture, History* (Cambridge: Cambridge University Press, 2000). The fact that the use of psychology and philosophy was largely unacknowledged, opened the door to revisionism, something we will touch on again at the end of this chapter. For the 'disciplinary presence of psychology', p. 187, he cites among others, empathy theory in Heinrich Wölfflin. He cites Martin Heidegger's 'Building Dwelling Thinking' as the culmination of historical revisionism. For the quote, see p. 188.

7 Giedion's historic progression Archaic (outside), Classic (inside), and Modern (outside and inside) has the whiff of Hegel's thesis, antithesis, and synthesis, as if with the development of the Modern spatial subject, we have reached the resolution and terminal point of history.

8 Le Corbusier, *Towards a New Architecture*, translated by. Frederick Etchells (New York: Holt Reinhart and Winston, 1960), the chapter titled 'Regulating Lines', pp. 65–71.

9 The symbolic and imaginary are not unrelated to Freud's word- and thing-presentations in his paper 'The Unconscious (1915)' for which see A. Richards and J. Strachey, eds., *Sigmund Freud: On Metapsychology* (London: Penguin, 1991), pp. 167–222.

10 See, for instance, 'The Direction of the Treatment and the Principles of Its Power (1958)', in *Écrits: The First Complete Edition in English* (New York: W.W. Norton, 2006) p. 513. 'It is not that easy to master the structure Freud isolated in the subject unless you distinguish therein the symbolic from the imaginary and the real'.

11 As nouns, the three orders are sometimes capitalised by Lacan's commentators but rarely by Lacan. Lacan sometimes abbreviated them as *SIR* (capitalised), which suggests class mastery or bondage/discipline games. It suggests that there is a degree to which one has to submit to psychoanalysis in order to accept its arguments. See Jacques Lacan, 'The Function and Field of Speech and Language in Psychoanalysis (1953)', in *Écrits op. cit.* pp. 197–268. See also an early translation and extensive commentary by Anthony Wilden as *Speech and Language in Psychoanalysis (1956)* (Baltimore: Johns Hopkins University Press, 1968).

12 Jacques Lacan, 'The Mirror Stage as Formative of the I Function as Revealed in Psychoanalytic Experience (1949)' in *Écrits op. cit.* Quotes pp. 76 and 78. Lacan's *italics*.

13 In Greek mythology, Narcissus dies because he sees his reflected image in the still surface of a woodland pond, and he wants to be it.

14 Lacan, 'Instance of the Letter in the Unconscious' (1957) in *Écrits op. cit.* pp. 414–15. The sign also has a referent. The word 'dog' (signifier) refers either to a dog or the thought of a dog. Its use may signify contempt (signified). It is beyond the scope of this text to untangle the complexity of the sign. It is a contested territory in the humanities. The critic Harold Bloom reckons that post-structural thought is forever conflating the difference between meaning and signification, for which see Harold Bloom, *Poetry and Repression: Revisionism from Blake to Stevens* (London: Yale University Press, 1976). Meaning has been under attack by structuralism since the work of Saussure. In Derrida, meaning as presence is always already deferred. Eisenman, following Derrida, attacks meaning, in his formal experiments with deconstruction. In Lacan, meaning is imaginary. You 'see' your meaning, feel its justifying presence, but all you pass on to your others is the significance of what you say.

15 See Claude Lévi-Strauss, *Introduction to the Work of Marcel Mauss* (London: Routledge and Kegan Paul, 1987), p. 16. He defines the characteristics of symbolic systems: collective and institutional (pp. 10–13). 'Mauss defined social life …, as a *world of symbolic relationships*' (p. 10). Cf. also the entry on the symbolic in Evans, *Dictionary of Lacanian Psychoanalysis* (London: Routledge, 1996) p. 201.

16 Ridley Scott, dir., *Alien* (20th Century Fox, 1979). The alien special effects were designed by biomechanical artist Hans Rudolf Giger.

17 Kant seems to be running unacknowledged in the background of Giedion as well. Immanuel Kant argued in *The Critique of Pure Reason* that space and time are preconditions for the material world of things and not directly part of it. Without the spacing and temporizing of things, which is a conception that we bring to the world, there could be no things as we know them. He posits *things-in-themselves* as the condition of things before they are individuated by our conceptual apparatus.

18 In order to interlink with each other, the three Borromean rings cannot be circles lying in a single plane but must be projections of ellipses rotated in space. They get their name from the coat of arms of the Borromeo family, although the symbol has been current since antiquity and is currently used in the logo of Ballantine Beer. For Koolhaas on Le Corbusier, see *Delirious New York: A Retroactive Manifesto for Manhattan* (New York: The Monacelli Press, 1978). He argues that concrete functioned in Le Corbusier's thought to turn even the wildest formal fantasies into reality. The Manhattan grid had the same function for the sober developers of Manhattan.

19 Lacan discusses Merleau-Ponty's *The Visible and the Invisible* in connection with the visual field in *The Four Fundamental Concepts ... op. cit.*, pp. 70ff.

20 Giedion, *op. cit.*, pp. 499–502 and 523–525. According to Giedion, *raum* does not enter architectural aesthetic discourse until Schmartzov introduced it toward the end of the 19th century (Adrian Forty reiterates this point in *Words and Buildings*). Although the word may not have been used in architectural discourse, arguably, space has always been represented in architecture.

21 The Archaic seen through Modern eyes is imagined in Jean-Luc Godard's film *Le Mepris* [translated *Contempt*] (1963) with Brigit Bardot and Fritz Lang (*playing himself, he is the Mies van der Rohe of film*), filmed on the rooftop of Adalberto Libera's Casa Malaparte. Also with Jack Palance, Michel Piccoli, and Giorgia Moll.

22 Leon Battista Alberti, *On Painting (Della Pittura)* (New Haven, CT: Yale University Press, 1435/1966); Adrea Pozzo, *Perspective in Architecture and Painting (Perspectiva Architectorum et Pictorum)* (New York: Dover, 1707/1989).

23 Colin Rowe and Robert Slutzky, 'Transparency: Literal and Phenomenal', *Perspecta 8* (1963), pp. 45–54; and Phyllis Lambert, *Mies in America* (Montreal: CC d'A, 2001).

24 The Klein Square was introduced into art historical discourse by Rosalind Krauss, for which see her 'Sculpture in the Expanded Field', *October* 8 (Spring 1979) pp. 31–44.

25 The asymmetries between the three orders are reflected in Freud's psychical apparatus (see figure 1.2). Its components relate to the imaginary and the symbolic orders: the unconscious and preconscious memory layers, sandwiched by sensory input and motor action at either ends. That from which the arrow emerges and to which it returns, but which remains unmarked by the diagram, may be the real, for it is quite strictly outside the apparatus.

26 Lacan has papers on Poe, Hamlet, de Sade, and James Joyce.

27 Lacan, *The Four Fundamental Concepts ... op. cit.* p. 45, his italics; Zevi, *Architecture as Space:... op. cit.* p. 77.

28 Cf. René Descartes, *Meditations on First Philosophy* (1641) and *Dioptrique* (1637) in Descartes, *Discourse on the Method and Meditations on First Philosophy* (Cambridge: Hackett Press, 1989) translated by. Donald A Cress. Cf. also, Lacan, *The Four Fundamental Concepts ...op. cit.* p. 44.

29 Cf. the poetics of silence and babble in Adrienne Janus, 'In One Ear and Out the Others: Beckett ... Mahon ... Muldoon', *Journal of Modern Literature* 30:2 (Winter 2007), 180–196. Lacan's engagement with Beckett is limited to a few comments, unlike his treatment of James Joyce, for whom *Finnegan's Wake* (1938) was, he argued, a way out of psychosis. A number of recent publications have put Lacan with Beckett. These include Rahime Çokay Nebioglu, 'Turning Language Inside Out in Beckett's *Not I*' in *Ankara Üniversitesi Dil ve Tarih-Coğrafya Fakültesi Dergisi* (Ankara University, 2018); Llewellyn Brown, *Beckett, Lacan, and the Voice* (Columbia University Press, 2017); Arka Chattopadhyay, 'Lacan and Beckett: Acts of Writing between Psychoanalysis and Literature' in *Samuel Beckett Today/Aujourd'hui* 29:1 (2017); Arka Chatto-

padhyay's PhD thesis *'Just enough still to joy': Beckett, Lacan and the jouissance of writing a little real* (Western Sydney University, 2016); and Suzanne Dow, 'Lacan with Beckett', *Nottingham French Studies* 53:1 (2014). For Beckett, see Samuel Beckett, *Not I* (1973) performed by Billie Whitelaw, the Royal Court Theatre, London, from which image 2.1 is taken; and *The Unnamable* (1953), the third novel in the trilogy *Molloy; Malone Dies; The Unnamable* (London: 1966), p. 352 for the figure of the tympanum.

30 *manque à être* translated as *want-to-be* by Fink and Sheridan and as *lack of being* by Evans. See Dylan, *op. cit.*, pp. 16, 95. We go with *lack* because that is how *manque* is translated elsewhere in Lacan's text. You only want what you lack. Both quotes from Lacan, 'The Direction of the Treatment and the Principles of Its Power' in *Écrits, op cit.*, p. 251.

31 Lacan, *The Seminar of Jacques Lacan, Book VII: The Ethics of Psychoanalysis 1959–1960* (New York: Norton, 1992), p. 139.

32 Giedion compares history to relativity theory. Each age has to reconstruct its own history. 'Today we consciously examine the past from the point of view of the present to place the present in a wider dimension of time, so that it can be enriched by those aspects of the past that are still valid'. Giedion, *Space Time and Architecture: The Growth of a New Tradition* (Cambridge, MA: Harvard University Press, 1967), p. 7. Lacan says something similar, 'History is not the past. History is the past in so far as it is historicised in the present', in *The Seminar of Jacques Lacan, Book 1: Freud's Papers on Technique 1953–1954.*

33 And, like the real, it comes with a threat. It threatens to undermine his conceptual edifice of space. 'It is possible to give physical limits to space, but by its nature, space is limitless and intangible. Space dissolves in darkness and … infinity. To become visible, space must acquire form and boundaries either from nature or by the hand of man'. Giedion, *op. cit.*, p. 494.

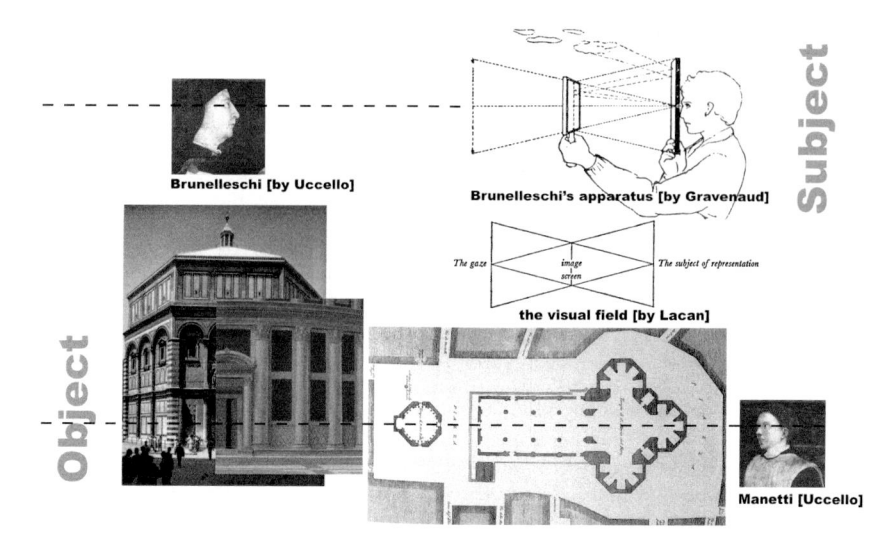

FIGURE 3.1   The distribution of the seeing subject in the visual field.

3

BRUNELLESCHI AND THE VISUAL FIELD [DESIRE AND SPACE]

Lacan said the unconscious was structured like a language. We say space is structured like a picture. We do not know how the Renaissance architect Filippo Brunelleschi (1377–1446) invented perspective (unlike Leonardo, he left no sketchbooks, he sculpted models from turnips); all we have is the account by his biographer Antonio Manetti, writing 20 years after his death, of how, in the second decade of the 15th century, he demonstrated it to the good people of Florence.

Brunelleschi painted a picture of the Florence Baptistery on a square wooden panel from a position standing inside the central portal of the Florence Cathedral so that it framed his view. According to Manetti, the panel evinced the fine skill of a miniaturist and had the 'effect of reality'. He drilled a 'pea-sized' hole at its vanishing point. He asked a participant to stand in the position he had stood when he painted the picture and view the Baptistery through the

DOI: 10.4324/9780429022845-3

peephole with the painted surface facing the Baptistery. He gave the participant a mirror and had him/her lift the mirror up to view the picture, then drop it to view the Baptistery. Up and down. First a view of the Baptistery, then a picture of the view of the Baptistery. The role of the mirror seems to have been to demonstrate the perfect fit between the view and Brunelleschi's picture of the view.[1]

It is not known how Brunelleschi painted the picture or what it looked like. In *The Origin of Perspective*, Damisch argues that it was one of a transformation series of paintings that included the three extant anonymous 15th-century *Ideal City* panels. In the panel at Urbino, which includes a Baptistery-like building with an open door, he finds evidence of a pinhole at the vanishing point. The pinhole is located on the open door as if someone were about to step out into the piazza to view the painter. It is not known how he got the idea that the painting could be organised by the geometry of perspective with a vanishing point that positioned its painter/viewer. The most peculiar bit of the demonstration was the mirror, which I have shown would *not* have achieved the desired effect of verisimilitude. Given the geometry of reflection, which includes the position of the eye point, the angles of incidence and reflection, plus the relative sizes and positions of the mirror and panel, the mirror would never have been able to align the view and the picture of the view. The mirror – by alternating between them – would have accentuated their differences, accentuated the lack of fit between picture and reality.[2]

It seems that the mirror had a symbolic rather than a practical function. The mirror was perhaps necessary to announce the optical model that underlies the geometry of perspective. A generation later, when Alberti published the first theoretical account and codification of *construzione legittima*, he described the picture plane as a transparent section through the pyramid of vision formed by the eye at the point of convergence of radiating sight lines (the apex) and the viewed object at the base, with Brunelleschi's square panel capturing the image at the intersection.

The mirror was also exotic. In the early 1400s, it was a rare and expensive item. Its presence was necessary as an alluring surface, a source of fascination and desire. No one can walk past a storefront without glancing at their image. Behind the allure of the well-formed image – and perspective is nothing if not the definition of the well-formed image - lies the fascination we all have with our own image, the allure of identity. Lacan calls it captivation, we are captured by our image.

There are several lessons to extract from this drama between the participant viewer, the view of the Baptistery, and the painter Brunelleschi, about the difference between view and picture, perception and representation, self and other, and finally, identity desire and authority. The relations enacted in this drama are encoded in every perspective. They will explain the hegemonic position of perspective in architecture and other realist practices. Identity first. Perspective makes a direct appeal to the ego. In effect, Brunelleschi asked his participant to put on a Florence Baptistery mask, and we can assume s/he experienced the same 'look, its *not* me!' frisson of identity we experience when, on the way out the door to a fancy dress party, we glance at the mirror. The demonstration was a staged enactment of identification with a building.

The identity of the ego

> ... this experience sets us at odds with any philosophy directly stemming from the *cogito*.
>
> *(p. 75)*

> It suffices to understand the mirror stage ... *as an identification*, ...: namely, the transformation that takes place in the subject when he assumes an image ....
>
> *(p. 76, Lacan's italics)*[3]

In 'The Mirror Stage as formative of the function of the I as revealed in psychoanalytic experience' (1949), Lacan argues that the formation of the ego is modelled on what happens when the enfant sees itself in the mirror and identifies with it. It is probably the paper in *Écrits* which is most referred to in the visual arts and architecture. We mentioned the mirror stage as the inauguration of the imaginary order, which is the register where the ego is most virulent. Ego and identity are closely related in Lacan's text. We do not construct the ego, we assume an image. It was his first paper, an early version of which was published in 1937. It is one of his most explicitly spatial papers. Identity is defined as the self-image, the image you have of yourself. It puts the ego in the imaginary register, with all the doubt this casts upon the ego as a source of knowledge, even though the ego polices the threshold between inner liquid world of unconscious desire and outer geometric world of optic reality. It is Lacan's answer to Freud's paper 'The Ego and the Id' (1923), in which Freud describes the ego as the reflective outer surface of the id.

> This jubilant assumption of his specular image by the [child]... – still trapped in his motor impotence and nursling dependence - ...seems to me to manifest... the symbolic matrix in which the *I* is precipitated in a primordial form, ...before language restores to it,... its function as subject.
>
> *(p. 76)*

> This development is experienced as a temporal dialectic that decisively projects the individual's formation into history: the mirror stage is a drama whose internal pressure pushes precipitously from insufficiency to anticipation – and which manufactures for the subject, caught up in the lure of

spatial identification, the succession of phantasies that extends from a frag-mented body-image to a form of its totality that I shall call orthopedic – and lastly, to the assumption of the armour of an alienating identity, which will mark with its rigid structure the subject's entire mental development. Thus to break out of the circle of the *Innenwelt* into the *Umwelt* generates the inexhaustible quadrature of the ego's verifications.

(p. 78)

The enfant subject sees itself as a well-formed image at a time when its body is still experienced as disorganised and outwith its control. It sees itself moreover with a continuous contour that distinguishes it from what it is not – space and other objects – at a time when it has not yet clearly separated itself from its mother. The subject makes the first distinction between self and other in terms of the image, which shows it to be a whole object. It is, moreover, out there in the world. Typically it responds to its image with *jubilation* in the adoring gaze of its mother. Hereafter, Lacan writes, the subject is caught in a drama between insufficiency and anticipation, the reality of the self that is never what it might be in relation to an ideal image of what it could be.

Although it is presented as a narrative of development with the before-after form of a temporal dialectic, the mirror stage is not a stage that we pass through but a stage as in Shakespeare's 'all the world's a stage'. We continuously re-enact the mirror stage as one of the structures of subjectivity, in which the subject is put before an image of itself.

That the image is the basis for identity and that identity is a surface phenom-enon is perhaps demonstrated by the reality television show *Big Brother*, in which the architectural plan of the house is opened out to the camera's gaze as a kind of anamorphic opposite of the perspectivated space of Teatro Olympico. The surfaces are reflective, the inhabitants talk to the camera as if to a mirror instead of to each other; and all topics of conversation revolve around who they *really* are, and what they *really* mean. The armoured ego projects an external world where it verifies itself inexhaustibly. This extreme ego talk indicates that the contestants are operating in an extreme imaginary order.

The desire of the subject

In *The Four Fundamental Concepts of Psychoanalysis*, Lacan presents an extended dis-cussion of what he calls the *visual field*. It is not the only place he discusses desire, but it is where he discusses it in visual terms and hence in terms that assimilate to the space that architecture makes. It is where he published his diagram of the visual field. He argues that vision for the subject is an effect of its unconscious desire to be seen by others, in Lacan's terms, to be in the centre of someone else's picture. We want to be at the vanishing point. *The Four Fundamental Concepts …* was the eleventh annual seminar, but it was the first seminar published and it was published before they were formatted as *The Seminar* series. The thrust of his argument is that neither the physiology of the eye nor the geometry of perspective projection – what Lacan calls 'geometral optics' – are adequate to explain the phenomenon of vision. Perspective geometry is only half the story. In order for the world to be visible to me, I must also be visible to others. It is not enough to open my eyes and let the light flood in. I must be in it for others too. Like my unconscious, my visibility is an inter-subjective effect of the presence of others. In the ideal city, the Baptistery door must be open.

This argument is built from several positions in an extended four-chapter section called 'Of The Gaze as *objet petit a*'. It is not a linear argument, more like several parallel strands with a cumulative effect. He does not discuss Brunelleschi's demonstration, but he does discuss Holbein's *The Ambassadors* (1533) as a dialogue between the optics of death and desire; and in *Seminar XIII*, he discusses the perspective in Velasquez's *Las Meninas* (1656). In this section, Lacan introduces one of the key components of the psychic apparatus, *objet petit a*, the little other (*autre*), to distinguish it from the big Other. *Objet petit a* (usually shortened to *objet a*) appears in a number of contexts in Lacan's text, with a number of functions. It is the object of desire, the cause of desire, the object of the drive; the gaze is the manifestation of the object in the visual field. The discussion of vision is framed by the discussion of repetition, the compulsion to repeat, which is the hallmark of the drive. We will endeavour to unpack this complex argument by reference back to Brunelleschi's demonstration as a kind of worked example, and it will repay us by going some way towards explaining the compelling nature of the demonstration. We will return to the drive again in Chapter 5 on politics, society, and the city.

Lacan's intention paradoxically is to drive a wedge between perspective and vision. The blind understand perspective. Lacan cites Descartes' treatise on optics, in which Descartes explains vision on the analogy of a blind man who uses a cane to detect objects in his path, the way the sighted use sight lines. The blind understand what sight, vision, and perspective are and what it is to be seen; they have no trouble navigating the visual world and using optical concepts. Like the sighted, the blind have a visual field. What they

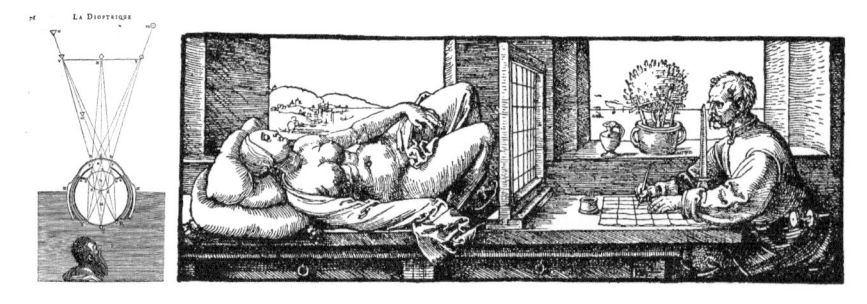

FIGURE 3.2 Two studies of visual desire: Descartes' *Cogito* constructs the visual world *a priori* + Durer's painter draws a perspective from sight.

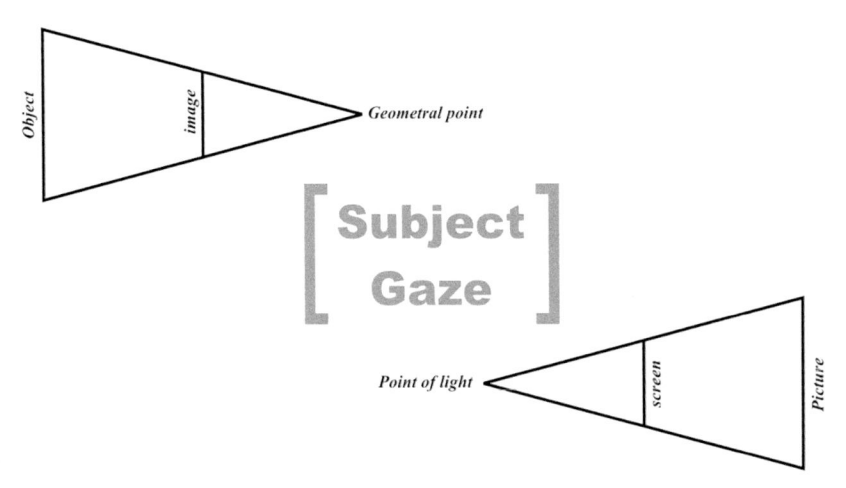

'The relation of the subject with the organ is at the heart of our experience. Among all the organs with which we deal, the breast, the faeces, etc., there is the eye, and it is striking to see... p.91

FIGURE 3.3 Object image Point | Point screen Picture: Lacan's diagram of the visual field is an *operational montage* of two triangles. One is a geometric projection from point to object; the other is an optical projection from light source to picture.

cannot do is see. Which means that the visual field of the subject comes from elsewhere than the subject's perception. The lesson of perspective, in so far as it is the model for the visual field, is that we are invisible in our own visual field. The only way we appear in our visual field is as a blind spot, which is tantamount to an unconscious blot on the centre of consciousness. It is like the hole in Brunelleschi's picture, which was necessary for viewing the object and positioning the subject, even as it obliterates the focal point of the picture. Descartes seems to have tacitly recognised the inadequacy of the perspective model when he modelled his seeing *Cogito* as a sentient presence within a black box. The optical geometry is there but the subject is blind and the centre is empty. The subject needs to come out of the black box and be made visible by appearing to another subject.

Lacan's diagram is a montage of two perspective projection diagrams: two pyramids of vision projecting in opposite directions from eye to object and laid on top of each other. Lacan begins by explaining them separately.[4] The surface at which they intersect is the site of both an image and a screen. Lacan calls it an 'operational montage'. The first triangle, with the 'geometral point' at the apex and the baseline at the object and intersected by the image, is essentially the conventional perspective diagram. It describes perception, but paradoxically, the image is essentially a plotting of points, as anyone who has ever constructed a perspective from plan and section will know and has little to do with visual phenomena. The second triangle, with the point of light at the apex and the

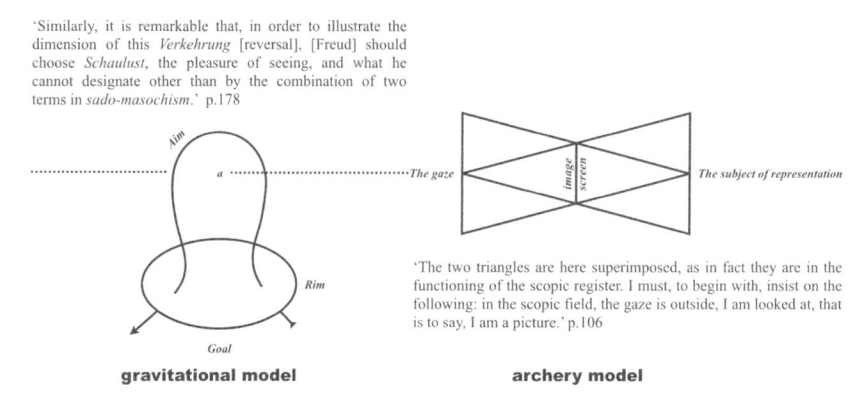

FIGURE 3.4 Lacan's diagram of the drive as a flow of signifiers + Lacan's diagram of the visual field as a negotiation between two cones of vision, one emanating from the subject of representation, the other emanating from the gaze of others, in which the desire of the subject appears as a picture.

picture at the base, intersected by the picture-producing screen, is effectively the diagram of a slide projector aiming at the lecturer. It produces pictures on a screen. This second triangle must be included in order to account for vision. Brunelleschi's demonstration – with our viewer looking out at the Baptistery and via the mirror, seeing a picture of the view of the Baptistery projected back onto him/her – matches it closely.

When Lacan montages the triangles, the point of light is condensed with the object to produce the gaze, and the geometral point is condensed with the picture to produce the subject. The subject and the gaze are now opposite each other, the way eye point and vanishing point are opposite each other in perspective. The gaze stares back. The visual field is shown as a triangulation of images, which describes the coincidence between my vision and my visibility. My visibility, and in particular, the visibility of my desire, is a question of the gaze – or the vision of others – rather than simply that I am bathed in light. In the Durer engraving of an artist using a gridded screen to draw a perspective of his model, he forgets that he is staging his lusty desire for all the world to see.[5]

> I must, to begin with, insist on the following: in the scopic field, the gaze is outside, I am looked at, that is to say, I am a picture.[6]

My visibility is tantamount to *I am a picture*. At this point, it would help to explain what Lacan means by a picture and to distinguish picture and image. I make this distinction in *Brunelleschi Lacan Le Corbusier*.[7] Lacan does not make this distinction, but it is implicit in his argument and he uses 'image' and 'picture' in different positions in his diagram; we have already touched on it in Brunelleschi's demonstration. Perception is a matter of having images. The image relates to the imaginary order. It is proper to a subject in the sense that no one else can have my images or my views. The picture is a visual signifier. The picture is the image of an other, in so far as it is lifted out of experience and communicated back to the subject through photographs, paintings, descriptions, and other socially constructed codes that constitute representation. When we say space is a picture, we mean it is socially constructed. In the demonstration, the role of the mirror was to match the participant's view of the Baptistery (i.e., the subject's image) with Brunelleschi's view of it (his picture). The picture belongs in the symbolic order; the image belongs in the flesh. In order for someone else to have my images, I need to run them through the symbolic circuit. Hence, in Lacan's diagram, the subject is the subject of representation, not perception.

Lacan continues.

> This is the function that is found at the heart of the institution of the subject in the visible. What determines me, at the most profound level, in the visible, is the gaze that is outside. It is through the gaze that I enter light and it is from the gaze that I receive its effects. Hence it comes about that the gaze is the instrument through which light is embodied and through which – if you allow me to use a word, as I often do, in a fragmented form – I am *photo-graphed*.[8]

The operational montage makes me a visual signifier for others and for myself, i.e., I am a part of someone else's picture, by 'graphing' me with light, thereby *instituting* me (*or installed the way you may be installed in a room*) in the field of visual signifiers. The subject is put in relation to an other, on account of which it has its visibility. Lacan's visual field is the field of visual signifiers, within which the subject articulates its desire.

We can see that the subjective and the phenomenological are different. The subjective account of vision is about the symbolic support for visual experience – my vision and my visibility to others; it is not about how or why or what we see (physiological); still less, what it is like to see (phenomenological). My visibility to myself is a question of my visibility to others, their images of me represented to me as pictures. There is the question of which is prior, image or picture, perception or representation, and it is here that phenomenology and psychoanalysis part company. Phenomenology assumes that perception is prior and can be accessed via a process of inward reflection. Psychoanalysis insists that all subjectivity is inter-subjectivity: two comes before one; my perception cannot exist without your representations; perception cannot exist without a prior syntax of representation that structures it. My originary perception such as it may exist, remains fleeting, inchoate, unknown and unusable to me until I map it into a world of representation. Remember the mirror stage: the mother supports the infant in the emergence of its ego, private experience embedded in the flesh of the subject is retroactively authorised and made significant to the subject through her adoring gaze. Psychoanalysis, unlike phenomenology, is a practice as well as a theory: in the analytic setting, which is the psychoanalytic laboratory, the inner self emerges through the subject's encounter with the other.

> Only the subject – the human subject, the subject of the desire that is the essence of man – is not, unlike the animal, entirely caught up in this imaginary capture. He maps himself in it. How? In so far as he isolates the function of the screen and plays with it. Man, in effect, knows how to play with the mask as that beyond which there is the gaze. The screen is here the locus of mediation.[9]

The subject is not simply captured by the allure of the image, the way a fish bites a lure. The subject maps itself on the picture, locates himself on it, and plays with image and picture (self and other) like a screen. Desire manifests visually by the drive to be made visible. In the subjective world, there is no other sense to *made visible* than *made visible to others*. In the present context, this desire is to be in the centre of someone else's picture, to be caught in their gaze. *Gaze* is the English translation of the French *regard*. It is also translated by the slightly more prosaic *look*. Look or gaze does not invoke the internal experience of seeing, but the externalised aspect of vision, in other words, what the subject sees of what others see. The apparatus defined by Gaze-image|screen-Subject puts the subject in the picture. We experience this frisson when we momentarily lock looks with a stranger.[10]

The gaze and the enigma ... death

In Lacan's treatment of visual desire in *The Four Fundamental Concepts*, there are two stories or anecdotes. The story of the glint of light and the story of *The Ambassadors*. I discuss them in detail in *Brunelleschi Lacan Le Corbusier*, and I flag them again because they are important in understanding how subject positions and object legibility function in relation to desire.[11] Lacan condenses object and other, *objet a* and gaze; they are the analogue of the vanishing point in a picture, the placeholder for desire like a lieutenant is a place holder for authority. We are aware of it at times when we feel that we are being looked at. The gaze, which never appears except as the hole in the picture through which Brunelleschi's viewer viewed him/herself, is the place where I and my objects become visible to myself and to others. The twin fantasies of perspective are that you are in the centre of the picture, in other words, in the other's vanishing point, when more than likely, the other does not see you. And that you are invisible in your own visual field so as to allow for the unimpeded legibility of your objects.

Lacan tells a story from his youth where, for teenage work experience, he is assisting Brittany fishermen. He feels that he is the centre of his *Boy's Own* adventure when really he is being tolerated by the local fisherman for whom fishing is their life and death livelihood. One of the fishermen says to him, 'see that glint of light', pointing to a tin floating in the sea, 'a witness to the canning industry which we were supposed to supply'. Lacan looks at the point of light, where upon the fisherman says to him, 'Well, it doesn't see you!'. Lacan had no place in that picture. Poor little rich boy. The point of light at once instituted Lacan in the field of vision and banished him to its periphery.

In Holbein's painting *The Ambassadors* (1533), an enigmatic phallus-like streak crosses the picture field of objects, disrupting it. It looks like something, but it is not clear what. It is about as close to 'creepy' or uncanny as renaissance pictures get. The ambassadors are posing with their exquisite objects, looking at us not the objects. More likely than not, we are looking at the objects, except for the streak that impedes our view and which from the proper angle, compresses into a skull. For Lacan, the lesson of *The Ambassadors* is that desire and the drives lead to death. *Beyond the pleasure principle* (Freud), which is the domain of desire according to which we accumulate our fine objects of wealth, taste, love, and distinction, lies the death drive. In the present context, the lesson of anamorphism is slightly different: it strips the picture of its likeness so that we realise that it is not just a picture but also a signifier. A picture of a phallus/skull is also a signifier of death. If there is an illusion of perspective (like Le Corbusier's 'Illusion of Plans'), it is the illusion that the picture of your object is *not* also a signifier signifying something else that you will never find by looking but only by analysis. In projective geometry, anamorphism is the general condition of projection, and perspective is the special case where projection is normal to the projective plane. It is only in this condition that the signifier of the object looks like the object. From the position of Lacan's glint of light, every projection is anamorphic. What is an altar from my position at the door of the cathedral is a streak from the position of an other. You approach the altar expecting love and salvation and all it is, is a stone. The altar is the anamorphism for something we would not recognise. It is not exactly death that haunts the picture, but signification. (The problem of the haunted house: every bump has too much significance.) Signification positions things syntactically but not within the tidy quadrature of the perspective apparatus.

Return to the mirror stage – externalising the image of the inner world

> These reflections lead me to recognize in the spatial capture manifested by the mirror stage, the effect in man, even prior to this social dialectic, ...
>
> *(p. 77)*

> The function of the mirror stage … is to establish a relationship between an organism and its reality, or … between the *Innenwelt* and the *Umwelt*.
>
> *(p. 78)*

The critical trope of the mirror stage is the generative move to the outside, a spatialising and externalising gesture. The infant subject is formed when it appears to itself as an image that becomes a picture out there, in the world, on a mirror, so that it can be reflected upon by itself and others. In developmental terms, once the subject is so externalised, its world will bifurcate into a world of others and a retroactively attributed inner world; prior to which infant and mother will have been part of the continuous flesh of the world, neither inside nor outside; and the infant an inchoate affair, un-named to itself, un-identified, un-formed, and if animated, animated by a pressure or drive to be visible, rather than any form of realised visibility. In terms of *The Four Fundamental Concepts* … written some 20 years later, the mirror stage is the moment when the subject becomes visible to self and others as a picture. Once it enters the subjective world as a picture in a mirror stage, the subject takes on a form, identity, and significance. This identity can be shared, manipulated, framed, reflected, deflected, dodged, faked, tagged, targeted, or tweeted.

Innenwelt-umwelt recalls the binary terms of Giedion's history, the architectural inside-outside, and we can see how it was possible for Giedion to slide between outside as in outside the house and outside the psyche (what Giedion called *cosmos*). And also to slide between outside the psyche and the real outside where signification and image-making fail. The mirror stage is where the spatial distinction inside/outside, upon which architecture depends for its sense, is crystalised for the subject. We can see how every architecture thereafter re-enacts the mirror stage for the subject, upon which depends the articulation of its *innenwelt-umwelt* and creates the frames that allow its identity and desire to be articulated. We shall return to inside/outside, in particular, the geometry of inside/outside, when we return to questions of Other space in the next chapters.

A vignette of desire

In that school yard ditty,

> I saw Esau kissing Kate.
> The fact is we all three saw;
> For I saw him,
> And he saw me,
> And she saw I saw Esau.[12]

A particular form of encounter, this *I saw Esau kissing Kate*, where desire and vision and others converge. The gaze = vision implicated in desire, in so far as it is an intersubjective encounter. You may not see me in the school yard, but if I kiss Kate, you will all see it.

Visual desire is the desire to be made visible to others. That is at least where the pleasure is. In psychoanalysis, desire is the defining trope of the human subject. Lacan says my desire is the desire of the other. He borrows this formula from Hegel. The 'of' is as ambiguous in French as it is in English:

- I desire the other (my lover, my friend, my mother);
- I desire what the other desires (I want what my lover wants);

- I desire the other's desire (I want my lover's love of me, I want my lover to love me);
- I want even to love myself as my lover loves me.

Even when I desire an object, that desire goes through others, although it should be clear that the desire for objects is a special case of desire for others, its inflated prominence today a consequence of consumer capitalism. In all four cases, it is a desire to have my desire recognised by others, which can be seen to be played out in Lacan's diagram for the visual field. I see you; I see you seeing me; you see me seeing you seeing me; and so on.

Architecture intervenes

A moment's reflection should make clear the central importance of perspective for architectural thought. After the demonstration, Brunelleschi designed the naves of San Lorenzo (after 1420) and Santo Spirito (1434 onwards), the two paradigm spaces of the Florentine renaissance, in which the Classical orders form a perspective grid that calibrates the distance from eye to altar. The art historian Rudolf Wittkower argued that these two spaces realised something that had never been realised before, a correspondence between picture and architecture such that it was possible to say that the perspective picture was the 2d representation of a 3d space, and architecture was the 3d representation of a 2d space. Wittkower is comfortable with the idea of 3d and 2d spaces, and 2d and 3d pictures.[13] Perspective also allowed Bramante, Brunelleschi's successor as renaissance innovator, to build the *tromp l'oeil* space of the choir of Santa Maria *presso* San Satiro (1480), as the technical solution to an otherwise irresolvable conflict between liturgy and a difficult site, and Palladio at Teatro Olympico (1580) to manipulate perspective to create one of the most uncannily scaled spaces in architectural history. Perspective made it possible for renaissance and post-renaissance architects to conceive of the exterior as an imaginary extension of the interior (Giedion's Classic space conception). I am thinking of Alberti's metaphor for perspective as a window in a wall (he was obviously thinking of fresco) and innumerable painted ceilings. It allowed Andrea Pozzo, the architect and master of *quadratura*, in a nod to Bramante, to present architecture as a process of creating new interiors as projections of existing ones.

The lesson of this chapter is that we use architecture to intervene in the visual field. The project of architecture is to manipulate our identity and desire by framing space. Architecture assimilates to a picture that allows the subject to be seen. Although Lacan does not say it (because he is not an architect), the desire to be seen is tantamount to the desire to be spatial. We are, in Lacan's discussion of the visual field, in the presence of the profound spatiality of the subject. It was Lacan's insight to realise that the optical world of objects and light in which the subject remains invisible to itself is not the same as the visual field of the subject. This *de facto* optical world becomes the visual field only when it is organised for

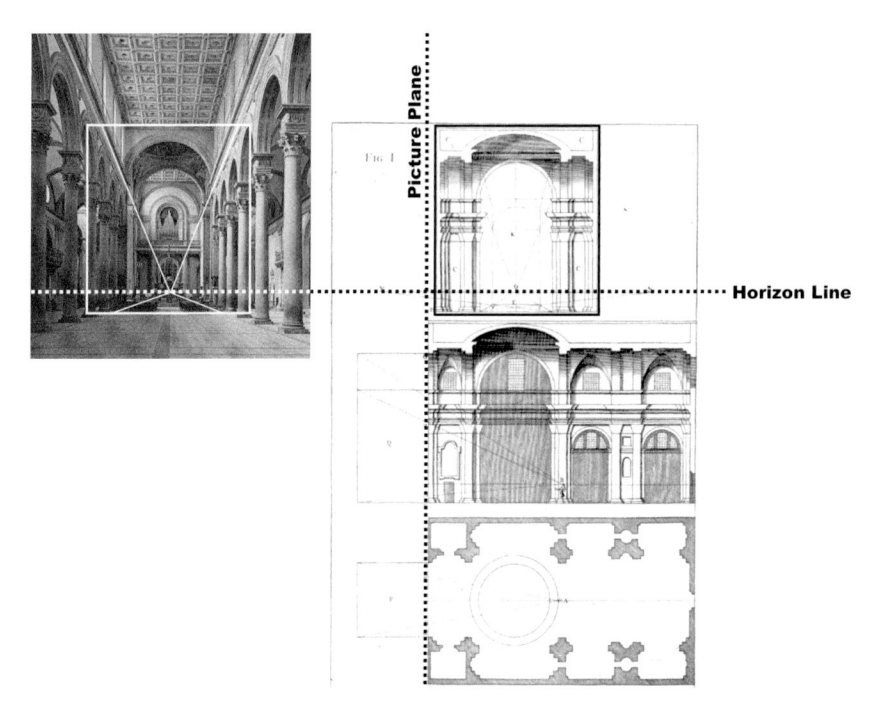

FIGURE 3.5 Pozzo and Brunelleschi: the visual projection of a nave.

the subject by its desire to be spatial. This desire – Lacan's gaze – is the place holder or home (*how do you house your desire?*) for the serial condition of objects. Lacan's diagram of the visual field approximates Giedion's dynamic interaction of inside/outside, what we might here call the modern field of desire. It also describes Giedion's reflective position in the modern. In the present context, it constitutes the geometry for how we situate our objects before us, which, at the same time, distances them from us, which speaks to something fraught and traumatic about desire, that it is never satisfied. (*Most people find it deeply disturbing to get what they want.*)

Although it is the cumulative unconscious of a civilisation to overlook the second triangle, the one that looks back, that speaks to our own visibility, it is possible to read both triangles into every perspective. In this sense, Lacan is simply doing what an analyst does in the analytic setting. He makes visible to the subject what was invisible to him/her before. In Brunelleschi's naves, the orders diminish in proportion as they recede towards the altar, as we would expect with any perspective; in one and the same gesture, the view opens out from the viewer at the door. The architectural rhetoric of the nave is perhaps the most explicit template for desire. The altar, distanced by the metric of the orders, holds the promise of salvation that is attainable if we could but traverse the axis whose length is measured in the column bays. Only you never get there because the altar turns out to be a stone and not salvation, and salvation lies elsewhere. And what we have accomplished instead is to place ourselves, now standing before the altar and suddenly aware that everyone is looking at us, in the centre of a picture orchestrated by architecture.

Manetti said that Brunelleschi produced the *effect of reality*. If Brunelleschi constructed a specular machine for producing the reality effect, we can ask exactly how did it work to effect reality. Panofsky and others have argued persuasively that the perspective picture looks nothing like what we see with two eyes, in motion, projected upon a sphere, with flickering alternating attention.[14] To my mind, what is more critical is that objects don't look smaller when they are far away, they just look far away. If you want them to look smaller, you have to put them in the picture. If perspective does not match reality we can ask what it matches. And what reality the machine produces. It enacts the continuous dialectic between image and picture: the unassailability of our own experience that always already runs up against the experience of others. It enacts the distancing between ourselves and our objects that is the hallmark of desire. Perspective seems so real and so natural because it conforms to our fantasy of desire, not because it conforms to reality. The perspective fantasy does not conform to reality, it is one of the constituents of our reality. Perspective positions our objects of desire in the centre of a picture in which we are seen to attain them. The object and its attainment is fantasy.

To conclude with emptiness

In his brief comments on architecture in *The Ethics of Psychoanalysis*, Lacan says that 'primitive architecture can be defined as something organised around emptiness' (he also mentions 'Palladio's theatre in Vicenza'); and that the assimilation of architecture to a framed picture – effected in the 15th century by the invention of perspective – underscored this emptiness. He is obviously referring to the hole at the vanishing point that is essential to vision but which blots out the most important part of the picture, which is where the subject's object is meant to appear. Here in *The Ethics*, he also relates emptiness to anamorphism, as if it were anamorphism that makes this emptiness appear in the picture. If the demonstration is a kind of mirror stage of viewing, in which the signifier is externalised as a picture, it comes at a price.[15] Something is lost in the assumption of the picture. If the image has a pre-symbolic fullness, all the fullness of velvety glorious lived experience, there is an emptiness at the centre of the picture, were our desire is visualised. It is a place where things vanish, corresponding to the emptiness at the centre of the subject.

In *The Four Fundamental Concepts*, Lacan calls it the – ø (minus phi) of desire and, with respect to Holbein's skullphallus, the absent phallus or minus phi of castration. There is a hole and what the hole frames is an absent object, not an object, but the negation of an object.[16] This absence appears in a number of places and guises in psychoanalysis. Freud called it the navel of the dream, the inscrutable *nothing* of the unconscious where the subject seems to emerge to itself as out of nowhere. When Lacan said that architecture and painting are organised around emptiness, he did not mean the emptiness of empty rooms. The picture of every room, empty or not, has two edges, an inner and an outer edge, which describe the inner and outer edges of visual experience. There is a pea-sized peephole, a blind spot at the centre of vision, 'a lesion, a locus of pain, a reversal...', where there is no picture, where the subject disappears into its unconscious desire, never articulated, never fulfilled. And there is an outer edge where Brunelleschi silvered the surface so as to reflect the clouds; where, into the closed inter-subjective circuit of private visual experience called into existence by the presence of others, a little bit of the real leaks in. In the next chapter on Rossi, the city, and the field of the Other, we will return to the question of how desire is spatialised in the city, which will lead us to re-evaluate the perspective apparatus.

Notes

1 There are two excellent interpretative treatments of Brunelleschi's demonstration. See Lorens Holm, *Brunelleschi Lacan Le Corbusier: Architecture, Space, and the Construction of Subjectivity* (London: Routledge, 2010), upon which this chapter is based, and Hubert Damisch, *The Origin of Perspective* (Cambridge, MA: MIT Press, 1994). Figure 3.1 is taken from my book.

2 See the diagrams in Holm, *op. cit.* Chapter 4 'Reading Manetti', pp. 77–102.

3 All page numbers in the text of this chapter refer to Jacques Lacan, 'The Mirror Stage as Formative of the I Function as Revealed in Psychoanalytic Experience (1949)', in *Écrits: The First Complete Edition in English.* Translated by Bruce Fink, Heloise Fink, and Russell Grigg (New York: W. W. Norton, 2006) unless indicated otherwise.

4 Jacques Lacan, *The Four Fundamental Concepts of Psycho-Analysis.* Translated by Alan Sheridan and edited by Jacques-Alain Miller (New York: W. W. Norton Press, 1981) p. 91.

5 Lacan, *op. cit.*, pp. 105ff. This is also how it is understood by James Elkins in his book on the effects of the visual field in visual culture, *The Object Stares Back: On the Nature of Seeing* (1997).

6 Lacan, *op. cit.*, p. 106.

7 Holm, *op. cit.*, 'Brunelleshi's apparatus delaminates a picture from its image...' p. 120. See diagrams pp. 60 and 88, and the extended treatment in Chapter 5 'Brunelleschi's Mirror' pp. 103–130.

8 Lacan, *op. cit.*, p. 106. Lacan's italics.

9 Lacan, *op. cit.*, p. 107.

10 There used to be an advert on the London Underground for a dating agency, in which a man and a woman are shown crossing paths on opposite escalators in a shopping mall. As one goes up and the other goes down, their gazes momentarily cross. Probably no one ever found true love in a shopping mall, but the truth of this advert is that the shopping mall is where visual desire manifests.

11 Holm, *op. cit.*, for *The Ambassadors*, see pp. 158–164; for the glint of light, pp. 136. Lacan, *op. cit.*, for the corresponding sections, see pp. 85–89, 94–95.

12 Iona and Peter Opie, eds., Maurice Sendak illustrator, *I Saw Esau – The Schoolchild's Pocket Book* (London: Walker Books, 1947/1992).

13 Rudolf Wittkower, 'Brunelleschi and "Proportion in Perspective"', in *Idea and Image: Studies in the Italian Renaissance* (London: Thames and Hudson, 1953) pp. 124–135.

14 Erwin Panofsky, *Perspective as Symbolic Form* (New York: Zone Books, 1991 (1927)). See also Ernest H. Gombrich, *Art and Illusion: A Study in the Psychology of Pictorial Representation* (Princeton, NJ: Princeton University Press, 1960), who takes the opposite position, he calls it 'common sense'.

15 Jacques Lacan, *The Seminar of Jacques Lacan, Book VII: The Ethics of Psychoanalysis 1959–1960* (New York: W. W. Norton, 1992) pp. 135, 140.

16 Lacan, *The Four Fundamental Concepts … op. cit.* p. 89 (castration) and p. 105 (desire).

FIGURE 4.1 The city is a theatre shadowed by the hand of the other.

4

ROSSI AND THE FIELD OF THE OTHER [PLANNING OR THE UNCONSCIOUS]

> History, that is, the unconscious, general, swarm-life of mankind, ...
> (Leo Tolstoy, *War and Peace* (1869))[1]

> The unconscious is structured like a language.
> (Lacan, *The Four Fundamental Principles of Psychoanalysis* (1964))

DOI: 10.4324/9780429022845-4

Architecture, the fixed scene of human events.

(Aldo Rossi, *The Architecture of the City* (1966))

The theatre was, for Rossi, the locus of the architectural imagination. It was the site for experimenting with architecture. It recalls the scientific theatre in Mantua and the anatomical theatre in Padua. The hand shadows Rossi's work, like the chorus in Greek tragic drama. It is an enigmatic witness and interlocutor, always present, its identity veiled, always more than the subject on stage. Rossi's city is always under revision in the way that language is always under revision by each instance of its use. In this chapter, we intend to read Lacan's concept of the field of the Other with Rossi's concept of the city. For Rossi, the city is a collective thing; we call the field of the Other, our commons.[2]

The purloined letter

I found this letter I wrote to my sister. It was amongst her things.

'Dear L,

Freud says that we map sex and death, or rather our encounters with sex and death, onto the places we inhabit. Hence the definition of what a place is. It is where we map sex and death, and what differentiates a place which is particular from space which is universal. In Freud's example, we do this by word associations with the places we inhabit. He provides a diagram of how this occurs, using an example from his own experience, where he forgets the name of the renaissance painter *Signorelli*, and remembers incorrectly, a series of people and place names including *Bosnia-Herzegovina*. There are other examples in Freud's text, which have more to do with places than names of places. He describes how going to visit the Parthenon for the first time made him depressed (he surpassed his father's limited aspirations), and how getting lost in Sienna made him anxious (sex, this time). So I was thinking of starting one of my history/theory lectures with this, and looking at how I might tie it into an account of New York in terms of its names, signs, billboards, etc. There is an important book on the city (*Learning from Las Vegas*) whose thesis is that the way signs are organised is a more significant feature of urban space than the shape it has. Information, not form. Or rather, information is form. I would link this to Freud's thesis and to my experience of Manhattan. Sex and death in Manhattan, Manhattan with its street numbers. Manhattan with all its memorable places.

Love Lorens'

That was 2005. I decided to continue the letter because it reminded me of a dream I used to have as a child.

'Dear L,

I used to have a recurring nightmare. I don't remember how old I was, but I had it often. In the dream I am on the Columbia campus. I am running up the steps of Low Library at night as someone is opening the glass doors to Butler Library in the distance. I am running as fast as possible because I can see there are two wolves behind the doors. I glance over my shoulder thinking, *please don't open those doors.* As soon as that person lets them out, and they bound after me, I start to lose my weight, and hence lose my traction and slow down. Not so the wolves, with their firm grip on reality. I would wake up just before they run me down. I never find out – never even asked myself before now – who that person is. S/he is simply a cipher for fate. I don't remember why I remembered the dream, but at the time, I was updating my sketchbook with a new signifier: what I call my signifiers – key things that people have said to me, principally Dad, that have stuck with me my whole life. I had a dream a few days ago that disappeared as I was waking, but must be a recurring dream because it seemed familiar. All that it (*my unconscious*) left me (*my ego*) was a single phrase *Say goodbye to an insignificant woman.* This was the phrase I was adding to my signifier list, when I remembered the Columbia dream. And I thought, *hmmm, maybe Columbia is one of my signifiers too.* It is the significant feature of one of my significant dreams, it was where we played as kids, and so on. In the Introduction to the American Edition of *The Architecture of the City* (*it's on page 15*), Rossi said that New York was an *analogous city.* The feature of the dream that attracted the most anxiety, was the distance from the wolves, a diagonal line drawn from the Butler Library entry on the central axis of the campus to where I was running up the upper right-hand corner of the Low Library steps (northeast corner). The next thing that came to mind was my painting of the steps of Widener Library that hung in mom's living room. That really oblique view. I realised that for me it was Harvard's version of Columbia's Low Library steps. I realised that I have been representing Columbia to myself in my dreams and my paintings all my life. The odd thing was that I was sure that the movers had lost that painting. I looked all over the house, I checked the manifest. We almost didn't take the painting with us when mom died but now that it was lost in transit, I was distraught. I asked the kids if they remembered it. O came in and said *oh, you mean the one in my room.* When I recently visited NY with the family, I took them to the site of the dream at night, and it seemed strangely denatured.

I now think these are the steps I want to be on, like the ones I painted at Harvard. I have always dismissed Columbia as an absolutely unattainable place. That it may be, but I realised today that it is in the centre of my world: I could never go there …. I would never go there …. I want to go there …. I want to go back to my wolves.

In *Inhibitions Symptoms and Anxiety* (1926), Freud distinguished internal and external objects. We fear external threats and either fight or flee. We feel anxiety over internal ones, the ones for which fight or flight does not work. Following Freud, Lacan argues that anxiety is a symptom of the proximity of the unconscious object. What is the object that so overtakes me from which it is impossible to flee? (*And who is the insignificant woman? is it Columbia? is it you?*) I have always wanted to be a professor at Columbia like K's dad, and I have always been too disaffected to go for it. I am afraid to let myself have what I really want and will die a narcissistic melancholic writing letters to my sister because of it. I would rather inhabit nostalgic memories of what I never allowed myself, than to stick my neck out. This object of desire is a long way from sex and death, but we can see how in this story, the object is signified by a place called Columbia, and perhaps we can accept on faith at least for the moment, that the object of desire is a proxy for sex and death, at least in so far as that object enters public discourse through a constructed place in the city.

I could describe my life in steps: New York, Boston, St. Louis, London, Dundee. These steps are my symptoms, hysteria written on the body of the earth. In the dream, what I want is always threatening to catch up with me. And I keep moving farther and farther away from what I want because I hope it will protect me from what I fear most, like Lady Macbeth compulsively washing her hands of a stain that no washing can remove. No distance I put between myself and New York seems to get rid of this want. And what do I want. I want to make my name in New York, where this want will catch up with me.

This want is no longer unconscious now that I have spoken it to you. What remains unconscious is the desire that drives this Ariadne's thread from one place to another, or as Lacan might say, from one signifier to another. How and why one thought followed another, is a mystery. They seem to have emerged randomly and from nowhere, one after the other, and threaten to disappear again: enumerating my signifiers, remembering the dreams, remembering the painting and losing it. Why these and not other thoughts? The truth of my psyche, what Lacan calls the *truth* of my *being*, lies in this mystery. This is the lack that I speak. This is the lack that marks me. It orients me with its mark.
Love Lorens'

Introduction

In the dream, a place in the city functions as the signifier of my desire, which, when made conscious, becomes a part of my history, which is the history I construct for myself. In *The Architecture of the City*, Rossi argues that 'the city itself is the collective memory of its people, and like memory it is associated with objects and places. The city is the locus of the collective memory' (p. 130).[3] Because his text alludes to the signifying condition of architecture, we can assume that *collective memory* is not a flowery way of referring to historic neighbourhoods and buildings but to how places become signifiers that figure in the histories of its many subjects. Rossi gets collective memory from the sociologist Maurice Halbwachs for whom collective memory is constituted of the field of material signifiers, including words, pictures, buildings, arrangements of streets,

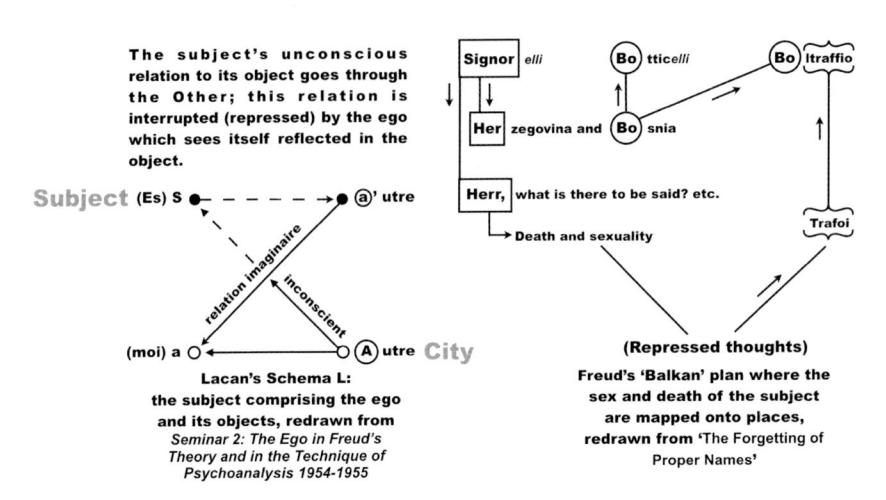

FIGURE 4.2   Lacan and Freud: the ego (*relation imaginaire*) and the unconscious (*inconscient*) distributed across the field of the city + the unconscious mapped across Bosnia-Herzegovina.

place-names, public and private archival records, newspapers, personal photographs, candy wrappers blowing in the wind, that constitute our world.[4] The city is the site of unconscious desire because it is constituted of the signifiers with which we construct our histories. Memory is the flip side of forgetting, and when we forget something, we commit it to the unconscious. We invoke Rossi to re-enter the subject of Lacan's unconscious. Lacan relates the unconscious to the phenomena of speech and language, and relates it to what he calls *the field of the Other*. This chapter will relate these concepts to the public realm of the city. In our Brunelleschi chapter, we acknowledged that seeing was not simply a matter of opening our eyes and letting the light flood it. Seeing was a signifying condition and we asked, in what sense is the subject instituted in the field of visual signifiers such that it can be said to see. In this chapter, we ask, in what sense is the subject instituted in the city such that it has an unconscious. Substitution, history, and the serial condition of objects will be thematic in this discussion.

Forgetting *Signorelli*

In *The Psychopathology of Everyday Life*, Freud recounts a conversation he had with a colleague in which he could not remember the name of the painter Signorelli, whose frescos in Orvieto he had recently seen, and instead remembered incorrectly the names of other painters and places. Most of us have had the experience where this *not* remembering is the provocation for calling to mind a series of other names or words that we know are not what we are looking for. They seem to substitute for each other. Freud is able to demonstrate that he forgot *Signorelli* because it had been associated in his mind, through a series of recent events and conversations, with sex and death, in particular the suicide of a sex-obsessed patient in Trafoi and the sexual practices of Turks. Freud draws a plan diagram of forgetting. It is a plan of northern Italian place names transformed by his unconscious. He could show that these signifiers were slippages and montages from *Signorelli*. He remembers *Herzegovina*, for instance, which is part of a slippage from *Signorelli* to *Signor* to *Herr*. He concludes that he was repressing disturbing thoughts about sex and death, which he associated with the signifier *Signorelli*, and these associations tugged this signifier underneath the taut surface of consciousness.[5]

Schema L

In *Seminar 2*, Lacan draws a plan diagram of the subject, which maps the relation of signifiers to repression. He calls it *Schema L*:

> This schema signifies that the condition of the subject, S (neurosis or psychosis), depends on what unfolds in the Other, A. What unfolds there is articulated like a discourse (the unconscious is the Other's discourse), whose syntax Freud first sought to define for those fragments of it that reach us in certain privileged moments, such as dreams, slips, and witticisms ….

> [The subject is party to this discourse], insofar as he is drawn to the four corners of the schema: namely, S, his ineffable and stupid existence; a, his objects; a', his ego, that is, his form as reflected in his objects; and A, the locus from which the question of his existence may arise for him.[6]

In Schema L, Lacan's formula for the subject (ego-unconscious) appears as four positions laid out on a version of the Klein Square (a pun and/or gloss on 'quadrature of the ego's verifications'). Like Lacan's diagram of the visual field, this diagram is both a map of the subject – its internal relations – and a map of the subject's external relations to the world of others. Speech comes to the Subject from the big Other or *Autre* (the unconscious line) but is blocked by the imaginary relation between the subject's ego and those with which it identifies. The ego is the agency of repression. The ego seeks confirmation of itself in the world by identifying with others. This imaginary relation interrupts a more direct route from Subject to Other. The subject's speech originates in the field of the Other and not in the ego, but it passes through the ego, which operates as a gate, letting some of it through and forcing the rest sideways upon a more circuitous and wayward path.

A short course on language and the unconscious

For Freud, the unconscious is absolutely different from consciousness. It is separated from consciousness by repression and is not simply what is temporarily forgotten or otherwise out of mind. Lacan's contribution to the unconscious is to attend to the inter-subjective linguistic setting within which the unconscious is operative. In the case of a dream, the significance of the dream in the life of the dreamer emerges through free association. This process involves language and other people because it involves speaking the dream to others.

The subject's unconscious escapes the ego because it involves what others do to the subject's words when they interrupt, interpret, punctuate, play, and react to them. The unconscious resides in the gap between what you think you say and what others think you said. Sometimes you don't say what you mean; the classic is a slip of the tongue, and you exclaim, *that's not what I meant!* Sometimes the message you send to others is not the message they receive. What you say goes out into the world, and you no longer have any control over it, and it comes back to you in forms that are sometimes unrecognisable.

The unconscious is not a language, but it is structured like one because it works through speech and because words have a life of their own. The unconscious depends upon two things: the signifying capacity of words and the way that the users of words are not able to control the way they signify. They form associative chains, open-ended substitution series, that link together of their own accord. Many of the signs of the unconscious, including dreams, slips of the tongue, witticisms, the punch lines of jokes, and bungled actions, are different sorts of substitutions that work without our intention (*Baltimore in the morning*) because they belong to the properties of words themselves when they are put to use in speech and writing and other forms of communication. In a solipsistic world with no others with whom to share your dreams, there would be no signification and no unconscious, or at least, it would be silent.

A short course on the field of the other ...

> The unconscious is the field of the Other.
>
> The subject's unconscious is the discourse of the Other.
> (*Lacan, The Four Fundamental Principles of Psychoanalysis (1964), p. 126*)

The unconscious occupies a particular place. It is a function of speech *between* subjects. It emerges in the subject's encounters with others. It is everything the Romantic notion of the unconscious is not: it is a dispersed field and not a sacred entity internal to the individual. Nor is the unconscious natural: it does not reside in the biology of the organism and will not be found by neuroscience, even though neuroscience may find correlative brain activity that we are not aware of in the same way that we are not aware of other bodily processes. Although we tend to regard the unconscious as immaterial – this is a ploy of the ego – the role of speech confirms its materiality. Speech exists as sound, it is shaped by the tongue, has sibilance and texture; it can be recorded, replayed, played over, projected, scratched, disfigured, or polluted. Signifiers are media and anyone who has struggled to write a book or design a building can attest to the intractable and intransigent nature of signifiers.[7]

In the paper 'The function and field of speech and language in psychoanalysis', Lacan distinguishes language from speech. Speech is a temporal or diachronic function; language is the simultaneous or synchronic field that allows speech to happen. The innumerable speech acts of individuals build the language field. Language evolves with speech, but at the moment of each speech act, language exists as the simultaneous field of speech possibilities. No one subject controls it (although nation states often try); we all contribute. Lacan says *field* because it is the ambient environment that precedes objects and within which we articulate them.

In *Seminar 2*, Lacan distinguishes big Other from little other to refer to the cumulative effect of signification on the subject. The field of the Other is not simply the field of others, which might refer to a multitude of people; it is the symbolic environment that gives them an orientation and a grammar. Lacan insists that the analyst must situate him/herself in the position of the Other, not the other. This position is one of the defining characteristics of the analytic setting. The little other is an other person, as in 'your significant other', a counterpart to the ego, what the ego sees of itself reflected in others and as such is inscribed in the imaginary order. For the analyst to place him/herself in the position of other is to play the relationship game. Analysis is about how the subject appears in the signifying world, not about how you appear to me, although how you appear to me has a contribution to make to this appearance.

In *Seminar 3*, Lacan writes, 'the Other must first of all be considered a locus in which speech is constituted'.[8] The Other is the locus or place of the subject's speech as opposed to the locus of the speech of an other person. The Other is the well-spring of signifiers that constitutes the subject's world. It has the capacity to coalesce into an agency or voice. It makes demands upon us (*Che vuoi?*). We address it as a locus from which our being emerges, as when we refer to personifications like 'the Law' or 'the Public' or 'Architecture'. Think of it as a cosmic mouth, an oracular voice, a witness. Think of Odysseus, or in popular culture, the Wizard of Oz. Speech and language originate in this collective place, and not in the subject or in its ego, and it is alienating. At that moment, when our ego loses control of our speech, with slips of the tongue, or when its significance runs away from us, with witticisms, this becomes apparent.

Other space

Lacan calls the Other a field because it is spatial. In an extraordinary paper, 'Secondary Virtuality: the anamorphosis of projective geometry', the architectural theorist Donald Kunze argues that Other space has the particular topological properties of the Mobius strip and Klein bottle.[9] The field of signifiers has the logic of a surface that intersects itself and hence fails to enclose, let alone distinguish one side from the other. Columbia is where my wolves are. Northern Italy is where Freud forgot Signorelli. This self-intersection appears in the 'twist' that gives Schema L its crossed form. The subject's ego has an investment in regarding the Other as outside it, but any attempt to so neatly position the Other runs into

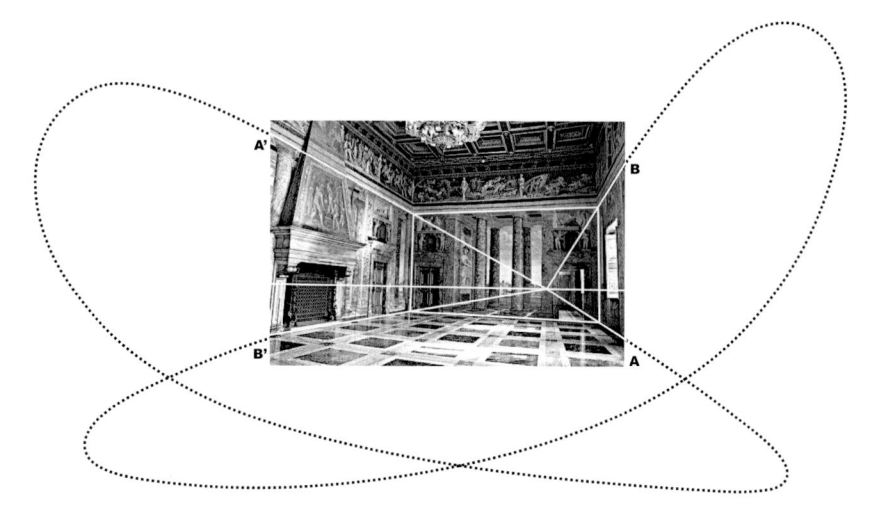

FIGURE 4.3 The visual field is a mobius strip. Both sides of the projective plane are continuous with each other. The projective plane is infinite. Projection lines leaving the picture plane on one side return on the other.

the problem that outside is already marked by inside and inside by outside. Kunze annotates it Insideout and Outsidein. The symbolic field of the Other is not out there beyond the window, not because it is in here (in my head), but because the subject and Other has a loopy logic that stymies the binary inside-outside logic that appears in architecture and the perspective apparatus of the ego. We experience this condition of *extimacy* as the uncanny – that quality of horror stories, the double, which we find so compelling and what Iain Borden *et al.* called in the context of the city, the strangely familiar.[10]

Perspective redux

Before we return to Rossi, we can ask what the field of the Other makes of perspective? We use the threshold of architecture to repress the field of the Other, whose main feature is its paradoxical continuities. If Lacan's diagram of the visual field is the formula for spatiality, at least the form of spatiality known by the desiring ego, we can read it together with Schema L, and make mischief with them. The a–a' axis of the Schema L corresponds to the perspective line of sight, from eye to altar, ego to other/object. We could call it, in a nod to Brunelleschi, the *mirror axis of reality*. In projective geometry, the projective plane extends to infinity. It must be infinite because the vanishing points are at infinity. The horizon line shown going off to the left returns from infinity on the right. The converging lines of the ground plane extend in depth without meeting but return from infinity with left-hand line returning on the right and the right-hand line on the left. Flatness and depth (picture plane and ground plane) are projections of each other on the projective surface. The projective plane has, like the Mobius

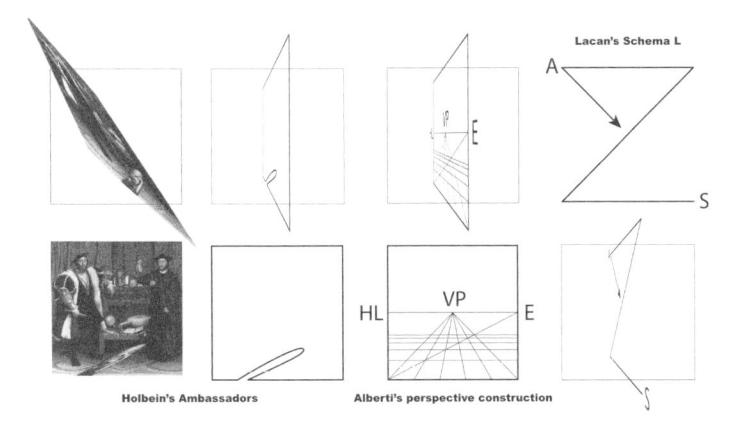

FIGURE 4.4 Holbein Alberti Lacan: The lesson of the *Ambassadors* is that Alberti's visual axis and Lacan's Schema L are anamorphisms of each other. Looking along the mirror axis of reality, S and A disappear. The symbolic trajectory 're-appears' when the ego arrives at a' and a' turns out to be a disfiguration in the visual field. The skull appears when the picture is turned sideways. If you were to extend the picture plane to infinity, the symbolic trajectory connecting S and A, subject and field of the Other, would be a continuous loop.

strip, the topological properties of the single-sided surface that loops but does not enclose.[11] You reach what appears to be the other side of the window by traversing twice around the loop and not by passing through its surface. There is no way to visualise this in a way that makes sense. The perspective window is simply a very local instance of this infinite single-sided field. This reading of Lacan's Schema L with the visual field does not destroy architecture's claim on space, but it limits the territory over which it roams.[12]

All signifiers point to other signifiers but not the way we expect them to. In Schema L, the Z trajectory from Other to subject forms a continuous loop. Subject and Other constitute a single social symbolic formation. The effect of repression by the egoic eye/I is to hold two domains separate that are a continuous surface by diverting attention from the reality of the signifier stream that constitutes the unconscious to the imaginary world of things. It uses architecture as its vehicle to rotate attention away from the single sided world where every projection is anamorphic, to the visual axis where every projection is the picture of an object. That is the formula for conscious desire. The sideways world of unconscious desire we would scarcely recognise. Perspective is the ego's short circuit to objects (things, places, people, whatever we objectify by placing them at the vanishing point). It leads to unhappiness because enjoyment is found in delay and not in the object. We cannot escape one for the other, we would not want to; unconscious and repression are part of the same psychical system.

We can read Rossi's theatre of the unconscious with Schema L. The city is the place from which flows the subject's speech. I am continuous with the city because I dream with it, and this dream is my history. We are attached to cities the way we are attached to our memories and histories and to the others with whom we share them. What interrupts this communication? What gets in the way? The ego of the subject sees its stupid existence reflected in monuments, flags, and other idiocies, and this identification (*dumbing down, we used to call it*) blocks more significant but circuitous constructions of self and other. The ego rallies around a church because it features in picturesque photographs, the brochures produced by developers who want the new shopping mall, tourist boards who want the new revenue, advertising agencies and other spivs because they cannot think of anything more important to say about the place. Meanwhile, we suffer.

The construction of the city

Rossi opens *The Architecture of the City* with a description of the city as the field of construction.

> The city … is to be understood here as architecture. By architecture I mean not only the visible image of the city and the sum of its different architectures, but architecture as construction, the construction of the city over time. I believe that this point of view … addresses the ultimate and definitive fact in the life of the collective, the creation of the environment in which it lives.
>
> *(p. 21)*

The Architecture of the City was published in Italian (1966) two years after the completion of Lacan's 11th seminar (1963–1964, *The Four Fundamental Concepts of Psychoanalysis*), one of his most comprehensive statements on psychoanalysis, and ten years before Gandelsonas wrote his paper 'From Structure to Subject' (1976) in which he argued that in order for architecture to have a subject, architecture must be reformed as a signifying structure like a language.

For Rossi, a key fact about the city is that it is always under construction. Imagine a time-lapse aerial view of the city: the cumulative effects of countless separate incremental acts of construction, an emergent order, a historic body flowing into the future that is the reflection of no one individual. Rossi's city is produced by innumerable acts of construction in the way that the field of language is produced by innumerable acts of speech. Everyone contributes to it, everyone is affected by it, no one is fully responsible for its outcome, and except in cartographic maps and city plans, it rarely forms itself into a unified figure.

Rossi's 'life of the collective' has affinities to the concept of the multitude posited by the political philosopher Paolo Virno.[13] The multitude is the life-swarm that resists being totalised in fictional – Lacan would say imaginary – unities like *the people* in *we the people* or *the people have spoken*, to which politicians appeal as if it were a singular and purposive character. Rossi's collective, like the multitude, eschews the armoured carapace of an identity (a single name, a single image, a policy of excluding others), but it is organised by a form of grammar that exceeds propinquity, which for Rossi is 'construction'. We are collective because we build the city, if not exactly together, then at least alongside each other, and this alongside has a grammar of construction that encompasses multiple forms of engagement and enjoyment, including a tradition of building and procurement (finance, planning law, contracts), and an infrastructure of spaces, paths, streets, and ideas, to which the collective has an attachment.

The construction of histories

> This assumption by the subject of his history, in so far as it is constituted by speech, is addressed to another, …
>
> *(p. 213)*

> What we teach the subject to recognize as his unconscious is his history ….
> *(Lacan, 'The Function and Field of Speech and Language …' p. 217)*

Lacan equates the subject's unconscious and history, and he treats the subject's history as a continuous process of construction not unlike the process of working, reworking, and working through that goes on in the analytic setting. This text is an example of working through, in which the same material is reformed with a shifted significance each time. Lacan may not say that the unconscious is collective in so many words, but he says it is inter-personal, inter-subjective, and trans-individual. The subject's history is constituted by his/her signifiers. It is *assumed* by the subject. *Assumed* is the word that Lacan used in the mirror stage (*the subject assumes an image*), which suggests that it is something donned like a coat or acquired like an opinion and, once assumed, has a transformative effect (the *Assumption of Mary*). It is not the same subject before and after the assumption of its history. This history is constructed by the subject in the act of speaking it to others. Your history is not simply what you say it is, but what I hear (which may not be the same as what you say) and how I respond to it. The subject's history involves recognition by the subject and by others (*what we teach* …). In retelling my dream, I recognise in it my unconscious.

This extended quote, abridged, indicates the form of this history, its materiality, and its dis-locatedness. Lacan's text is never so territorial as when he discusses the unconscious.

> The unconscious is the chapter of my history that is marked by a blank …: it is the censored chapter. But the truth can be found; most often it is written elsewhere. Namely,
>
> In monuments: that is, my body, … the hysterical symptom …;
>
> In archival documents too: … my childhood memories …;

> In semantic evolution: ... the stock of words, ... my own ... vocabulary, ... my style of life;
>
> In traditions too: ... the legends which, ... convey my history;
>
> And, lastly, in its traces that are ... the distortions, ripples, of inserting my chapter into the chapters surrounding it, ...;[14]

This blank produces signifiers. The signifiers in which this history is written are always material and always displaced of their mark. Whatever the subject comes to recognise as its unconscious is always already no longer unconscious. In this sense the unconscious is always elsewhere, and reconstructing a history is a game of catch up. The subject's history is what the subject remembers of its past (*dreams memories recollections*). It changes as the subject's encounters with others change. The subject's history is always in a dialectical relation to what the subject does not remember, and may remember at an other circumstance, or what others see to be shaping its actions. We take from Giedion the concept of orientation. A subject's history is not a matter of fact, but an orientation, what is stable is the continuity of the construction. Here is Rossi:

> All great manifestations of social life have in common... the fact that they are born in unconscious life. This life is collective ...
>
> *(p. 33)*

> The value of history seen as collective memory, as the relationship of the collective to its place, is that it helps us to grasp the significance of the urban structure, its individuality, and its architecture which is the form of this individuality.
>
> *(pp. 130–131)*

> The city itself is the collective memory of its people, and like memory it is associated with objects and places. The city is the locus of the collective memory.
>
> *(p. 130)*

Rossi is not the only urbanist to associate the city with memory (Patrick Geddes and Lewis Mumford),[15] but he seems to be unique in stressing the city as inscription and not artefact (archive and monument). The rules for the construction of collective memory are effectively the substitution of signifiers. This memory does not produce a history of the city, but a city history, a history written by its inhabitants using the city as its medium. If the architecture of the city is construction, we have to understand that a single environment is being constructed that is both material and symbolic. As a history, it has particular properties. It is always changing because it is always under construction, and it has a retroactive temporality.

Rossi locates collective life in the unconscious. He condenses history, collective memory, and the city, or at least argues that when we understand history as our collective memory, we understand its significance. The multitude is able to recognise its relation to a place when it recognises that its history is written in the city. They may not always agree (collective does not imply consensus), but these many histories will share the same field of signifiers. If we do not read Rossi this way, it is difficult to understand what he means when he says that the city is the locus of collective memory. By analogy, Rossi's city makes sense of the idea that Lacan's unconscious is a project of the multitude and an immersive environment to which we are both attached and alienated (*who is not alienated by the city?*), which goes on collectively cumulatively, incrementally, and if not automatically, at least without the intervention of any one subject. We want to be able to say, for political and urbanistic reasons, that Lacan's field of the Other – like Rossi's city – is 'the mode of being of the many'.[16]

The collective place of the subject

A collective social formation is not an object that many people jointly own, like a house; it is a multitude of individuals united by a common grammar that gives them coherence without identity. Coherence without identity is invisible. Each person may own a percentage of the house. The house exists independently of the owners. The field of the Other is collective in the sense that it is the common field of signifiers from which individuals and their speech and actions emerge, and although it is logically prior to the speech acts of individuals, it only exists as a cohering body of knowledge because of the continuous individual incremental contributions of subjects. The status of common land, such as it is known in the public life of British settlements, is common because of its legacy of use, not its shared ownership.

Linking Rossi's city of collective memory with Lacan's field of the Other is a tricky move because the psychoanalyst Carl Jung used the term *collective* to describe a form of unconscious that is antithetical to the Freudian and Lacanian unconscious, and moreover, Halbwachs appears to derive individual and collective memory from Jung's distinction between individual and collective unconscious. Jung's use of *collective* is different from Halbwachs' and Rossi's use. Jung's collective unconscious is populated by archetypal figures that are pre-existing and inherited by individuals, which comprise a 'collective impersonal universal nature'. He also describes it as 'objective'. For Jung, the collective unconscious is an object that we share like slices of a pie. For Rossi, collective memory is not one thing shared. Each subject constructs its own memory from a common field of city artefacts. They are collective – and also they cohere – because of the common field. This should be clear because, for Rossi, the flip side of collective memory is individual forgetting.[17]

The field of the Other has the potential to form the basis for our understanding of the collective life of cities, under which we subsume a number of political categories like public and private life, Arendt's concept of the polis, Virno's concept of the multitude. The field of the Other describes a form of intersubjectivity that could contribute to, but has been largely ignored by, the political critique of cities. The Other has the expanded explanatory power to bind the multitude of individuals to each other with a common field of signifiers, *and* not relinquish their claims of individuality to a larger social entity. And in particular, not relinquish their claims to that most personal aspect of the subject – its unconscious. This is how Rossi's city of collective memory functions. The field of the Other joins the common land and the intellectual commons as fields that we commonly use, and by using, reassert their common status.

Rossi on signification

> In order to be significant, architecture must be forgotten, or must present only an image for reference which subsequently becomes confounded with memories.

> *Forgetting Architecture* comes to mind as a more appropriate title for this book, since while I may talk about a school, a cemetery, a theatre, it is more correct to say that I talk about life, death, imagination.
> *(Aldo Rossi, A Scientific Autobiography (1981), pp. 45, 78)*

> It is strange how I resemble myself.
> *(the first sentence in Aldo Rossi, Three Cities: Perugia,*
> *Milano, Mantova (1984) p. 7)*

Architecture has to be forgotten in order to be significant: it has to be committed to the unconscious, which is the flip side of memory, where its significance is worked over, reformed, rearranged, condensed, displaced, as if we were asleep. In the dream, the significance of a place is reconstructed by its subject. That

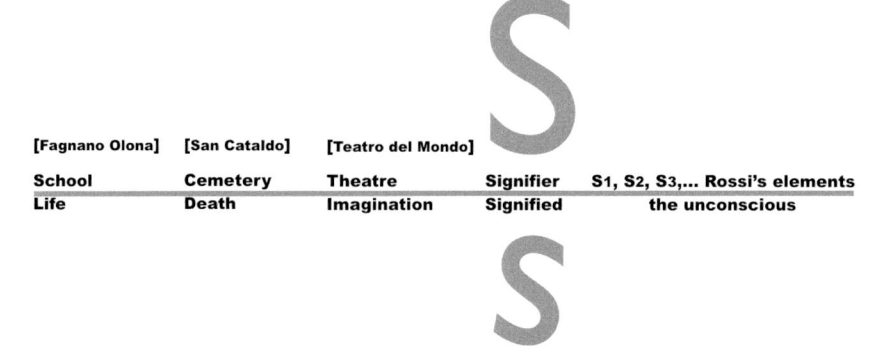

[Fagnano Olona]	[San Cataldo]	[Teatro del Mondo]		
School	**Cemetery**	**Theatre**	**Signifier**	**S1, S2, S3,... Rossi's elements**
Life	**Death**	**Imagination**	**Signified**	**the unconscious**

FIGURE 4.5 Rossi's architectural elements are his signifiers.

Rossi regards the architecture of the city to be a signifying field is indicated in scattered comments that accompany his text like a murmur. The school, the theatre, and the cemetery signify. Rossi puts architecture in a dynamic relation to its subject. Things are not significant *per se*, they are only significant for subjects. Signification works through a form of forgetting. When we speak, we do not dwell on the words but on their meaning. If we remember the structure of the sign, S/s, signifier over signified: signification involves forgetting the signifier – the school or other city signifier – so that it can rearrange itself in new sequences with other signifiers, to create new narratives. Something can only be significant if it functions within this structure. In a kind of inverse of Freud forgetting Signorelli, in order to access life, we need to forget *school*. Rossi seems to recognise that even the subject is in the signifying system as a signifier. Lacan said a signifier represents a subject to another signifier.[18] And Rossi says sometimes he is strange to himself (it is the sentence that opens a book of his projects) as if he realises that the signifier that he is to himself is the signifier of an other. This is nothing if not the spatial logic of the Mobius.

The analogical city

All cities are analogical cities. We live in the material city. The analogical city lives in us. In the 'Preface to the Second Italian Edition' of *The Architecture of the City*, Rossi introduces his vision of the analogous city with the example of a *capriccio* of Venice by Canaletto in which the Rialto Bridge (Venice) is flanked by Palazzo Chiericati and the Basilica at Vicenza (p. 165). It is not elaborated. It is briefly reprised in the prefaces to subsequent editions. The tenuous position of the analogical city in Rossi's text indicates its significance in this thought. It is lingering, marginal, secondary, introduced, … hence essential. Like the unconscious, it had to be introduced because nothing would make sense without it. Rossi's analogical city is like a super-real dream, in which one building substitutes for another to produce an other architectural scene (Freud called the dream *an other scene*). In the construction of the analogical city, we can expect like-for-like rules of substitution and close attention to reality in the details, especially at the joins.

The analogical city depends upon the serial substitution of objects; one building replaces another. Although Rossi does not specify the rules, we can glean them in his theory of types and his architectural elements. The type functions in Rossi's thought as the rule of substitution for the series of architectural elements that instantiate it. The type is 'a logical principle that is prior to form and that constitutes it'. The central plan, the linear plan, and the tower, constitute principles of organisation for form and use. The type remains 'constant', like Giedion's space conceptions, it is what does not change, but 'it reacts dialectically with technique, function, and style, as well as with both the collective character and the individual moment of the architectural artifact …' (pp. 40–41). Rossi's elements are particular instances of the type interpreted as architectural form:

lighthouses that can be towers or church spires or teapots, fly towers that can be office blocks or ossuaries, pediments that can be bridges, and so forth. They are more particular than the type. Rossi uses his lifelong project of drawing and photographing his elements to identify them as the signifiers that rework his own history. In effect, they are his signifiers. Mine may be different from his, but we all have them and they all form substitution series. His project is universal. He is building the lexicon of elements and their adjacencies. When these different components of his text are joined up, we get a picture of the city as the signifying field of its subjects that lifts claims – Rossi's, Freud's, Lacan's – about the city as unconscious out of the register of metaphor and make it operative.[19]

The city of the Other

We have to ask a fundamental question, *how do you occupy a city?*, except that we have travelled too far down our reading of Lacan with Rossi to accept an answer like *by walking through the city gates*. It depends upon what kind of field the city is and what kind of signifier the subject is. We enter the city when it enters our dreams. The city of the Other is the city of collective memory because it is the city in which it is possible for its subjects to write their histories. Its logic is the *ana*logic of the transformation series. It evinces a certain linguistic coherence, such that each subject can construct his/her history by the typological substitution of city elements; something stays the same so that something remembered can replace something forgotten. This history uses the city as its field – the shared signifiers of which bind its subjects to each other, to groups, and to places. This city of the Other is caught in a dynamic of forgetting and remembering, of repression and representation. The unconscious is a better model for the attachment of people to places than identification with landmarks. If identity is a strong force, then the unconscious is weak (*gravity is a weak force*), but it has the potential to be more effective in the long run for shaping communities. It is continuous and enduring in a way that identity is of the moment. This city of collective memory is not historicist. The heritage industry, a response to the tourist industry, falsifies continuity by commodifying it. (*Imagine imposing Shakespearean English upon our speech; it would destroy speech*). As compelling as it may seem, nothing could be less about the unconscious than historicism.[20]

The most obvious audience for this discussion of the city will be the agencies for planning policy and implementation, where the forms of the city are determined. Current planning discourse revolves around the identity, wellbeing, and sustainability of communities. These terms are never adequately understood in planning policy documents and they have been coopted by market forces to promote development.[21] We would like to see them address unconscious attachment instead. Henceforth planning applications will include a discursive section called *The Other*. It will answer the question, *how does this development contribute to the unconscious of the subjects of the city? what are the possible analogues of this place in the unconscious of its inhabitants? how does it figure in their collective memory?* Attachment is not a matter of individuals identifying with particular monuments, which is essentially the range of possibilities within which statutory heritage bodies like English Heritage and Historic Environment Scotland operate, but of how the inhabitants of a place use that place to communicate with each other. This addresses collective life: it is not an individual condition but a common one. And mostly, it will not be about the monuments but about all the things that pass under the radar because they are not subject to statutory controls: things that are too small, complex, ambiguous, ephemeral, unquantifiable, and difficult to value.

Planning applications will have to set out the principal signifiers of each new development and the principal signifiers that it replaces. It will have to demonstrate that these replacements conform to the linguistic and spatial rules of substitution that define the analogical city and their visual formal corollaries in montage. It is a problem of representation that we ought to be able to solve. It is not so simple as surveying landmarks, historic or otherwise. We need to be able to draw the forgetting Signorelli map for each place. These will be the site plans that accompany planning applications of the future. Substitution is universal because analogical cities are universal without relinquishing the particularities that define localities. One way to compile the lexicon of architectural elements and the grammar for change that define a particular place is through speculative design projects. Like Caneletto's real fictions, these projects will probably attend to the line of incision between context and substitution (*as any montage artist knows*). Planners will need to be trained as architects with a facility for design as an investigative and speculative process. This is what all architecture should be anyway if it is to rise to the challenge that the unconscious poses. Exploring *analogicity* is not about enumerating the elements of a place such as what a survey might do, but of condensing them into one thing that has the coherence and ambiguity of the analogical city.[22]

The lesson of Rossi is that the subject uses the city in all its heterogeneity (its spires and streets, its public lobbies and private windows, its architectural and urban elements and details, its pathways and spaces, beggars in doorways, field furrows and stone walls, street signs, traffic lights, shadows falling on thresholds, wind-born front pages, the distant roar of the football crowd, the storefront that changes ownership every two years, … *where are your wolves?*) to construct its history, such that an ethnography of the city is possible. I am thinking of ethnographies like de Certeau's practice of daily life; Benjamin's *Arcades Project*; Bruno Latour's online *Paris: invisible city*; Geddes' citizens' civic survey. These are different implementations of Halbwach's collective memory project.[23]

In the *Arcades Project*, Benjamin compiled a dossier of the newspaper clippings, films, novels, diaries, letters, neighbourhood legends, and old wives tales about the Paris Arcades – the memory of the Arcades. The control rooms of this city will be analytic settings – a network of them – in which the conflicts of individuals and places are addressed and not the observation rooms for CCTV *cameras*. What begins as ethnography of a place becomes the psychoanalysis that constructs a story. And if these proposals are too costly, or too time consuming, too complex, unreasonable, falsifiable, or fractious to work with the necessary expediencies of the procurement process, then at least we should stop pretending that development is good for people and acknowledge the violence and destruction of the planning and development process. Development is good for remote investors and politicians; it is almost always traumatic for the people being developed. It is doubtful whether development driven by investment opportunities will ever issue in anything other than trauma and whether planning policy driven by investment opportunities will ever do anything except destroy the city in the life of its inhabitants.

The shadow of a hand …

Sometimes incremental acts of construction coalesce into a single agency that blasts us like a clarion. The hand of San Carlone shadows Rossi's analogical city drawings, the theatres and *piazze*, as if it were the city, haunting itself. If the city is the field of the Other, this is the Other of the city; not an other city, but the city as the locus of all the fields, legal, geographic, and material, in which we articulate our desire. This is not the only place that the city appears ghostified. Patrick Geddes refers to ghost writing as a form of civic-urban discourse.[24] The colossal statue of San Carlone has been a 'progressive permanence' in the city of Arona since 1697. We don't know what it represents to Rossi, but it accompanies his thinking wherever it goes. It may be akin to the teapots and other objects incorporated into Rossi's drawings, disrupting their scale and easy reference to the world. It belies the cool extraction of the author from his/her work (*It is strange how I resemble myself*). Rossi might find the resemblance strange, or he might find himself strange. He raises the question: How do you put yourself in your city. How do you signify yourself? How do you go into the world of others as a signifier? You put yourself in your work by addressing it with your desire. When we find it there, it is uncanny because it seems to come from elsewhere. In the next chapter, introduced by Scott Brown/Venturi, we will look more closely at the city in the context of politics.

Notes

1 Leo Tolstoy, *War and Peace* (London: Penguin Popular Classics, 1869/1997), p. 666.
2 Portions of this chapter appeared in Lorens Holm, 'Aldo Rossi and the Field of the Other' in *Architecture and the Unconscious*, edited by John Shannon Hendrix and Lorens Holm (Abingdon: Routledge, 2016).
3 Page numbers in the text refer to Aldo Rossi, *The Architecture of the City* (Cambridge, MA: MIT Press, 1982).
4 Maurice Halbwachs, *The Collective Memory* (New York: Harper & Row Colophon Books, 1950/1980) and *On Collective Memory*, translated by Lewis A. Coser (Chicago and London: University of Chicago Press, 1952/1992). Halbwachs argues that price is an example of collective memory. The price of a commodity reflects the entire history of the production of the commodity, market practices and labour relations, international trade relations, and the like. Price is a symbolic construct of the money

system, without which it would not exist. There is no requirement that collective memory be held in whole, or even in part, in the minds of individuals, only that it be made operational through use.

5 Sigmund Freud, *The Psychopathology of Everyday Life: Forgetting, Slips of the Tongue, Bungled Actions, Superstitions and Errors (1901)*, Translated by Alan Tyson (New York: W. W. Norton, 1960). Freud's map appears in 'Chapter 1 The Forgetting of Proper Names' on p. 5.

6 Schema L is published and discussed in several texts, including *Seminar 2 (1954–55)*, 'Seminar on "The Purloined Letter"' (1966) and 'On a Question Prior to Any Possible Treatment of Psychosis' (1958) from whence this quote in *Ecrits: The First Complete … op. cit.* pp. 458–459. Note that Fink has translated the diagram: Other = *Autre* = A; other = *autre* = a.

7 The philosopher Jacques Derrida insisted upon the material nature of speech in his program to deconstruct the hierarchy that values speech over writing, signified over signifier. Speech, like writing, is a form of inscription. For a synopsis of this argument, see Jonathan Culler, *On Deconstruction – Theory and Criticism after Structuralism* (Ithaca, NY: Cornell University Press, 1982), in particular, the section 'Writing and Logocentrism', pp. 89–110. For the full treatment, see Jacques Derrida, *Of Grammatology*, translated by Gayatri Spivak (Baltimore, MD: Johns Hopkins University, 1976).

8 Lacan, *The Seminar of Jacques Lacan, Book III: The Psychoses 1955–1956* (New York: W. W. Norton, 1993), p. 274. Lacan, *The Four Fundamental Concepts … op. cit.*, p. 129, 'the locus of speech and, potentially, the locus of truth'.

9 Donald Kunze, 'Secondary Virtuality: The anamorphosis of Projective Geometry', in *Architecture and Culture* 8:3+4 (November 2020).

10 Iain Borden, Joe Kerr, Alicia Pivaro, and Jane Rendell, eds., *Strangely Familiar: Narratives of Architecture in the City* (London: Routledge, 1996).

11 Ground plane and picture plane intersect at the axis of perspectivity, for which see Desargues theorem (1648). A good guide to projective geometry and topology for non-mathematicians is A.D. Aleksandrov, A.N. Kolmogorov, and M.A. Lavrent'ev, *Mathematics: Its Contents, Methods, and Meaning*, trans. K. Hirsch (Cambridge, MA: MIT Press, 1963), in particular vol 3, part 5, chapter XVII 'Non-Euclidean Geometry' and part 6, chapter XVIII 'Topology'. For mathematically minded readers, see Rey Casse, *Projective Geometry: An Introduction* (Oxford: Oxford University Press, 2006) and H.S.M. Coxeter, *Projective Geometry* (New York: Springer-Verlag, 1987).

12 In *The Object of Psychoanalysis: The Seminar of Jacques Lacan, Book XIII: 1965–1966*, trans. Cormac Gallagher (unpublished manuscript for private use only, n.d.), Lacan discusses the paradoxical geometry of perspective and other typological figures. See in particular Seminar 16: Wednesday 4 May 1966 – on perspective including discussion of perspective, cross-caps, projecting one plane (picture plane) onto another (ground); the eye point in Alberti, Vignola, Durer; the horizon line. And Seminar 17: Wednesday 11 May 1966 – on *savoir* (knowledge), perspective, and *Las Meninas*.

13 For which, see Paolo Virno, *A Grammar of the Multitude: for an Analysis of Contemporary Forms of Life* (New York: Semiotext(e), 2004). See also Virno, 'Three Remarks Regarding the Multitude's Subjectivity and Its Aesthetic Component', in *Under Pressure: Pictures, Subjects, and the New Spirit of Capitalism*, edited by D. Birnbaum and I. Graw (Frankfurt: Sternberg Press, 2008).

14 Jacques Lacan, 'The Function and Field of Speech and Language in Psychoanalysis (1953)', in *Ecrits, op.cit.*, p. 215.

15 See, for instance, Patrick Geddes, *Cities in Evolution: An Introduction to the Town Planning Movement and to the Study of Civics* (London: William & Norgate, 1949) p. 170. 'Town plans are thus no mere diagrams, they are a system of hieroglyphics in which man has written the history of civilisation …' And his student, Lewis Mumford, *The City in History: Its Origins, Its Transformations, and Its Prospects* (1961) '… the great city is the best organ of memory man has yet created'. Rossi quoted Mumford, *The Culture of Cities* (1938), 'mind takes form in the city and urban form conditions mind …'.

16 In *A Grammar of the Multitude*, p. 75, Paulo Virno defines the multitude as 'the mode of being of the "many"'.

17 There is a good synopsis of the collective unconscious as it appears in Jung's text in Wikipedia, at https://en.wikipedia.org/wiki/Collective_unconscious (accessed July 2021), from where the quotes were taken as a secondary source. The Lacanian unconscious is immersed in the languages of its subjects and could not exist without their use; it does not – as does Jung's – exist independently of the languages of subjects and transcend them. Jung also acknowledges an individual unconscious which emerges in the analytic setting. The Freudian and Lacanian unconscious does not admit of a hierarchy of two. For each subject, the unconscious process comprises a stream of signifiers, although the signifiers of which they are constituted are heterogeneous and from many fields.

18 Jacques Lacan, *The Four Fundamental Concepts … op.cit.*, p. 207 in a chapter on alienation in the field of the Other.

19 For Rossi's analogical city and his theory of types, see a series of recent publications by Cameron McEwan, including 'Analogical Syntax: Form and Association in Three Projects by Aldo Rossi', *Scroope: Cambridge Architecture Journal:* 28 *Concinnitas* (2019), pp. 74–77; 'Linguistic Surface: The City Is the Locus of the Multitude', *Lo Squaderno:* 48 *Surfaces and Materials* (2018), pp. 13–16; 'Drawing the City – Writing the City: The Analogue as a Linguistic Form' *Drawing: Research, Theory, Practice* 3:1 *Drawing on Text* (2018), pp. 29–45; and 'The Analogical Surface: City, Drawing, Form and Thought', *Drawing On: Journal of Architecture Research by Design: 2 Surface and Installation* (2018), pp. 18–31. See also the discussion of Rossi's types and Rossi's elements in my paper 'Aldo Rossi and the Field of the Other', in *Architecture and the Unconscious*, edited by Hendrix and Holm (Routledge, 2016).

20 Rossi identifies historic artefacts in the city that have become 'pathological' (as opposed to propelling) permanences; these calcified, mummified artefacts have lost their signifying status and no longer support our capacity to articulate our unconscious in our encounters with the city.

21 See, for instance, the Ministry of Housing, Communities, & Local Government, *National Planning Policy Framework*, latest revision Feb. 2019; and the Dundee Local Development Plan 2019, both available online. These documents set as their goals the well-being of inhabitants, but they are not able to theorise and hence reconcile the conflicting demands of well-being and development. For example, in 'Section 12. Achieving well-designed places' of the former document, paragraph 127:
> 'Planning policies and decisions should ensure that developments:
> (c) are sympathetic to local character and history, …
> (d) establish or maintain a strong sense of place, …
> (f) create places … which promote health and well-being, …'.

22 Cameron McEwan develops a graphic strategy for thinking *analogicity* in his paper, 'Architecture, Multitude, and the Critical Project', *Architecture and Culture* 8:3+4 (November 2020).

23 Michel de Certeau, *The Practice of Everyday Life*, trans. Steven Rendall (Berkley, CA: University of California Press, 1984); Walter Benjamin, *Arcades Project* (Cambridge, MA and London: Belknap Press of Harvard University Press, 1999); Bruno Latour, *Paris Invisible City* at http://www.bruno-latour.fr/virtual/EN/index.html (1998); Patrick Geddes, *Cities in Evolution: An Introduction to the Town Planning Movement and to the Study of Civics* (London: Ernest Benn/ Williams & Norgate, 1968/1915).

24 Lorens Holm, ed., *The City Is a Thinking Machine: Patrick Geddes and Cities in Evolution* (Dundee: Geddes Institute for Urban Research and the University of Dundee, 2016) in 4 volumes. See *Volume 2: The Geddes Archives* with caption notes by Lorens Holm, in which is reproduced Geddes lecture notes on phantomography, the city as ghost writing.

FIGURE 5.1 Venturi and Nolli: learning from Las Vegas or commerce trumps space.

5

FRAMPTON AND SCOTT BROWN/ VENTURI [THE SOCIAL INSTITUTION OF THE CITY OR THE DEATH DRIVE]

> The manipulative bias of such ideologies [new urbanism] has never been more openly expressed than in Robert Venturi's *Complexity and Contradiction in Architecture* (1966) wherein the author asserts that Americans do not need piazzas, since they should be at home watching television. Such reactionary attitudes emphasize the impotence of an urbanised population which has paradoxically lost the object of its urbanization.
>
> (Kenneth Frampton, 'Towards a critical regionalism')[1]

Most architects go to Rome. Le Corbusier went to the Acropolis. Denise Scott Brown and Robert Venturi went to Las Vegas. When they return, they montage

DOI: 10.4324/9780429022845-5

a tourist picture postcard onto the Nolli plan of Rome. They place one of the most commercial forms of picture upon one of the most hallowed city plans in western architectural discourse.[2]

The Nolli plan represents Rome as if it were a continuous extended plastic surface that wraps around *piazze* and moves in and out of churches. Postcard Las Vegas is a city of road signs. Scott Brown/Venturi replace an expanding and contracting room with an infrastructure of information. What is important about Las Vegas are not spatial qualities but quantities of information: its densities, the direction of flow, how much static there is. To the European avant-garde, Scott Brown/Venturi were building within a landscape whose salient feature was its lack of information, collective or otherwise, no traces of past or future. They were compensating for an amnesiac landscape.[3]

Las Vegas is the paradigm car city. Scott Brown/Venturi made no attempt to conceal their appeal to popular culture, which here means not vernacular culture but culture *overwritten* by advertising and entertainment. The threat is that this commercial car culture will overwhelm Rome. One of the visual effects of the montage is to flip the Nolli plan vertically to make it into a sign that advertises itself as a fun tourist destination.

That Frampton understood Scott Brown/Venturi's gesture as an attack on the political value of the city is clear from the way he castigates Scott Brown/Venturi for saying that Americans do not need *piazze* because they have TV. They fail to recognise the role of the city as the locus for the public life of politics. Without defending Scott Brown/Venturi or ameliorating the critique, we see in their work the tacit recognition of something else: the recognition that as regards architectural thinking on cities and political life, the conventional political categories of public and private are shadowed by the instrumental categories of individual and collective.

This chapter will follow a line of political thinking on cities, architecture, and the togetherness of people sketched out in Vitruvius' account of the primitive hut in *The Ten Books on Architecture*, Aristotle's *Politics*, and Arendt's reading of Aristotle in *The Human Condition*. It will read these texts against Freud's account of the death drive in his late text *Civilization and Its Discontents*. It will conclude with Lacan's discussion of *Civilization* ... in *The Ethics of Psychoanalysis*. It is the intention of this chapter to sketch the political role of architecture and, in so doing, shift the focus of architectural discourse from the political relation of public and private to the social relation of individual and collective. I want to understand how architecture gathers people together into what I will call discourses.

The dialectic of individual and collective

Vitruvius

> Therefore, because of the discovery of fire, there arose at the beginning, concourse among men, deliberation and a life in common. Many came together into one place,...[4]

(p. 77)

… then, from the construction of buildings they progressed by degrees to other crafts and disciplines, and they led the way from a savage and rustic life to a peaceful civilisation.

(p. 85)

Vitruvius' account of the primitive hut in *The Ten Books on Architecture* tells the story of the birth of architecture from its pre-architectural origins. Primitive men (Aristotle's breeding pair) live in the forest until driven out by a catastrophic fire. 'Men, in the old way, were born like animals in forests ….' (p. 77). Once the fire had run its course, the forest dwellers congregate in clearings around the scattered embers. These are the first campfires, catastrophe domesticated. 'In this concourse of mankind, … they fixed words ….' (p. 79). 'And so they generated conversation with one another' (p. 79). Once gathered into groups around these originary hearths, they invented language so that they could speak to one another and, once speaking, decide to build homes. Architecture is born with language and fire. Architecture is different from the rude burrowed shelters of primitives, the way language is different from the barking of animals. The trace of speech – what accompanies it as its permanent trace – is writing; and in his extraordinary narrative, Vitruvius presents construction, the construction of architecture, as the writing that accompanies concourse. Not writing on the walls, but walls. For Vitruvius, language constitutes the life in common, and Vitruvius equates language with speech and the construction of architecture. These are the symbolic activities that bind us to each other. Henceforth we will use Rossi's term *construction* and not *building*, to indicate when architecture builds buildings as well as the social order of civilisation.

Aristotle and Arendt

Observation tells us that every state is an association, and that every association is formed with a view to some good purpose …. The association that aims to embrace all other goods, the highest good and the 'most sovereign' association is the state. This is the association which we call the state, the association which is 'political' ['political' = 'the association that takes the form of a *polis* (state)' for which see the translator's footnote].

(Aristotle, The Politics, para. 1252a1)

The *polis*, properly speaking, is not the city-state in its physical location; it is the organisation of the people as it arises out of acting and speaking together, and its true space lies between people living together for this purpose, no matter where they happen to be …. It [the polis] is the space of appearance in the widest sense of the word, namely, the space where I appear to others as others appear to me, where men exist not merely like other living or inanimate things but make their appearance explicitly.

(Arendt, The Human Condition (1958), pp. 198–199)

We are all what Aristotle called statesmen: men and women of the state. There is a long line of thinking in architectural and political discourse that equates the city-state or *polis* with the site of public life and politics. This equation has its clearest contemporary statement in the political philosopher Hannah Arendt's reading of Aristotle. The architects Pier Vittorio Aureli, George Baird, and Kenneth Frampton are largely responsible for maintaining her work in architectural discourse.[5] The agora or marketplace in Aristotle's Athens was originally the space for commerce, intellectual thought, and political debate at a time when democracy was still a new form, perhaps still so new it was not yet fully recognised as a new social form. They were working it out as they built it. In *The Politics*, Aristotle argued that the polis was the natural home of man, the political animal. He argues that there are four forms of association: the breeding pair (Vitruvius' primitive forest dweller, pre-fire, pre-linguistic), the family, the village, and the state (a kingdom is simply a large family ruled by a despot/father). The *polis*, whose inhabitants meet as equals to publicly stage conflicts of interest, is the social condition of democracy. And the agora is its form. When Aristotle defines man as a 'political animal' motivated by virtue, and distinguishes this political animal from the simple animal – what the political philosopher Agamben will call bare life (*zoe*) to distinguish it from a qualified life (*bios*) – he makes a similar distinction to Vitruvius' distinction between the purposive concourse of men brought together by speech and construction, and the primitive condition of the barking twig-gathering solipsist whose togetherness is random.[6]

Aristotle also distinguishes the form of life that is bare (*zoe*) from the form of life that is political (*bios*). In Aristotle's teleology, the state, like every community, exists for an end, which is – for Aristotle – necessarily a good end. It is the end of a thing that defines its nature. The end of the state is the good life of man. Indeed, it is only in the state that man can live the good life. Man is political by nature and the state is where he realises his nature. The state is the environment that subjects build for themselves, which allows their nature its full development. In this sense, the state is natural, although its ends are the good life, not the bare life. Aristotle makes two points about the state that will be critical for our argument. For Aristotle, speech is the critical component of the state, which is where the social life of man reaches its most complete form. And the state, as a form of association, is logically – not temporally – prior to the breeding pair and the family. It is prior because it is self-sufficient, whereas the breeding pair and the family are not.[7]

In *The Human Condition* (1958), Arendt argues that the city is the formal paradigm for democracy. Frampton singles out two key ideas from Arendt: 'space of appearance' and 'the togetherness of people'. The city or *polis* is the locus for both. In the togetherness of people (Vitruvius's *concourse* and Aristotle's *association*) lies our political power (*unity is strength*). The space of appearance is where we make our views public, hence the space where they can be scrutinised and reflected upon and the conflicts between them debated. We appear with our views so that we remain accountable to others. This happens in Aristotle's agora and the debating chamber. It happens in the boulevard and piazza, both of which appear as architectural forms in the plans of cities. It is unclear whether concourse in social media, in which the author of a view remains hidden from public view, meets the criteria for Arendt's space of appearance, and for this reason, whether social media is a supplement to public space in politics or the undoing of politics. In a series of oppositions that cascade under Aristotle's distinction between state and household, Vittorio Aureli, reading Arendt and Aristotle, distinguishes politics and economics in classical thought – politics is a public relation between people of the state, and economics is a private relation within the household – and hence the social form of the *polis* from the management of city growth. Aureli criticises contemporary planning practice as a form of household management of the continuous process of urbanisation, rather than what it should be, the formal articulation of settlements for public debate.[8]

Freud

> The existence of this inclination to aggression, ... disturbs our relations with our neighbour and ... forces civilisation into such a high expenditure of energy. In consequence of this primary mutual hostility of human beings, civilised society is perpetually threatened with disintegration.
>
> *(Freud, Civilisation and its Discontents, p. 49)*

> [T]he inclination to aggression is an original, self-subsisting instinctual disposition in man, ... that ... constitutes the greatest impediment to civilisation. ... [C]ivilisation is a process in the service of Eros, whose purpose is to combine single human individuals, and after that families, then races, peoples and nations, into one great unity, the unity of mankind. [9]
>
> *(Freud, Civilisation and its Discontents, p. 59)*

The architectural discourse on public and private life is shadowed by another discourse that runs parallel to it but is rarely invoked in political or architectural contexts. It speaks more directly to the togetherness of people. One of the most ambitious attempts to articulate the relation of individual to collective is Freud's account of the death drive in *Civilisation and its Discontents* (1930). In its ambition, it exposes the ambiguities that dog originary thinking. Freud made three definitive statements on the drives (or instincts as they appear in English translations). We will look at *Civilisation ...*, 'Instincts and their Vicissitudes' (1915), and *Beyond the Pleasure Principle* (1920) in this chapter, and will refer to them again in the next.

Freud wrote *Civilisation and Its Discontents* when the long shadow of a war he would not live to see was already cast upon Vienna but whose symptoms were already everywhere around him. He is putting his finger on, not political disagreement between social groups with conflicts of interest but a form of social disintegration. When we look at the continuous state of conflict since the Second

World War, combined with the eroding of natural habitats and environmental quality, we begin to wonder if Freud got the model right. In *Civilisation and Its Discontents*, Freud puts the drive in opposition to civilisation, as indeed does most of the literature emanating from *Civilisation* …. This is Freud's final statement on the drive and as an architectural proposition, his most definitive. Freud sketched the idea that civilization was an edifice imposed by human subjects upon themselves in order to control their instincts. Civilisation is thus frustrating, masking discontent but a necessary form of sublimation. He argues that our natural inclination for aggression against others will tear civilisation apart.[10]

The drive resides in the individual and civilization appears as the ties that binds individuals into collective social formations. Freud does not elaborate these ties, but we can assume that they include the great social institutions that regulate life, chief among them language and what Lacan's colleague at L'Ecole Freudienne de Paris, Michel de Certeau, called the practice of everyday life, but also the law, construction, money, religion, and the arts. We are bound to each other by ties that are material and symbolic, like co-housing arrangements, marriages, mortgages, rental agreements, housing associations, neighbourhood associations, professional associations, guilds, food banks, sports clubs, gun clubs, gun control laws, labour laws, construction and construction contracts, local development plans, pension schemes, shared risk, and our weekly Tesco run. Lacan says in the *Ethics of Psychoanalysis* that we experience reality through our social relations. Civilisation imposes a symbolic infrastructure upon subjects that reigns in our drives, without which we would expend ourselves in a kind of objectiveless fighting and fornicating. The 'inclination to aggression' resides in each individual and threatens to break those binds.[11]

There are passages in *Civilisation* … where Freud puts the death drive in opposition to love or Eros rather than civilisation (a return to the thinking in *Beyond the Pleasure Principle*). Eros here is not the narcissism of the individual (self-love and hence aggressivity to others); it is the love of others, shorthand for the social field that constitutes civilisation. We are bound to each other, mostly in unconscious ways or ways of which we are largely unaware, because they work through mechanism of language rather than intention. In terms of Vitruvius, Eros is near to 'concourse among men'; Eros has the form of speech and construction, which draw people together. Although Freud seems to equivocate, Eros appears to reside between individuals in the social field rather than – like the drive – in the individual. And the drive, even when placed in opposition to Eros, seems to be not an other component of the social field, one social pressure among many, but something real that lies outside it, other to it, in the individual.

In *Civilisation* …, drive theory is presented within a dialectic between the collective, whose locus is civilisation, in all its particularity and universality, its creation and constructivity (Rossi defined *the architecture of the city* as *construction*) and the individual, which lies outside it, and is the locus of aggression to others. We know it as a form of deaf, dumb, and numb repetition that undoes all that is civilisation and all that it signifies. In his argument, drive plays the role of what is simple and pre-significant *vis-à-vis* a civilisation that is constructed and signifying. Freud puts *civilisation* in the singular: it is a collective fiction, a fictional collective. *Discontents* is plural: reality is a multitude of individuals. A fictive unity is put in dialogue with a real multitude. As if we are all naturally individuals, the reality of the body, my body different from yours. And we share a fiction that we are a civilisation, and what civilisation is protecting us against is our own nature.[12]

Freud distinguishes *Trieb* or drive from *Instinkt* or animal instinct. This distinction is similar to Aristotle's distinction between political and simple animal, between the qualified and the bare life, except that in his argument, drive – not instinct – is put in the position of the individual with respect to civilisation. Any argument about origins that depends upon the distinction between man and nature can be deconstructed. We shift the argument to the dialectic between collective and individual social formations and allow that they are both nature, in order to sidestep these hazards. It is man's nature to construct civilisations, in the sense that Aristotle can say man's nature is to be political, and Mumford that man's nature is to be technological.

Freud opened *Civilisation and Its Discontents* with the account of a conversation with a novelist friend who proposes that what unites people is a feeling of inclusiveness that he calls 'oceanic'. Freud dismisses it as infantile and illusory. It seems to be an odd way to introduce a study of civilisation, until you realise Freud's point that there are two ways we seem to be bound to each other into civilisations: the so-called oceanic *feeling* of togetherness which is illusory, and the social ties that really bind us. The oceanic feeling is illusory because it resides in the imagination of the individual as opposed to the ties between individuals. It is an individual social formation as opposed to a collective one. The paradox is that the oceanic feeling is comforting but useless; and the latter – the ties that really bind – efficacious but onerous.

A short course on the drive

The theory of the drives is psychoanalysis at its most speculative. It is where psychoanalysis is most ontological, at once reductive and universalising, and perhaps most removed from the behaviour of individuals. For this writer of architectural narratives of the human condition, it is also the most compelling. Freud describes the drive as a stimulus-response mechanism; an itch of the body that needs a psychical scratching. The deaf and dumb stimulus of the body cross over and become 'psychical representatives' in the consciousness of the subject. The drive is the flywheel of the psyche and the horizon where the deaf dumb real of the body crosses over into the inter-subjective world to become consciousness: in our terms (not Freud's), a bio-mechanical threshold located in the individual (natural) and producing signifiers (civilisation). It is at the threshold between the real and the symbolic worlds. We know that such a horizon must exist.

It can't not, but we also know that empirical science will never find it because we are always on one side of that threshold, and it was the genius of Freud that he could comprehend such an object of thought and recognise that it must exist. In Freud's thought, the drive represents – if not the irreducible kernel of biology in each subject then at least – the irreducible confrontation of the subject with its biology. It acknowledges the biological substructure to subjectivity. There is more architectural work to be done on the drive, its constructed nature, its necessity for a site, its imposition of hard labour upon the psyche, and its seemingly intractable spatial, temporal, and material nature.

In 'Instincts and their Vicissitudes' (1915), Freud's first paper on the drive, Freud writes 'an instinct appears to us as a concept on the frontier between the mental and the somatic, as the psychical representative of the stimuli originating from within the organism and reaching the mind, as a measure of the demand made upon the mind for work in consequence of its connection to the body'. Freud argues that to understand the drive it has to have four components: pressure, aim, object, and source. The drive has a 'motor force' or urgency that drives behaviour, it has an aim which is 'in every instance satisfaction [relief from stimulus]', an object or 'thing [the scratch] in regard to which … the instinct is able to achieve its aim', and it is associated with a bodily source or organ 'whose stimulus [the itch] is represented in mental life by an instinct'. These are the erogenous zones of the body.[13]

In *Beyond the Pleasure Principle* (1920), Freud puts the death drive in opposition to pleasure. We have already seen this binary thinking in *Civilisation …* where the death drives are put in opposition to civilisation. The drives went through a number of iterations in Freud's thought, but they never lost their binary structure. In *Beyond …* Freud argues that there are two forms of drive in opposition to each other, life drives or Eros and death drives or Thanatos, but he argues that these drives are not actually equal and opposite; rather, the death drives lie beyond the life drives as if they were the end point of the drives. Beyond – or underlying – pleasure, which is the driver for all that is creative and procreative, lies the death drive and the destruction that is also innate to subjects. Underlying all we do for life, love, happiness, and construction; lies aggression, repetition, and death. Architecture and its perspective apparatus operate in the zone of pleasure; but beyond it, perhaps as an inevitable consequence of the satisfaction that is pleasure, lies the enjoyment of the drive to death. This is not another way of referring to the perversions: the death drive is not about taking pleasure in causing pain (sadism) or in receiving it (masochism), but the compulsive way that the pursuit of the good life inflicts unhappiness upon ourselves and others. Rossi could write: *Architecture. Bar. Death.* Le Corbusier could say in his last text, published posthumously, 'The law of life: death'. And in another discourse altogether, the economist Joseph Schrumpeter, argued that the defining trope of capitalism is creative destruction and Marshall Berman, following Marx, could say of capitalism, 'all that is solid melts into air'.[14]

Lacan reading Freud

Civilisation is not a fiction, but it is, to borrow Lacan's term, symbolic, which distinguishes it from other sorts of fictions that are imaginary, like the oceanic feeling, and from the opacity of the material world. In *The Four Fundamental Concepts of Psychoanalysis* (1964), Lacan argues that Freud's concept of the drive is as much a symbolic construct as is civilisation. This is not the place to unpick the detail, but Lacan argues that Freud's four components constitute a *montage*. What links them is the compelling nature of the assemblage and not logic or cause. As architects, we are familiar with this sort of compelling but not logical assemblage. Think of Vitruvius' treatment of the Parthenon as an assemblage of architectural elements governed by proportion. Lacan also draws attention to the fact that Freud cannot articulate the recursive 'circuit' or trajectory of the drive, in effect driven behaviour, without recourse to the linguistic forms of the active, reflexive, and passive verb forms. Note that for Lacan, the drive is a path, it is spatial, even if it simply returns in itself. Lacan takes Freud's English translators to task for translating both *Trieb* and *Instinkt* as *instinct*, thereby blurring a critical distinction in Freud's thought between what is constructed and what is the natural behaviour of animals. The distinction between drive and instinct will always be contested, but drive is behaviour explained through language, and instinct is behaviour explained through zoology.[15] According to Lacan, Freud's individual – the locus of the drive – is as much an artefact or construct of civilisation – as is civilisation. The subject of psychoanalysis, takes the form of a speaking being (Lacan's *parle-être*), an individual availing itself of a collectively held linguistic culture, and it must already be bound into civilisation, in order to articulate itself as an individual.

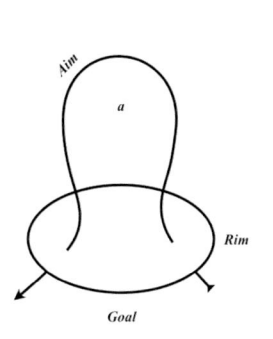 

The drive is a return journey **The spatial typology of Vitruvian concourse**

FIGURE 5.2 Lacan's diagram of the drive + learning from Vitruvius, the first concourse involved speaking and building around a campfire.

It is worth drilling into these points in a little detail. Freud's active, reflexive, and passive – *to see, to see oneself, to be seen* – seems to produce subjects and objects (*I saw Esau kissing Kate*). To see (an object; as there is as yet no sense of a subject, it might be better to say an object is seen). To see oneself (to make oneself an object of vision for yourself (the subject appears for itself, a kind of mirror stage). To be seen (to make oneself an object for others, at which point one's subjectivity is now fully emerged in relation to others). We could generalise the template to define architecture as the Vitruvian drive to subjectivity, part of the on-going practice of humanising ourselves: to build, to build one's self, to be built by others, within the field of the city. In *The Four Fundamental Concepts* …, Lacan diagrams the drive as a flow of signifiers that form a 'circuit' or return journey around the object and return to the site on the body. This is his spatial interpretation of the active-reflexive-passive progression of voices with which Freud articulates the recursive temporality of the drive. It is also one of the key moments where Lacan's structuralism replaces Freud's biologism. For Freud, the goal was the relief from stimulus (scratch the itch); the comparable aim in Lacan's reformulation is the trajectory or aim of signifiers. Lacan puns the word *aim*. For both, the pleasure is in the repetition.[16]

Freud related the drive to the theory of psychosexual development, the oral, anal, phallic, and genital stages, and to neurotic and perverse modes of sexuality.[17] In Lacan's thought, there are four part-drives mapped onto the body by their corresponding part objects, the breast, faeces, gaze, and voice. We have discussed the gaze and voice, whose sites on the body are the eye and hear. In chapters 2 & 3, we also gave them architectural locations. Note that the sites all have a rim structure. They are openings.[18] Unlike Freud's stages of development, which are unified with maturity in the genital stage, Lacan argues that all drives are partial – the four never reduce to or add up to an originary unity, nor are they ever more than partially representations of the sexuality of the body – and all drives lead to death. All drives are death drives, not because we are inherently destructive, nor even that we are mortal – the aim of life is death – but because death like sexuality are effects of the symbolic order (*the way inflation is an effect of capitalism?*). Whereas instinct in animals is satisfied in reproduction, sexuality in humans is not satisfied by reproduction and is not regulated by instinct but by this quite particular arrangement of the symbolic order in which the body is an assemblage of these symbolic parts/part-objects. The denatured signifier replaces the nature of the body.[19]

In *Brunelleschi Lacan Le Corbusier*, I used the drive to understand the relation of the Parthenon to architecture and to Le Corbusier's career. I argued that the Parthenon functions in architectural discourse as the unassimilable object that has to be disowned by architecture in order for architecture to be spatial. It is the traumatic object that drives Le Corbusier's prodigious production of projects, all of them signifiers circumnavigating the Parthenon without ever being it. We will see in the next chapter that what organises the driven life may become pathological when it becomes collective. The drive and desire are closely entwined concepts and Lacan uses *objet petit a* to name the objects of both. The aim of desire is the object, which it never attains. The aim of the drive is to flow around the object. The Lacanian Hegelian philosopher Slavoj Žižek uses the simile of the warped space of a gravitational field around a void. They describe different relations of *objet a* to the subject. The object of desire is always absent to the subject. It is absent because possession is always deferred. The enjoyment associated with desire is the enjoyment of delay, as in Marcel Duchamp's window construction *The Large Glass or the bride stripped bare by her bachelors, even* (1915–1923), which he called a *delay in glass*. The object of the drive is a void, absence is itself the object about which the signifiers flow (in another context altogether, Eisenman distinguishes the absence of a presence from the presence of an absence). The enjoyment of the drive is repetition. In neither the structure of drive nor desire is the object possessed or attained.[20]

We need to bring this detour back to the question of civilisation and man's nature.

Rereading the concourse of Vitruvius

The same retroactive logic of origins at work in Freud's account of civilisation and in Aristotle's account of the state is at work in Vitruvius' account of architecture. In a trope in '… Vicissitudes' that is not unlike the emergence of architecture as discourse in Vitruvius, the drive appears in each individual at the 'frontier between the mental and the somatic', where opaque body process emerges as representation to the psyche. In Freud, the subject has to invent an unbound individual (*an oxymoron?*) in order to explain itself by reference to an origin. Civilisation has to expel this fictive individual in order to be civilisation; thereafter, this individual persists as a kind of absent presence that haunts civilisation. This individual is a construction but is asked to play the role of an origin. It appears as an outsider banging at the gates but turns out to be internal to the logic of civilisation. The logic is spatial, but it is masked by temporal language. It appears in Derrida's deconstructive reading of phenomenology as a meaning that is always already deferred, an absent presence that has haunted western philosophy since Plato. It appears in the political philosopher Giorgio Agamben's account of the origins of the concept of the law and the force of law, in the state of exception or emergency that is precisely the moment when the power of the law is revoked. It appears in one of Lacan's few short statements on architecture, *architecture, like painting, is organised around emptiness.* This individual is not the origin, but the *negated present* (Derrida's formula) of civilisation. Civilisation constructs this absent destructive figure at its centre and then tries to disown or repress or incarcerate it in order to be civilisation.[21]

We don't need to look far to see how pervasive this celebration of the individual is in popular and intellectual culture. It is two steps: individual is conjoined with nature; nature is celebrated as origin. It is the subtext to the return to nature espoused by the great American men of letters, Ralph Waldo Emerson and Henry David Thoreau, who championed the individual against the pressures of society. It is articulated in the justification of civil disobedience, in which the individual stands against a corrupt state. It is one of the subtexts that drive American gun laws; you are only an individual because you can defend your way out of any situation, in particular one involving big government. It is the subtext to every car advert that montages car and owner into an impossibly beautiful place in New Zealand. Car ownership equates to freedom of the road and freedom of the road to freedom to leave the city. This is paradoxical because the road is one of the most rule governed environments, and the city was where the civil rights of individuals were written. It is the subtext for any aesthetic theory that derives beauty from nature, including Vitruvius, who sought to derive the proportions of the orders from the human body.[22]

Western intellectual culture puts the individual in a hierarchical relation with the collective, in which the individual is first, the collective second. The individual is natural, or at least closer to nature, which is the guarantor of purity, priority, and honesty. The collective is an artifice, a complexity, a fall from the originary condition of the individual. The collectivised individual is older, worn out, cynical, and seduced. Not a Parthenon, but a shopping mall. The Parthenon is the architecture object before it is compromised by the concept we call space. It is so purely architecture, it is not architecture. In the collective, the nature of the individual is polluted by the hand of man. The individual can be one or many, but when the many becomes a collective, the collective exists not in individuals – the site of nature – but in the scaffolding between individuals, the site of civilisation. As soon as we introduce the scaffolding that binds individuals, what had been unsullied by the hand of man becomes mired in signifiers. The many ones become bound together into a single complex, and this complexity begins to compromise the original singleness and purity of the many. It introduces the possibility of confusion, differences of opinion, and conflicts of interest.

The upshot of Lacan's argument is that the subject never existed as individual outwith the conceptual curtilage of the subject that invented it. This individual that is the indexical sign of nature was always already an invention of a socialised collectivised individual that invokes it in order to explain itself. Animals are always already organised into groups, whose individuals operate as part of larger communication relays. The lesson of Lacan's rethinking of Freud's concept of the drive is to reverse the hierarchy between nature and civilisation.[23] It took the most civilised men of letters in American culture to invent this natural individual who has to flee the bounds of civilisations in order to know thyself. It took an advertising agency, staffed by humanities graduates who wrote their dissertations in American romanticism, with offices in the Seagram Building, commissioned by an automotive manufacturer, advised by their legal team, to invent this subject that drives a car all the way to New Zealand.

In Vitruvius, civilised people construct a pre-linguistic individual to exclude in order to make concourse among speaking subjects intelligible. The subject cannot experience itself as individual until it is part of a larger linguistic entity. A civilisation styled as a social group modelled on the family, i.e. a grouping around a campfire or hearth but in reality, a grouping of many families, and no longer an extension of the breeding pair, who now have language, in other words, a linguistically constituted group who have moved beyond the yelping of animals, invent a pre-social formation, the unattached wandering yelping forest-bound fire-harassed individual, in order to make intelligible to themselves their current condition of concourse. Plurality comes first; subjects are always already a plurality. The many subjects come into being with speech and architecture; the many subjects are already civilisation, already civilised. Speech and architecture are the linguistic infrastructures that bind subjects; the negativity they contain, which threatens them from the inside, is the retroactive construction of an absent presence. The biological body is natural, but the driven individual we attach to the body is no more natural than the collective formations with which we bind them.

Architecture binds individuals because projects are – in Arendt's terms – bigger than what any one person can construct and they outlast the mortality of individuals.[24] There is an analogous relation between language and architecture: Vitruvius' *parle-être* talking around their campfire and the Vitruvian hut that they build and habit together. We are bound to each other by concourse and by the project. Language is a form of construction that binds us, only we tend not to recognise it as such because we live in a linguistic environment, it is our air, it is all around us, as opposed to a crafted artefact that we place before our eyes and hands. Hannah Arendt talks about the importance of work (*Victorian good works*) which put things into the world that outlast us and distinguishes work from labour that is completely exhausted each day in survival (*the drive is labour*). She critiques Marx for flubbing this distinction.[25] Work produces civilisation and its enduring artefacts. The distinction between labour and work maps onto Aristotle's forms of association. According to Aristotle, the breeding pair and the family exist to meet the needs of daily life. The state is an enduring work. Although it may seem that our speech disappears like labour, gone without remainder as soon as it does its job, and writing – writing unlike speech, leaves a trace – is a slim artefact, speech and writing put ideas into the world which are as constructional and artefactual as building. Lacan's student, the analyst and philosopher Felix Guattari argues for an ecology that preserves non-corporeal beings like ideas as well as living beings. People congregate around ideas as much as they congregate around buildings and campfires.

In Vitruvius, we witness the dual emergences of the symbolic code of architecture from instinctual twig gathering and the symbolic code of language from instinctual barking. We witness the emergence of the symbolic body in drive theory. Like the Parthenon, it is an assemblage of objects. We are bound by these codes into collective social formations without which we could not articulate ourselves as individual subjects. These codes define our subjectivity; their emergence from a deaf and dumb instinctual condition mark the horizon of our subjectivity. The effect of the drive is reductive. The death drive is a disintegration of these social codes into repetition, which is not the same as instinctual twig gathering, although in some cases, they may look similar. Instead of symbolic distinctions, repetition that destroys them. If desire depends upon the articulation of difference, the death drive depends upon the proliferation of the same. In the context of desire or object choice, which is a symbolic activity that cannot be understood outside the social codes that construct desire and its choices, the death drive appears as greed. Greed is the disintegration of desire into a form of proliferation. Greed increases as choice decreases. Greed increases with the proliferation of identical signifiers: 25 different toppings of pizza which are all really just pizza; cars with hundreds of interchangeable options and colours and configurations of lights and grills and vents and repayment plans, all of which are just Mondeos. In 'Homes for America' (1967), Dan Graham reproduces the endless identical variations for the same suburban home – his critique of Levittown – each model with an anodyne name and colour. This is not Vitruvius' primitive hut updated – in other words, a condensation of architectural discourse into a single simple form – but its negation by the proliferation of objects driven by commodity capitalism. It is going in the opposite direction to civilisation. Our subjectivity emerged with the emergence of Vitruvius' hut, and we witness it disappearing again in the numbing repetition of 'Homes for America'.[26]

The death drive is not a return to the primitive, or to the animal; nor even to the non-organic; although it may sometime look that way, and indeed, Freud sometimes seems to describe it that way. It is a break down or corruption of the symbolic order when we no longer think it is functioning for us and we no longer see its importance or significance. It is when concourse becomes chatter. It is when we forget that the overriding significance of speech is to bring us together, even when we are arguing with each other. Or the primary reason for construction is to bring us together, to collect us, even when we are building walls that separate. Or when we get so carried away with what we want that we forget that the objects we acquire are only steppingstones to an Other place, what analysis calls desire. Most of these wants are fanned by the advertising industry, which has become the 5th estate.

Wo es war soll ich werden or desire is an ethical position

In *The Ethics of Psychoanalysis*, Lacan argues that desire is an ethical position. In a nutshell, be true to your desire, which means seek it in the field of the Other, not in the acquisition of objects. In *The Four Fundamental Concepts …*, Lacan focused on Freud's '… Vicissitudes' paper. In *The Ethics …*, he turns to *Civilisation and Its Discontents*. He seems to interpret the ties that bind as injunctions, as if the flip side of a moral code is a taboo in which we collude. And oddly, he focuses on the relatively short passage where Freud evokes the neighbour. Freud says that most people would sooner enslave and torture their neighbour as love them. Lacan points out that Freud, like all good neighbours, hates his (*who doesn't?*).[27] Freud is horrified at the prospect of loving his neighbour, loving his neighbour simply because it is his neighbour, loving his neighbour as he would love himself (*a stranger, an other, what happens if de Sade is the neighbour?*). Freud wrote

Civilisation ... as an individual, subject – like all of us – to the almost impossible demands imposed upon individuals by civilisation, and not from a position outside it. (One of Lacan's tropes is to remind us that Freud was subject to his own psychoanalytic claims and this fact must be the basis for authoritative readings of his work.) *The Ethics* ... is the text where Lacan addresses moral experience. In the opening chapter, where he seems to be casting his net, collecting evidence, he says something is 'imposed' upon us by transgression, it leads to 'the origin of a higher complexity, something to which the realm of civilisation owes its development'.[28] He is referring to the myth of originary transgression and guilt that binds us (Freud's *Moses and Monotheism*).[29] He relates it to 'the logos' (language, the law, the law of language). He then segues into a discussion of one of Freud's most enigmatic statements about the relation of ego and id, *wo es war soll ich werden*. Strachey's translation, followed by Lacan's:

> *Where id was, there ego shall be. It is a work of culture – not unlike the draining of the Zuider Zee.*
> *(Freud, New Introductory Lectures on Psycho-Analysis (1933) transl. by Strachey)*

> ... it is in the locus *Wo* (Where) *Es* (the subject devoid of any *das* or other objectifying article) *war*, (was – it is a locus of being that is at stake, and that in this locus), *soll* (it is a duty in the moral sense ...) *Ich* (I, there must I ...) *werden* (become ... be born of this very locus in so far as it is a locus of being).
> *(Lacan, 'The Freudian Thing' (1956))*

Or what is less tortured:

> Where it was, there I must come to be as a subject.
> *(Lacan, 'Science and Truth' (1966))*

I is the subject's signifier for itself. For Lacan, it is the moral duty of the *I* to inhabit the position of unconscious desire and not ego. In this context, Lacan's intent seems to be to shift Freud's opposition individual-civilisation to ego-unconscious, as if the locus of the unconscious was civilisation and the locus of civilisation's destruction was the ego. An individual unconscious, with a collective locus. It is about where we position the subjectivity to which *I* refers. It is a duty to itself and to others.[30] Desire is realised when it is subjected to the linguistic order that emerges in concourse with others. The project of architecture is to read this order in the city, to find its form in the city. Freud's Eros is asked to do a lot of work here. Freud's Eros segues to Lacan's unconscious desire; it is Vitruvian concourse that binds us into social groups, and it cannot quite disentangle itself from the love of *love thy neighbour*. It is not too much to say that for Lacan, the field of the Other, in which unconscious desire is articulated, is the paradigm of social grammar and the most fundamental form of togetherness (Arendt). It is akin to other terms in architectural and political discourse including collective memory (Rossi, Halbwachs) and class consciousness (Marx).

It cannot be overestimated how pivotal this enigmatic statement is. For Lacan, it is the textual detail upon which the whole Freudian edifice hinges – Freud's Copernican revolution – and Lacan returns to it time and again in different texts.[31] It was the last sentence of one of Freud's lectures on the ego and the id. This lecture was published in *The New Introductory Lectures on Psychoanalysis* (1933).[32] *The New Introductory Lectures* was a late summatory work. Freud was 77. Lacan described it as Freud's 'last will and testament'. According to Peter Gay, Freud described it privately as 'coarse work, intended for the multitude'.[33]

In Strachey's translation, Freud appears to promote the ego, and Anglo-American ego psychology, which is anathema to Lacan. It appears in the *Standard Edition,* which is the authoritative translation of Freud's work. In Strachey, it is the work of culture (civilization?) to replace the id or locus of unconscious desire with the conscious agency of the ego. Freud's simile about draining the Zuider Zee seems to support it. It suggests that the unconscious is an artefact available to scrutiny by simply uncovering it, like Jung's collective unconscious. Strachey's translation goes against what Lacan regards to be the central tenet of Freud's thought, the importance of the unconscious. In Lacan's text, unconscious desire (like meaning in Derrida's text) is always deferred. We follow our desire by following the linguistic path marked by our speech (the project of analysis), but we never arrive. Desire is a trajectory not a destination. It is our ethical duty to be attentive to our unconscious desire by following our speech, staying on the path (the Z path of Schema L) and not repressing it. Lacan defends his translation by pointing out that Freud did not use the article *das* with *Es* or *Ich*. *Das Es* means id, *Das Ich* means ego. Without the article, *Es* means it and *Ich* means I.[34]

What is important about Lacan's reference to *wo es war soll ich werden* in the context of *Civilisation* …, is that it puts unconscious desire central to the ethics that binds civilisations. Ethics is about framing a course of action within a code of conduct that is articulated with respect to others.[35] It puts ethics between civilization and the death drive, and ethics is about how the one relates to the many. The same ego that injuncts us to love thy neighbour is the ego that drives civilisations apart. Lacan turns to the hating and hated neighbour, only to return – through the speaking subject – to a collective social form. The desire of the individual is individual not collective, but it depends upon a common field. My desire does not speak to me in isolation, although my ego pretends that it does; it is articulated with respect to others. I do not know my desire until it is articulated to others so that they can respond to it. Desire is thus an ethical position that entails the care of others. We either remain isolated in our want of objects, or we accept the moral duty to ourselves and to others that the inter-subjective condition of desire imposes upon us. It is the difference between Vitruvius' original individuals wandering in the forest, and groups organised around speech and construction. It shadows Aristotle's teleological argument (to which Lacan also refers) that the end of man – the good to which s/he strives – is to be a statesman.

Summary

We opened this chapter with Frampton's accusation that Scott Brown/Venturi celebrate a form of urbanism – the motor suburb – which is as anathema to political consciousness as it is to collective memory. There is a long line of thinking that argues that the political function of the centralised city is to draw people together. We reviewed two parallel thought threads on cities/politics and on individual/collective. It was filtered through architecture. Vitruvius' story of the origin of architecture provided a model for thinking the emergence of language and construction out of the gathering of people. Although they do not reference Vitruvius, both Aristotle and Arendt reading Aristotle, identify the *polis* or city state as the site for the emergence of politics because it is in the 'togetherness of people' that power is founded. In Arendt, this space for the appearance of political power has the urban form of the agora and its subsequent analogues in the debating chamber, the piazza, the boulevard, Speakers' Corner.

Arendt argues that the *polis* is, above all, a symbolic environment not a 'physical location'. You take it with you wherever you go. In a gesture that puts polis and politics in opposition and prioritises politics over polis – a trope that Derrida would recognise as similar to the prioritisation of speech over writing in the western philosophical tradition – it is easy to see how polis becomes the site for politics and is then disregarded as attendant upon but non-essential to politics, not its essence. If, following Vitruvius and Rossi, construction accompanies speech as the permanent trace of concourse, and the construction of the city as the permanent trace of the subject's history, then the polis as a permanent material trace of discourse – political or otherwise – is not portable. The *polis* is symbolic and material.

Freud's discussion of the drive in the context of civilisation, shifts the terms of discussion from the political relation of two special interest groups in conflict, what we might call the binary paradigm of politics, to the relation of the individual to the collective. This is perhaps implicit in Arendt concept of togetherness. Freud is important firstly – and we may as well say it – because he has a way of bringing theory down to earth: society, however it is configured, means that you actually have to love the very person you spend most of your time avoiding. Thank architecture for party walls. Lacan's interest in *Civilisation and its Discontents* focused on Freud's discussion of the neighbour, not the drive. Secondly, it puts the discussion of social organisation in the register of ethics. It allowed Lacan to say that the ethical imperative is not love thy neighbour, but put your *I* in the symbolic field where your desire is, this, in the context of civilisation and its threatened demise by the rapacious drives of the individual.

Lacan neutralises the priority of individual over civilisation, by arguing that the drive cannot be thought of as originary. The subject bound by civilisation constructs the individual that is home to the drive in order to exclude it. It confirms Aristotle's point about the priority of the state. This other that we exclude in order to be civilised, has the loopy *extimate* spatial logic that we encountered in the field of the Other, the logic of intimate exteriority and exterior intimacy. The individual may be against civilisation, but it is socially constructed, so that the threat comes from within civilisation. It is internal only to the extent that we impose the dichotomy of inside/outside upon it, an architectural logic we hope to supersede with construction. Lacan's insistence that desire is an ethical duty is tantamount to saying that the Other is our commons, that what we hold in common, what holds us together, our cohesion, is the field of the Other. The grammar of the many is the linguistic structure of unconscious desire; it is represented in the Z-trajectory from Other to subject. Lacan uses the term Other (capital O) in so far as the unconscious field has the capacity to coalesce into a figure that addresses the subject and makes demands upon it, like civilisation. We have presented the drive as an individual social formation and the subject of desire as a collective one, which is a simplification, but it will suffice, this subject of desire with a driven individual residing inside it like an irreducible kernel.

Statesmen and consumers

We are statesmen and consumers. We are consumers, but we need an urban praxis that will enable us to reclaim our statesmanship. When Marx argued that capitalism would create the conditions for its demise, he did not take into account the irresistible nature of the death drive. Capitalism seems so natural because it produces the economic and social relations that most closely approximate the death drive; we call these relations consumerism. When, in *The Urban Revolution* (1970), the Marxist philosopher Henri Lefebvre produced his genealogy of cities and argued that the current iteration, the industrial city, which is in a dialectical relation with agricultural production, was in a crisis phase, he knew this next phase was 'planetary', but he was not yet able to name the consumer city and trace its signs and characteristics. We don't yet know if the consumer city is the industrial city in crisis or the next step in a genealogy. When in *The Right to the City* (1968), Lefebvre argued that we have a right to the city because it is where we articulate our subjectivity with others and that it is not simply a 'visiting' right, a right to visit, but – to borrow Heidegger without permission – a dwelling right, the city is where our being is, he did not take into account the fact that this subject of the city is a consumer, and that even when we live in the city, it is difficult to do anything with it except visit, sample, taste.[36]

If there are architectural typologies that define the consumer city, they are the shopping mall and the motor suburb. That the mall and the suburb function pathologically in the contemporary city should be clear from the way that they isolate us in our demand for objects rather than construct forms of engagement. They keep us locked away from our subjectivity. There are consumers, but there is no consumer *society*, as such, in the way that Lefebvre can understand urban society as an effect of the industrial city, in a dialectical and productive relation with it. Mall and suburb constitute junkspace typologies where we witness the power of capitalism to endlessly reconfigure the world. In the mall and the suburban home, the world is wholly inside (no Archaic outside, no imaginary outside, no symbolic interaction between the two). In the mall, everything – even extreme sexuality – is vanilla. There is only one tense: shopping time now. In the mall and the 'convenience' home with its touch-button appliances, everything is designed to reduce the distance between you and your objects. Shopping therapy is an avoidance mechanism. Scott Brown/Venturi's TV is a grace note indicating a necessary attendant state of distraction. Like Graham's vanilla houses, the mall tends to repeat the short-circuit to objects rather than delay it; it dissolves ideas through repetition rather than condensing them. It promises infinite variety and universality, but it delivers the degradation of the same. The shopping mall destroys signification by destroying difference.[37]

In order to appreciate the pathological nature of the mall and suburb typologies, we need to look at their relation to fantasy. The drive is accompanied by the fantasy image of the individual attaining its object. It is aided and abetted by an advertising industry which functions as an external image production machine. The drive expelled to the internal outside of civilisation, returns as fantasy. We all have objects and we all have fantasies about objects we don't have. When the fantasy becomes a discourse, in other words when it becomes collective and concretized as architecture, it becomes a pathological form in the city. It becomes pathological because the fantasy starts organising reality and not the other way around. We will return to these points in the next chapter when we introduce Lacan's treatment of capitalism as a discourse.

Conclude

What is emerging from this reflection is a social typology of cities, which we hope to develop in future research. This brief sketch will suffice. The city of politics such as it is currently conceived is organised around spaces of enclosure that match the formation of politics as an assemblage of special interest groups. It is celebrated in concepts like collage city.[38] It is not exactly the agora model celebrated by Arendt, which is a heterogeneous accumulation of spaces and objects. The consumer city is organised around pathological objects that concretise certain ego fantasies of independence and possession. Scott Brown/Venturi's information city, which may or may not be identical to the consumer city, is organised around densities and flows of information – infrastructure. None of these typologies are mutually exclusive.

We take the term *pathological* from Rossi, who used it to define historical presences in the city that no longer functioned to organise the city or its social life.

He argued that they are calcified, mummified. The mall and suburb are simply the counterpart to the debating chamber and other political forms. More enlightened perhaps but no more structurally adequate to the task of organising collective life, which appears, rather, to be organised by a poetics of construction.[39]

The city of the Other, which we do not know yet, is organised round the appearance of desire. We can only access it through the other cities, but we know it is there because it has a particular character. This city and its community is – paradoxically – organised around emptiness, the hole in the picture from which the vanishing point is removed; think of it as the charged void because the object of desire is always delayed and turns out to be a nothing that leads elsewhere and to others. To my mind, the salient spatial feature of the agora is its emptiness. The project is still about togetherness, but it is the togetherness of the multitude around a charged void, not the charged monument or the charged enclosure, or the charged shopping mall. The field of the Other shadows the public realm with a different form of organisation for togetherness – we called it a knot – more akin to the grammar of the multitude introduced into political discourse by the political philosopher Paolo Virno, the mob, the swarm, than the imaginary stable unities of the conventional political city. It raises questions about ethics, the good, and what is natural, with which we began this chapter. This city is not against people wanting things and shopping for them. It simply does not organise its communities around the fantasy of attaining them, as opposed to accepting the fantasy as a fantasy and recognising the reality of delay; recognising that when you arrive at the altar, it is a stone, and that love and salvation are elsewhere.[40]

If this text has a political bias, it is the conviction, perhaps now looking simultaneously conservative and radical, that the public space of the city is the foundation of political life. If this text is against something, it is against the particularly virulent form of capitalism that addresses the individual exclusively and is wont to tear apart the ties that bind us into civilisations. We do not, however, share the opprobrium that Frampton pours on Scott Brown/Venturi. Their iconic picture, now looking more prophetic than ever, marks the individual and the collective as opposing social formations: the many dispersing along the information highway alone; the one drawn into a unity with others by the city. The public realm of politics is replaced by private distraction. What modern architects love about Rome more than its historical forms, is its public social life. Being public is hard work, and sometimes all we really want to do is flub out in front of the telly. Lacan's reading of Freud's account of the drive put the social nature of the individual against the anti-social nature of its wants. It is a dialectic between an ego with its fascination with the image of the individual body that is animal and an always already incomplete subject that is attentive to unconscious desire.

Scott Brown/Venturi were set up as the antagonist in this argument, but they got at least one thing right. The many is not the same as the public. They shift the architectural agenda from public-private to collective-individual. They saw the forces of dispersal and put it into architectural and urban discourse by identifying a city typology to which it corresponds. They opened the way for articulating the possibility of a city discourse, even if they were not able to articulate it themselves. For at least one future, we will need analytic tools that will allow us to map the city as a field of lines of dispersal and convergence of individuals – aloneness and togetherness – and that this may be a more relevant way to read the city than public-private, figure-ground, for which current analytic tools are designed. Instead of using these binary logics, we should attend to a logic of knotting.[41] They also anticipated the media world; they saw that it is now part of the urban arena and we have to work with it. We will need ways to think hybrid platforms for togetherness. We read their iconic picture as a challenge. There may be other ways to design for information space than the motor suburb. Their point is that the life in common (Aristotle), the togetherness of people (Arendt), concourse (Vitruvius), and construction (Rossi) are not reducible to the public space of the city and that architecture still has a job to do if it wants to configure these collective social forms in ways that instrumentalise them for the public good.[42]

Notes

1 Kenneth Frampton, 'Towards a Critical Regionalism: 6 Points for an Architecture of Resistance', in *Anti-Aesthetic: Essays on Postmodern Culture*, edited by H. Foster (Seattle: Bay Press, 1983), p. 25.
2 The cover image of Robert Venturi, Denise Scott Brown, and Steven Izenour, *Learning from Las Vegas: The Forgotten Symbolism of Architectural Form* (Cambridge: MIT Press, 1972/1986).
3 An amnesiac landscape for Americans of European descent. In the neo-noir movie *Momento* (Christopher Nolan, director, 2000), an amnesiac awakes and has to recover his past – not his memory – by writing post-it notes to himself. The post-it note is one of the icons of information delivery. The European post-modern avant-garde celebrated the work of Scott Brown/Venturi because of its amnesiac and surface like qualities. For the European reception, see Antonio Sanmartin, ed., *Venturi, Rauch, & Scott Brown* (London: Academy Editions, 1986), in particular his introduction.
4 All page numbers in this section are from *Vitruvius: On Architecture, Books I–V*, translated by Frank Granger (Cambridge: Harvard University Press, 1998).
5 Pier Vittorio Aureli, *The Possibility of an Absolute Architecture* (Cambridge, MA: MIT Press, 2011); George Baird, *The Space of Appearance* (Cambridge, MA: MIT Press, 1995); Kenneth Frampton, *Labour, Work and Architecture: Collected Essays on Architecture and Design* (London: Phaidon Press, 2002).
6 Aristotle, *The Politics* (Harmondsworth: Penguin Classics, 1962/1982). The title translates 'things concerning the polis'. The nub of our argument resides in pp. 55–60, paragraphs 1252a24–1253a29. According to the translators Sinclair and Saunders, Aristotle was unknown to Republican Rome, so we should not expect Vitruvius to refer to him. The historian Kitto says that there is no direct English translation of *polis*; it approximates *self-governed community*. Cf. H.D. F. Kitto, 'The Polis' reprinted from *The Greeks* (1951) in Richard LeGates and Frederic Stout, eds., *The City Reader* (London: Routledge, 1996), pp. 44–48. In the television programme 'Ancient Greece: The Greatest Show on Earth' (BBC4 Sunday 11 March 2018), the classicist Michael Scott argues the extraordinary thesis that the Athenians used theatre to work out the basic forms of democratic governance. Giorgio Agamben, *Homo Sacer: Sovereign Power and Bare Life*, trans. Daniel Heller-Roazen (Stanford, CA: Stanford

University Press, 1998). For the discussion of the classic distinction between bare life, or life itself or natural life (*zoe*) and a qualified or political or legal life (*bios*), see pp. 1–12; a summary of its critical convolution pp. 181–188.

7 Frederick Copleston, S.J., makes this point clearly in his history of philosophy, and it is worth backing it up. Cf. *A History of Philosophy: Volume I Greece and Rome; Volume II Augustine to Scotus; Volume III Ockham to Suarez* (Doubleday Image, 1985), p. 351. 'The State is prior to the family and to the individual in the sense that, while the State is a self-sufficing whole, neither the individual nor the family are self-sufficient'. And 'The Platonic-Aristotelean view of the State as exercising the positive function of serving the end of man, the leading of the good life or the acquisition of happiness, and as being *natura prior* (to be distinguished from *tempore prior*) to the individual and the family, has been of great influence in subsequent philosophy'.

8 Frampton quotes Arendt ['space of public appearance' and 'the living together of people'] in the chapter 'Architecture in the Age of Globalisation', pp. 344–389 in *Modern Architecture: A Critical History*. For Aureli, cf. Aureli, *op. cit.*, chapter 1 'Toward the Archipelago: Defining the Political and the Formal in Architecture', and esp. pp. 2–11. Copleston makes similar points in his discussion of Aristotle, *Ethics*, for which see Copleston, *op. cit.* pp. 343–344.

9 Both quotes from Sigmund Freud, *Civilization and Its Discontents (1930)*, translated by Joan Riviere and James Strachey and edited by M. Masud and R. Khan, *International Psycho-Analytical Library* (London: Hogarth Press and Institute of Psycho-Analysis, 1975).

10 These themes are picked up in, e.g. Felix Guattari, *The Three Ecologies* (London: Athlone, 1989/2000); Herbert Marcuse, *Eros and Civilization: A Philosophical Inquiry into Freud*; Norman O. Brown, *Life against Death*, and Nancy Julia Chodorow, 'Beyond Drive Theory: Object Relations and the Limits of Radical Individualism', *Theory and Society* 14 (1985): 271–319, which discusses these two latter texts. See also the short film Amanda Zachem, *American Psychosis* (2017), narrated by the journalist Chris Hedges, accessed on Vimeo 18 March 2019 at https://vimeo.com/293802639. Hedges argues that the anxiety of living together is creating a form of psychosis characterised by excessive consumerism and illusory political visions.

11 I first began thinking about the categories individual and collective and about how collective life is organised and constituted during the strike action over the Universities Superannuation Scheme in early spring of 2018, which – to my mind – was about how risk was shared across a group of individuals, rather than carried by individuals.

12 Sigmund Freud, *Beyond the Pleasure Principle* (London: Hogarth Press and Institute of Psycho-Analysis, 1920/1974); *Civilization and Its Discontents* (London: Hogarth Press and Institute of Psycho-Analysis, 1930/1975).

13 Sigmund Freud, 'Instincts and Their Vicissitudes (1915)', in *Sigmund Freud: On Metapsychology: The Theory of Psychoanalysis*, edited by A. Richards and J. Strachey (London: Penguin, 1991), pp. 113–138; quote p. 118, the components pp. 118ff.

14 Le Corbusier, *The Final Testament of Pere Corbu: A Translation and Interpretation of Mise Au Point*, translated by Ivan Zaknic (New Haven, CT: Yale University Press, 1997), p. 83. Joseph A. Schrumpeter, *Capitalism Socialism Democracy* (London: Routledge, 1942). In his reading of Marx, Schrumpter is describing the necessity for capitalism to continually renew itself. Marshall Berman, *All That Is Solid Melts into Air: The Experience of Modernity* (London: Verso, 1983). This reading of Faust, Baudelaire, and the Communist Manifesto is about the destructive effects of modernity, by a New Yorker. See also Karl Marx and Frederick Engels, *Manifesto of the Communist Party* (1848) p. 16. 'The bourgeoisie cannot exist without constantly revolutionising the instruments of production, … and with them the whole relations of society. All fixed fast-frozen relations, … are swept away, all new-formed ones become antiquated before they can ossify. All that is solid melts into air, all that is holy is profaned, and man is at last compelled to face with sober senses his real conditions of life, and his relations with his kind'.

15 Jacques Lacan, 'The Subversion of the Subject and the Dialectics of Desire in the Freudian Unconscious (1960)' in *Écrits: The First Complete Edition in English*, translated by Bruce Fink, Heloise Fink, and Russell Grigg (New York: W. W. Norton 2006), pp. 671–702.

16 See Jacques Lacan, *The Four Fundamental Concepts of Psycho-Analysis*. Translated by Alan Sheridan. Edited by Jacques-Alain Miller (New York: Norton Press, 1981), p. 178 for the diagram of the drives as a return journey; and p. 179 'If the drive may be satisfied without attaining what, from the point of view of a biological totalization of function, would be the satisfaction of its end in reproduction, it is because it is a partial drive, and its aim is simply this return into circuit'. He quotes Heraclitus 'To the Bow (*Biós*) is given the name of life (*Bíos*) and its work is death', p. 177.

17 For which see Sigmund Freud, 'Three Essays on the Theory of Sexuality (1905)', in *On Sexuality: Three Essays on the Theory of Sexuality and Other Works*, edited by Angela Richards (London: Penguin, 1977).

18 In Lacan's text, the four partial drives (and their objects and sites on the body) in order of development are oral drive (lips, breast), anal (faeces, anus), the scopic drive (gaze, eye), invocatory (voice, ears). Evans, *Dictionary of Lacanian Psychoanalysis*, the entry on 'drive (pulsion)' p. 48 has a handy table.

19 Jacques Lacan, 'Position of the Unconscious (1960–64)' in *Écrits: The First Complete Edition in English*, translated by Bruce Fink, Heloise Fink, and Russell Grigg (New York: W. W. Norton, 2006), p. 719, 'Speaking subjects have the privilege of revealing the deadly meaning of this organ, and thereby its relation to sexuality. This is because the signifier as such, whose first purpose is to bar the subject, has brought into him the meaning of death. (The letter kills, but we learn this from the letter itself.) This is why every drive is virtually a death drive'.

20 For Lacan's reading of Freud's 'Instincts and their Vicissitudes', see Lacan, *The Four Fundamental Concepts, op.cit.*, chapters 13 'The Deconstruction of the Drive', pp. 161–173 and 14 'The Partial Drive and Its Circuit', pp. 174–186. For my treatment of the driven Le Corbusier, see Lorens Holm, *Brunelleschi Lacan Le Corbusier: Architecture, Space, and the Construction of Subjectivity* (London: Routledge, 2010) Chapter 8 'Space and the Drives: the Parthenon and Le Corbusier', pp. 175–203.

21 Jacques Derrida, 'Différance', in *The Margins of Philosophy*, translated by Alan Bass (Chicago: University of Chicago, 1982), pp. 1–27; Giorgio Agamben, *State of Exception* (Chicago and London: University of Chicago Press, 2005); Jacques Lacan, *The Seminar of Jacques Lacan, Book VII: The Ethics of Psychoanalysis 1959–1960* (NYC: Norton, 1992). Derrida uses a similar formula to account for how Marxist thought continues to haunt philosophical thinking, especially after the fall of the wall for which see: Jacques Derrida, *Specters of Marx: The State of the Debt, the Work of Mourning and the New International*, translated by Peggy Kamuf (London: Routledge, 1993/1994).

22 See, for instance, Thoreau's *Walden, or life in the woods* (1854). The conjoining of the individual with nature extends to the law. Typically, the law attaches to the individual. The law distinguishes human or natural rights from legal rights. Life and liberty and the pursuit of happiness are natural rights. The right to drive a car or own a gun are legal rights or privileges (in the case of gun ownership, Americans seem to confuse legal and natural rights). Natural rights originate in human nature and legal rights originate in governance. In the *United States Declaration of Independence* (1776), Thomas Jefferson distinguishes inalienable and alienable rights and argues that the former are self-evident. 'We hold these truths to be self-evident, that all men are created equal ....' They need no argument or testing. In *Rights of Man* (1791), Thomas Paine argued that human rights originate in nature, and these natural rights pertaining to the individual cannot be granted by charter or by any government because to do so would imply that they could be revoked by charter. They are simply defended or not by the government. In what seems an extreme extension of the idea of natural rights, David Harvey argues that the right to the city is a natural right.

23 This is a Derridian trope. Derrida argued to reverse the hierarchy that defined what he called the logocentrism of western philosophy, which sought always to elevate speech (pure originary) over writing (artificial, material, delayed, corruptible).

24 Hannah Arendt, *The Human Condition*. (Chicago: University of Chicago Press, 1958) part 1 'The Human Condition' pp. 7–21, and in particular, p. 8 'Labour assures not only individual survival, but the life of the species. Work and its product, the human artifact, bestow a measure of permanence and durability upon the futility of mortal life and the fleeting character of human time.' and p. 19 'The task… of mortals lie in their ability to produce things – works, deeds, and words – which would deserve to be… at home in everlastingness, so that through them mortals could find their place in a cosmos where everything is immortal except themselves.'

25 Arendt, *op. cit.*, for example, pp. 305–306, where Arendt talks about the elevation of *homo faber* (work) over *animal laborans* (labour) and how Marx has to justify the later by misrepresenting it as the former.

26 Dan Graham, 'Homes for America' in *Art in America* (January 1967). 'Homes …' was an anthropological project. A sampling of the names of the house types: the sonata, concerto, overturn, ballet, prelude, serenade, nocturne, and rhapsody. A different anthropological project, but one that leads to a similarly death drive vision of American homes, is Jason Griffith and Alex Gino's *Manifest Destiny: A Guide to the Essential Indifference of American Suburban Housing* (London: Architectural Association, 2011).

27 Jacques Lacan, *The Seminar of Jacques Lacan, Book VII: The Ethics of Psychoanalysis 1959-1960*. Translated by Dennis Porter. Edited by Jacques-Alain Miller. (New York: Norton, 1986/1992) pp. 185–187; the passage Lacan quotes is found in Freud, *Civilisation …*, the full discussion of the neighbour, pp. 45–53, 49.

28 Lacan, *The Ethics of Psychoanalysis*, *op. cit.*, transgression, guilt, death, superego, logos, the signifier, a higher complexity, pp. 2–7.

29 Freud, *Moses and Monotheism (1939)* trans. Joan Riviere and James Strachey, ed. M. Masud R. Khan, *International Psycho-Analytical Library* (London: Hogarth Press and Institute of Psycho-Analysis, 1951).

30 Jacques Lacan, *The Seminar of Jacques Lacan, Book VII: The Ethics of Psychoanalysis 1959–1960*, translated by Dennis Porter and edited by Jacques-Alain Miller (New York: W. W. Norton, 1992), pp. 5–7 for moral duty; 184–186 for Freud the neighbour.

31 In addition to the *Ethics* … see the five papers published in *Écrits*: 'The Freudian Thing or the Meaning of the Return to Freud in Psychoanalysis' (1955), 'The Agency of the Letter in the Unconscious or Reason since Freud' (1957); 'Position of the Unconscious' (1960–64); 'Science and Truth' (1966); and 'The Subversion of the Subject and the Dialectics of Desire in the Freudian Unconscious' (1960) in *Écrits: op.cit.* For an extended discussion of this phrase, see my *Brunelleschi Lacan Le Corbusier*, *op.cit.*, pp. 66–69.

32 Sigmund Freud, *New Introductory Lectures on Psycho-Analysis (1933)*, translated by James Strachey and edited by M. Masud R. Khan, *International Psycho-Analytical Library* (London: Hogarth Press and Institute of Psycho-Analysis, 1974), p. 80, the end of lecture XXXI 'The Dissection of the Psychical Personality'.

33 For which, see Peter Gay, *Freud: A Life for Our Time* (London: Dent, 1988), p. 369, quoted in Wikipedia, accessed 25 August 2019 at https://en.wikipedia.org/wiki/Introduction_to_Psychoanalysis#cite_note-12

34 Cf. Lacan, 'The Freudian Thing or the Meaning of the Return to Freud in Psychoanalysis' in *Ecrits: … op. cit.*, pp. 347–348.

35 For a succinct discussion of the ethical code as the code of others, and hence the action of the individual with respect to the many, see Jane Rendell, 'Hotspots and Touchstones: From Critical to Ethical Spatial Practice', *Architecture and Culture* 8:3+4 (November 2020).

36 Henri Lefebvre, *The Urban Revolution*, trans. Robert Bononno (Minneapolis, MN: University of Minnesota Press, 1970/2003), p. 2. 'I use the term "urban society" to refer to the society that results from industrialization, which is a process of domination

that absorbs agricultural production'. For the crisis, see pp. 15–18. For 'planetary society and the 'global city' cf. p. 17. What Lefebvre calls *urban society*, I call *urban consciousness*. See Henri Lefebvre, 'The Right to the City' in *Writings on Cities*, edited by Eleonore Kofman and Elizabeth Lebas (Malden, MA: Blackwell, 1968), pp. 147–159. 'The *right to the city* cannot be conceived of as a simple visiting right or as a return to traditional cities. It can only be formulated as a transformed and renewed *right to urban life*. It does not matter whether the urban fabric encloses the countryside and what survives of peasant life, as long as the "urban", place of encounter, priority of use value, inscription in space of a time promoted to the rank of a supreme resource among all resources, finds its morphological base and its practico-material realization .... As a hundred years ago, although under new conditions, it gathers the interests (overcoming the immediate and the superficial) of the whole society and firstly of all those who *inhabit*'. Lefebvre's italics. See also David Harvey, 'The Right to the City', *New Left Review 53* (2008), pp. 23–40. 'The right to the city is far more than the individual liberty to access urban resources: it is a right to change ourselves by changing the city. It is, moreover, a common rather than an individual right since this transformation inevitably depends upon the exercise of a collective power to reshape the processes of urbanization. The freedom to make and remake our cities and ourselves is, ... one of the most precious yet most neglected of our human rights'.

37 This paragraph is a condensation of a public conversation with the psychoanalyst David Bell, held during the launch of the book John Shannon Hendrix and Lorens Holm, eds., *Architecture and the Unconscious* (Abingdon: Routledge, 2016) at UCL, 08 December 2016. We borrow junkspace from Rem Koolhaas, 'Junkspace', *October: Obsolescence A Special Issue* (2002), pp. 175–190. Rossi used the term pathological. The *permanences* or permanent elements of the city were either propelling or pathological according to whether they play a living role in shaping the city and our understanding of it or were effectively isolated and dead. We use pathological in a slightly different way, except that the shopping mall and the motor suburb are forms that keep us locked away from our subjectivity. Cf. Aldo Rossi, *The Architecture of the City*, trans. Diane Ghirardo and Joan Ockman (Cambridge, MA: MIT Press, 1982), pp. 59–60.

38 Colin Rowe, and Fred Koetter, *Collage City* (Cambridge, MA: MIT Press, 1978). *Assemblage* city is more to the point.

39 Rossi distinguishes urban elements that are propelling from those that are pathological, but he does not put this distinction so explicitly in relation to collective life.

40 For the community organised around nothing as an ethical position, see Roberto Esposito, *Communitas: The Origin and Destiny of Community*, translated by Timothy Campbell (Stanford, CA: Stanford University Press, 2010) who opens with the statement that what the members of a community hold in common is nothing. For the grammar of the multitude as a political position, see Paolo Virno, *A Grammar of the Multitude: For an Analysis of Contemporary Forms of Life*. Translated by Isabella Bertoletti, James Cascaito and Andrea Casson (Semiotext(E) Foreign Agents Series. New York: Semiotext(e), 2004). Cf. also, Paolo Virno, 'Three Remarks Regarding the Multitude's Subjectivity and Its Aesthetic Component', in *Under Pressure: Pictures, Subjects, and the New Spirit of Capitalism*, edited by Daniel Birnbaum and Isabelle Graw (Frankfurt: Sternberg Press, 2008). Virno rehabilitated the concept of the multitude for political discourse and made it respectable. It has affinities to Arendt's togetherness of people: in both texts, the context is power. The multitude is a stuff word, as opposed to a thing word. It is like a murder of crows, a shrewdness of apes, a parliament of owls, a multitude of people. He argues that the multitude is organised – it has a grammar – even though it may seem unruly. He argues that what it is always put in opposition to, by politicians in their appeals for support – 'the public', or 'we the people' or 'the man on the street' – are fictions of the politician's discourse. There is no people as such, there are only multitudes with different organisations.

41 Lacan was interested in the loopy logic and topology of knots, which he explored in his late work, in relation to discourse and social ties. See, for instance, Jacques Lacan, *The Seminar of Jacques Lacan, Book XX: Encore - on Feminine Sexuality, the Limits of Love and Knowledge 1972–1973 (Encore).* Translated by Bruce Fink. Edited by Jacques-Alain Miller (New York: W.W. Norton & Company, 1998) 'Rings of String' pp. 118–146.

42 An earlier version of this text appeared as 'The City Is a Critical Project – A Poetics of Collective Life', *arq: Architectural Research Quarterly* 23:2, (2019) with Cameron McEwan.

DDT. Pesticides. Exxon Valdex (1989). Oil spills. Deep Water Horizon (2010). Water pollution. Air pollution. Acid rain. SO2. Smog. Ozone. CO2. Carbon. Carbon trading. Carbon credit. Carbon footprint. Social capital. Cultural capital. Natural capital (oxymorons, all). Acid rain. Acidification. Overpopulation. Population explosion. Extinctions. Endangered species list. Gorillas. White rhinos. Elephants. Snow tigers. Bees. Songbirds. Bees. Great Barrier Reefs. Rainforests. Deforestation. Desertification. Glaciers. Permafrost. Methane. Diversity. Biodiversity. Brundtland Report (1987). Rio Earth Summit (1992). Lead. Mercury. Carcinogens. Nuclear waste. Halflifes (sic). Fallout. Chernobyl (1986). Climate change. Kyoto (1997/2005/2008/2012). Global warming. 1.5 degrees. Extreme... weather/flooding/wildfires. Doha (2012). Ocean acidity. Sea levels. Recycling. Cycling. Sustainability. Resilience. Whole foods and smart cities (as if you could make a city smart by wiring it up). Paris (2015/2020). Industrial farming. Antibiotics. Antibiotics in beef. Antibiotics in rivers. Plastic. Plastic bottles. Microplastics in the air water soil. Plastics in the stomachs of beached whales and drowned albatross. Climate change. Climate Crisis

FIGURE 6.1 The headlines.

6

TO CONCLUDE WITH CLIMATE CHANGE [DISCOURSE AND THE ETHICS OF PSYCHOANALYSIS]

'If there's an intelligence there, I want it to know that there's an intelligence here'. In the cult sci-fi horror flick *Phase IV* (1974), ants attain a collective intelligence that allows them to threaten human civilisation. It was caused by sunspots. Unable to respond with a collective intelligence of our own, we turn, predictably, to science. The backdrop to this little drama is a new suburban settlement in Arizona advertised as paradise, but which will only ever be desert. It turns out that the ants are retaliating against the way we are destroying the environment. In this film, we have all the key elements of the death drive in contemporary commodity capitalism. The failure of our collective intelligence compensated by science, the grim reality of squanderous development screened by a public imaginary aided and abetted by advertising. All of it overshadowed by an anxiety

DOI: 10.4324/9780429022845-6

whose locus seems to be the natural world, an anxiety which we have learned to live with. The ants win.[1]

In 2014, Foster + Partners Architects completed the design of a new city in the United Arab Emirates. On their website, 'Masdar City combines state-of-the-art technologies with the planning principles of traditional Arab settlements to create a desert community that aims to be carbon neutral and zero waste'. Its anchor institutions include the Masdar Institute of Science and Technology partnered with MIT, and the headquarters of the International Renewable Energy Agency (IRENA). It appears that the Emirates has decided that sustainable development will be the next global industry after oil, and they plan to become its centre. If the planning of Masdar was about sustainability rather than globalisation, the developers would have built on a brownfield site rather than encroach upon a mangrove swamp next to a desert airport; and they would not have based its infrastructure on the personal driverless car, which simply perpetuates a well-known form of individual that is not in a position to conserve resources through collective forms of organisation. There will be some potentially good things here if the city is completed (narrow walled streets, passive ventilation), but they missed an opportunity to explore new forms of environmental consciousness, perhaps even environmental consciousness at a planetary scale, rather than perpetrate a familiar form of commercial globalisation.[2]

Environment and damage

We need to sketch the ethical position for architecture in an age of climate change. Architecture is complicit in climate change, and not only because the suburb has provided 20th century discourse with the signifier for wasting the surface of the earth. In a nutshell, the ethical duty of architecture with respect to climate change is *not* to build sustainable settlements, which makes good sense and we should do anyway, but to explore new forms of collective space for building environmental consciousness. Architecture has the power to give form to the togetherness of people; it needs to exercise that power by bringing people together in ways that build *sustaining* societies, which in this context means to build societies in which it is possible to make sensible decisions about sustainability. In the terms that we developed in the last chapter, to build the *space of appearance* for environmental consciousness and reflection upon our lifestyles, in other words, an ethics of togetherness and a morality of renunciation.

To understand this ethical demand, we need to position climate change with respect to the human subject, at least in so far as climate change is presented to us in the popular press. This will be a brief sketch of climate change, which, while not drilling deeply will, hopefully, touch the landmarks in this difficult terrain.

Most of the public discourse and private discussion about climate change is mendacious and hypocritical. While most people except climate change deniers, accept that we are the causes of climate change, no one is willing to trace the

The death drive as it appears in land development within commodity capitalism. A montage of cold war and environmental paranoia.

FIGURE 6.2 The death drive as it appears in contemporary commodity capitalism: two scenes from the film *Phase IV.*

consequences for us – the human subject – of this fact. The fact that we are the cause of climate change makes it significantly different for us than if we were not the causes of it. For instance, it is remarkable how little expressions of guilt appear in public discourse. Given the human agency in climate change, you might expect there to be quite a lot of guilt.

We need to shift the terms of the debate. Climate change is the latest in a long line of names for the damage we have been doing to the environment. We have been knowingly damaging our environment since the 1960s. That's 3 generations, 11 presidents (USA), 11 prime ministers (UK), 16 prime ministers and 10 presidents (France), and approximately 10 CEO's of Exxon.[3] Rachel Carson published *Silent Spring* in 1962. Sir Frank Fraser Darling gave the Reith Lectures, *Wilderness and Plenty*, on BBC 4 in 1969. Greenpeace was founded in 1971. 'Gimme some truth' was released in 1971. At about the same time, Rowan and Martin's *Laugh-In* did a skit in which road companies starting on the east and west coasts meet triumphantly in the middle after having completely concreted over America. *An Inconvenient Truth* was released in 2006. In 2015, a team of RSPB researchers was surprised to discover that the beaches of one of the most remote islands in the South Pacific was covered in plastic debris. It made international news in 2017.[4]

Environmental damage takes successive forms in the public imaginary, as different aspects of the damage are studied by scientists and reported by the media. The damage appears in the news under a new name each time, and each time we pretend that it is the first time. What is essentially the repetition of a condition appears in the form of a discovery or an accident. We treat the damage as new

38 million pieces of plastic on Henderson Island

FIGURE 6.3 This scene is an architectural failure – a failure of our platforms for collective intelligence. We occupy the beaches of the world with our junk space typologies.

when it is a repeat of what happened yesterday. We spend the summer chucking garbage out of the house, and we pretend surprise by the tip in the garden. The repetition is supported by a genealogy of not knowing. We know we are harming the environment, but we pretend to not know. We pretend it is something happening *to* us, as if we are victims, rather than something caused *by* us. It is a collusion of amnesia.

This pathology of not-knowing is aided and abetted by a pathology of outsourcing. We outsource our responsibility for the damage we do by turning to technological solutions to repair it. This outsourcing involves two acts of refusal: we refuse to acknowledge the collective nature of the problem, and we refuse to look inward to our individual complicity. We turn away from our responsibility for environmental damage by diverting attention from the human agency for environmental damage to the technological solutions that allow us to go on doing the damage we have always done. We seek an external solution to an internal problem. Instead of looking inward to the agency of individuals, we look outward to more climate science, which under the circumstances, is a mechanism of denial and avoidance. What prevents us from political action is not a lack of information but an incapacity to recognise the truth of our own agency, which is aided and abetted by commodity capitalism that we find irresistible.

In the popular satiric anti-war film *Apocalypse Now* (1979), Lieutenant Colonel Bill Kilgore (Robert Duvall) and the boys have just firebombed a beachside settlement on the Pacific coast of Vietnam, now they are going surfing. Meanwhile,

Lieutenant Colonel Bill Kilgore (Robert Duvall) and the boys have just fire-bombed a beach head, now they are going surfing. Then Martin Sheen (left) will continue upstream to find a madman.

FIGURE 6.4 The death drive condenses domestic bliss and wanton destruction into a single phrase.

Captain Benjamin L. Willard (Martin Sheen) continues upstream to find a madman. *I love the smell of napalm in the morning* condenses into a single linguistic image, a certain form of domestic bliss [coffee] and our capacity for wanton destruction of the environment [napalm]. It is funny because it captures our upbeat complicity in a global disaster. I want *this* [clean air, clear water, green land], but I want *that* more [a frictionless-fly-to beach holiday, a bigger car, a few less socialists], and to get it I am prepared not to see the consequences [grey air, water, land]. Coppola's film was an attempt to work through the traumatic effects on the American psyche of the Vietnam War, for which a generation of Americans is indebted. The humour of Kilgore's quip, uttered with such conviction continues to resonate. What is so striking is the tacit co-habitation of not-knowing and knowing. Kilgore remains blissfully unaware of knowing. In what is a textbook example of the unconscious, his knowing is only evident to others.[5]

Because we harm ourselves when we harm the environment, environmental damage is a form of self-harm. Environmental damage constitutes an epidemic of self-harm of a scale and universal scope unseen in the history of epidemiology. The health crisis of modern life is not obesity (WHO) but self-harm. Imagine a zombie movie with a cast of 7.442 billion and rising. Self-harm through environmental damage is the *style* of our lifes (sic). It is concealed in our lifestyles, cloaked like a hidden heart, at once within and beyond our grasp. Everyone is afflicted. Self-harm thorough environmental damage is the new normal.[6]

The fact that environmental damage constitutes a form of self-harm puts it within the curtilage of psychoanalytic thinking. The fact that the damage is aided and abetted by a cluster of pathologies – repetition of the new, knowing/ not-knowing, turning away, outsourcing responsibility – raises the psychoanalytic stakes. The ethical project for architecture is bound up with psychoanalysis.

It is not the damage *per se*; damage does not always raise ethical issues. The ethical project revolves around the knowing and pretending not to know. We dissimulate all the time to the people we know: our family, neighbours, colleagues, and most important, to our selfs (sic). We never quite tell all. We always hold something back and keep something in reserve for later. The place we are not allowed to dissimulate is in the analytic setting. We need to stop avoiding the truth about ourselves and what we want with this world, even if it hurts. We need to ask ourselves what do we want in/from/out of this world of destruction.

We seem to be confronted by the prospect of an orgy of renunciation. The smallest carbon footprints are found in favelas. Kilgore will have to give up coffee unless it is locally grown. Most of us will have to give up meat. And fresh greens in winter. New Yorkers will have to give up air-conditioning (most of New York was built without it). Most of us will have to give up attending sustainability conferences and other overseas holidays. Most of us will have to move house or jobs in order to stop commuting. This will pose problems for double income households. Most of us will have to give up both cars. Most of us will have to stop breeding. Most of us will need to move out of our semi and into the city centre.

If we really wanted, we could stop damaging the environment today. We would just stop. The promise of an analytic approach to climate damage is that it will lead to an understanding of the sense in which it is true that we can stop the damage and how we can face the moral dilemma if we choose not to. We damage the environment either because we want to or because – irrespective of what we want – we cannot help it. This psychical fact is the central source of pain and suffering in the climate debate; it is too big and too complex to acknowledge, but it never goes away. In the analytic setting, the subject is never allowed to say 'he made me do it'. We are always faced with choices, and we always choose. In psychoanalysis, the subject takes responsibility for its choices. What the analytic position does not allow is to continue to avoid our responsibility by outsourcing it to science or pretending it is new.

We have shifted the terms of the debate from climate change to environmental damage. Not only is climate a subset of environment, and change this year's subset of damage; but climate change is an objective category and we want to put the terms of the debate more securely within the remit of human agency. It is our environment and we are damaging it. Not all change is damage and sometimes damage is accidental, but most change is wilful damage. It may be too late to stop climate change (that is a question for earth scientists), but it is never too late for us to stop damaging the environment. Also, it gets us out of a scrap with climate change deniers. Whether we are the cause of climate change (we are), we are nevertheless damaging our environment and pretending it doesn't matter. Even if its effects are minimal (they are not), or if they are absorbable without a trace by the earth's ecosystems (they are not), there is still an ethical question about why we are knowingly destructive. Most of the time, we do not knowingly participate in violence, even if its effects are negligible or benign. It matters from an ethical position.

We also shifted the terms of the debate from man versus nature to individual versus collective. Instead of man damaging nature, individuals are damaging their capacity for togetherness. This follows our reading of *Civilization and Its Discontents*, and puts the damage within the territory of the death drive. The individual is the site of the drive. For the purposes of this argument, we accept the position – by no means uncontested – that the individual is the site of agency. Whether you buy a bigger car or a President implements a national energy policy, at a certain point, an individual makes a decision, which raises again the question of what it wants. And here is the particular analytic form of the problem: if the damage is an individual social formation, the failure to stop the damage is a collective one. Just to be clear about the collective failure: it is not that collective forms like the United Nations Framework Convention on Climate Change (UNFCCC), the Earth Summit Rio de Janiero 1992, Kyoto Protocol 1997, Cancun Agreements 2010, Paris Agreement 2015, fail to succeed in the aims that they have set for themselves; they may or may not, that is a different question. What we have *not* done is collectively address the drive of individuals – their profligate expenditures. Individuals cannot address the drive alone, only individuals acting together can.

We shift the terms to individual versus collective because we hope to be able to think our way out of an impasse that politics does not seem able to address. In the public debate, we are often asked to address a problem (climate change) that is collective because it is cumulative and shared, with a solution that is individual (a change in lifestyle). That is obviously not going to work, and not only because I am not going to renounce my lifestyle unless you do too. It is an impossible demand because there is simply no symmetry between a cause that is individual and incremental (the drive) and a damage effect that is cumulative and collective. The individual has to change, but the solution is collective. In any case, it is not a political problem in a conventional sense because it is not about the public resolution of a conflict between special interest groups, one declaring itself for damaging the environment, the other against damaging it. It is not us against them. We are all doing it, and we are all denying it. Even Shell Oil publicly professes to be green. If there is a political conflict, it is a conflict between individual and collective interests.

For Lacan, the drive wreaked havoc with ethics, and one of the problems he faced was how to remain true to Freud's thoughts and have an ethics for psychoanalysis. It has to be stressed how diametrically opposite drive theory is to the narrative of progress that dominates positivist thinking. The death drive runs counter to most understandings of life, whether from biology or the humanities, as the pursuit of happiness of the individual and the propagation of the species. It runs against ethical imperatives to do good in the world. Instead of progress, repetition. Instead of better life, death. The death drive matches the particulars of our encounter with the environment: the not knowing, the turning away, the disavowal, the repetition compulsion. It acknowledges the wilful and the inevitable nature of this damage, and the particular form of enjoyment we derive from it. We all enjoy the smell of napalm in the morning, even if we don't think we do. No one sets out to destroy the environment, but it seems to be the consequence of the good life. If there is a real of environmental damage, it is our nature. It is not the damage to soil, air, and ocean – that's just more reality, messy, problematic, and unreliable – but our own not-knowing nature. We go on doing what we always do, and the same not-knowing keeps repeating under a different name. If we could understand the drive, we might be able to assimilate it. By assimilate it, I mean name something that we don't even know exists, let alone recognise; and describe it, rearticulate it, reshape it, move it to other purposes. This text may not change a condition, but it will change the way we talk about it, which is the first step to changing it.

Other psychoanalytic approaches to the environment

Most psychoanalytic approaches to climate change focus on the relation of man to nature. In 'How Is Climate Change an Issue for Psychoanalysis', the sociologist Michael Rustin sees climate change in terms of the opposition between advocates of rationalist modernisation who are aggressive to nature and advocates of environmentalist conservation who are reparative. These approaches often draw on Melanie Klein's work in object relations, which is one of the ways that she developed Freud's opposition between death and life instincts in *Beyond the Pleasure Principle*. She understood these as the paranoid-schizoid and the depressive positions. Klein was one of the few post-Freudians that Lacan respected. According to Klein, the paranoid position marks an aggressive position in the enfant's relation to his/her mother. In the depressive position, guilt replaces aggression, and reparations begin. These are developmental stages that the infant passes through; they are also psychoanalytic structures that define the subject's relation to others throughout its life.[7]

Our approach is broadly in line with the position outlined by the psychoanalysis Donna Orange in *Climate Crisis, Psychoanalysis, and Radical Ethics*, although her focus is broader. She addresses the social injustices and suffering of climate change with the psychoanalytic conditions of narcissism, mourning, and trauma. She looks at how shame and envy configure our responses to climate change. The intention expressed in the tone of her writing is to call analysts to action. She says 'I will argue that psychoanalysis as a profession, and psychoanalysts as individuals, need to make three significant changes to embrace the ethical turn in the face of the climate crisis: (1) from double-mindedness to single-mindedness; (2) from narcissism to community; and (3) from elitism to solidarity'. She makes practical suggestions like fly less and use the internet instead, and live simply, which we regard to be part of the problem because they channel environmental consciousness away from the critical problem – raising consciousness through togetherness – to ineffectual household solutions. What could have been a powerful critique is compromised by trying to do good in the world.[8]

By shifting the debate from man against nature to man against his own nature, we open up the possibility for intervening in our nature. We reject Rustin's position that the man-child is aggressor to a victimised mother-nature and look instead at how the subject constructs itself through architecture. The subject is a collective social formation attached to a collectively constructed individual. Remember Lacan's formula ego-unconscious. To call the subject *collective* reflects the fact that desire is unconscious and therefore is fundamentally awaiting completion by others. This always awaiting completion by others is the human condition. The difference between our positions lies in the question of what is unconscious. For Rustin, what is unconscious is a destructive phantasy (the paranoid schizophrenic position), which, if it could be brought to consciousness may lead to greater awareness of what drives us to destroy. For us, it is the largely conscious formations of the ego that are the cause of damage. By attending to the unconscious as unconscious, we argue the opposite. For Lacan, unconscious desire is a linguistic process that never shows its cards. We are attached to each other and to places, above all unconsciously. Unconscious desire is not made conscious to the subject, it is a path the subject follows by being attentive to others. We hope to find paths that are more caring of the natural and social environments.

We reject the man versus nature approach on a number of grounds. Most of us don't trash nature; but we all love the smell of napalm in the morning. Secondly, it uncritically accepts that there is a nature to which we stand as aggressors. From the position of man, there never was a nature untouched by the hand of man just as there never was a natural man. More importantly, this position, man versus nature, irrespective of its merits, is of no help to a project on the ethics of architecture because the first relation that architecture has is to its subject, the occupant, and any relations to other objects, like nature, are secondary.

What is critically different in our approach is that we are returning to a critical moment in Lacan's text, *The Ethics of Psychoanalysis*, where he invokes Freud's *wo es war, soll ich werden* as an ethical response to the injunctions imposed upon individuals by civilisation. If there is an ethical commandment in the analytic setting, it is to be true to your desire. The *thou shalt not* ... is not ethics but repression. The injunction is the form of the ego repressing desire. We need not more repression, paradoxically, but less. The way to deal with the drive is to reposition its object, not contain it; instead of erecting cladding around a repressive consumerism, an architectural strategy for containment that will only further isolate and individuate subjects, we must give voice to our desire by speaking to others. In *Civilization and Its Discontents*, Freud argued that 'civilization is a defence against our own instincts' (p. 34) as if the walls of the city were there to protect us against our nature. Freud also argued that 'civilization is built up upon a renunciation of instinct' (p. 34) as if we need to renounce something to be civilised. To speak in terms of defence and renunciation is the ego speaking. If we need to renounce something, it is the ego; if we need to defend something, it is our capacity and means to construct our unconscious.[9]

Discourse

If we accept, at least as a theoretical proposition, that we write our individual histories in the city, then we ought to be able to understand construction as a form of discourse. This is at least how we understand Rossi's construction of the city and – at a different scale – Vitruvius' originary concourse. Lacan developed his theory of discourse in his late seminars in order to elaborate in a precise and determined way the social bonds that bind individuals into civilisations. He elaborated four discourses, principle among them the discourse of the master, and sketched a fifth, the discourse of the capitalist. If we begin with the discourse of the master, we ought to be able to see how construction functions as a form of discourse that brings people together in the material environment of the city. It is significant that he developed the theory of discourse in a context where he also examined the relation of the subject to science and technology, nature, and media ecology, and coined a new term, *alethosphere* to name the increasingly technological status of the subjective sphere in which truth (*aletheia*) is revealed to the subject through discourse. This late work, much of it published recently, is now the focus of scholarship.[10]

When Lacan proposed the master's discourse in *Seminar XVII* (1969), he was interested in the way in *The Politics*, Aristotle distinguishes the 'know-how' or craft of the slave from the knowledge (*episteme*) of the master. The discussion is framed by knowledge and truth. The slave is 'the support of knowledge'. Philosophy, the paradigm of a master discourse, advances by 'stealing slavery of its knowledge, through the manoeuvres of the master'. 'It is all about finding the position that makes it possible for knowledge to becomes master's knowledge. The entire function of the *episteme* insofar as it is specified as transmissible knowledge … is always borrowed from the techniques of craftsmen …. It is a matter of extracting the essence of this knowledge in order for it to become master's knowledge'.[11] The master's discourse is modelled upon Hegel's dialectic of master and slave. The master rules the slave; the slave is dependent upon the master for his life, but the master is dependent upon the slave for his enjoyment without which his life is not worth living. 'By virtue of this forced labour, the slave ends up, at the end of history, at this point called absolute knowledge'.[12] The master's discourse is also the template for Marx's class struggle, in which the dynamic of power and dependency implicit in discourse applies to the multitude.

That the representational practice of perspective is a master's discourse should be clear from Brunelleschi's demonstration. In that little drama staged between Cathedral and Baptistery before the good burghers of Florence, Brunelleschi's master signifier – his perspective panel – addresses the know-how of an existing studio practice that had been approximating perspective to produce new knowledge, new subject, and new object. The difference between know-how and knowledge is not one of exactitude or of imposing a law. There is no reason to think that Brunelleschi's panel was more exact than existing studio practice. And it took another generation before Alberti codified perspective with a geometric law. The difference between the master discourse and the slave practice is authority. Aristotle inscribes the slave in the family; the master is a man of the state. It took Brunelleschi's demonstration to authorise the practice as knowledge, give it a name, and take it out of the 'family' of studio practice and put it in the public realm. In the demonstration, we witness the emergence of a new form of subject, one that sees the way Brunelleschi sees, or more precisely, that sees the way Brunelleschi represents what he sees. Brunelleschi and his viewer are equally subjects of the discourse. Both are subject to this new view. The subject is an effect of discourse, not the other way around (*you are what you build*). It also produced a new object of desire for the subject: the vanishing point, the lynchpin of perspective, which appears in the demonstration as a little hole.[13]

Central to any concept of the city as the locus of discourse is the operation by which information becomes knowledge for subjects. This is what discourse does. The city exists as an inexhaustible field of information with varying densities, flows, and textures, what Lacan calls 'the battery of signifiers, which we will refer to as the sign S2'.[14] [Figure 6.5] In *Seminar XVII*, Lacan differentiated know-how and *episteme*, the latter authorised by a master discourse. Two years later, in *Seminar XX*, Lacan makes a similar distinction between information and knowledge. 'There is no information that stands up unless it is shaped for use'. Lacan is making a number of points. Knowledge is already informed by the signifier ('the function I grant the letter in relation to knowledge'). The value of knowledge is its use value to subjects.[15] Information becomes knowledge with the intervention of the signifier that represents a subject to another signifier. In the master's discourse, the S2's are information – the entire field of facts that constitute the city – and S1 organises that field into the discourse form called knowledge. One of the most interesting – *avant la lettre* – projects for a city discourse, whose function was to transform information into knowledge, was the proposal by the planner Patrick Geddes for a so-called Outlook Tower. Every town was proposed to have an Outlook Tower, which was a combination of a viewing platform and a display for local knowledge. It was a new civic institution. The distinction between information and knowledge was raised but not fully addressed by Scott Brown/Venturi in Las Vegas. Geddes insisted that the city was first and foremost a knowledge environment. Town plans were 'hieroglyphs', if we could but read them. If for Vitruvius, building is a form of writing, for Geddes, inhabitation is a form of reading. Each settlement would become, by addition of an outlook tower, a spatial and temporal apparatus for self-knowledge. By an ongoing process of citizen surveys, citizens organised into survey groups, information about a place would be gathered by its inhabitants and organised into intelligible narratives of identity and desire for display so that each inhabitant could find out about themselves through the place they live and its relation to the world, what we might call, the truth of the place and its subjects.[16]

Discourse has always been central to Lacan's thinking on the subject, but only in the later texts does the development of the master discourse become central to his thinking on the social bonds between subjects. In early texts

S1   the master signifier
$ the subject, barred or marked by language
S2   the signifier chain or field of information retroactively appearing as knowledge to
     the subject
a   objet a, surplus enjoyment

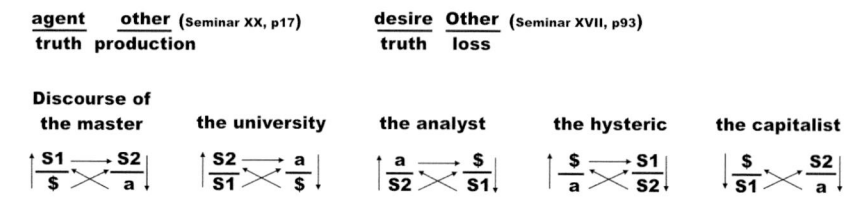

FIGURE 6.5   Lacan's four discourses + the discourse of the capitalist.

like *Seminar II* (1954), where he states 'the unconscious is the discourse of the Other',[17] discourse is described as a circuit, 'a small circuit' and related to repetition. '[I]t is the discourse of the circuit in which I am integrated. I am one of its links. It is the discourse of my father ..., in so far as my father made mistakes that I am ... condemned to reproduce'. A discourse is the enduring traces of a relationship.[18]

In *Seminar XVII*, it takes a precise form. Lacan calls discourse (he is referring to the master's discourse) a 'fundamental form', a 'signifying structure', 'it subsists in certain fundamental relations', and although discourse is 'a necessary structure that goes well beyond speech' and can 'subsist without words', it is a linguistic structure and its development by Lacan is a demonstration of the fundamentally linguistic nature of social urban relations.[19] Discourse is an apparatus comprised of four places: the agent, other, product, and truth. An agent, representing a truth, addresses an other, and produces an object. These four places are occupied by four 'functions': the master signifier S1; the signifier chain or knowledge S2; the barred or incomplete subject marked by language, $; and *a*, what in this context he calls 'jouissance', and which we know as *objet a*, the object of desire, more an empty place holder than an object.[20] 'S1 [the master signifier] is the point of departure for the definition of discourse'.

Discourse 'subsists' in 'the fundamental relation ... the relation of one signifier to another [the metonymic chain of one signifier displacing another, the metaphoric relation of one signifier signifying another]. And from this there results the emergence of what we call the subject – via the signifier which, as it happens, here functions as representing this subject with respect to another signifier'. The master signifier represents a subject to another signifier. The subject emerges through the process of representation in discourse. It is represented along the signifier chain like Chinese whispers, which is what makes Descartes' *I think therefore I am* an endless source of fascination for Lacan. S1 intervenes in S2 to produce knowledge. 'Knowledge initially arises at the moment at which S1 comes to represent something [the subject $], through its intervention in the field defined [S2] ...'[21]

The four discourses are produced by rotating the four elements, in the same order, a quarter turn each time, around the square of places. The master's discourse, with which Lacan begins, puts the master signifier in the agent position, signifying a subject $ placed beneath the bar of signification and addressing knowledge S2 as other. It is other because it is knowledge that will have been information. If there is a truth to the discourse, it is the truth of the subject. The discourse apparatus brings subjects, others, and objects together in four different ways. Through the discourse apparatus, signifiers represent subjects and produce objects; this double trope of the signifier Tomšič calls parallax.[22]

We have reproduced Lacan's diagrams for the four discourses, but we do not have space put them to work in all the different social encounters necessary to explicate them. Suffice it to say that most planning is masters discourse, what de Certeau called the 'view from above': Haussmann imposed axial boulevards (S1) upon the medieval practice of Paris (S2). Most bottom-up community action, like Kowloon Walled City, built largely within the planning lacunae of the city of Hong Kong, is hysterics' discourse in which the subjects' desire (*a*) is written on the body of the building ($) as a response to the repressive nature of the planning apparatus (S1). The discourses are critical analytic frames applicable to any social formation (and not mutually exclusive categories of social formation). Benjamin's *Arcades Project* constituted a counter discourse (*analysts or hysterics?*) and site for resistance to the master discourse of Haussmann. Lacan said that the analyst's discourse is fundamentally subversive because the analyst puts the subject's desire (*a*) in the place of the agent addressing the subject $. Lacan used the university discourse, in which knowledge S2 is in the place of the agent concealing a master signifier S1, to critique the role of the university in the unholy alliance between science and capitalism. Knowledge often conceals a hidden agenda – its truth, the master signifier – to produce student consumers ($).

Lacan's discourse apparatus forms an open circuit. There are two vector sequences that define discursive relations between the functions occupying the discourse places. These are the arrows. In the master's discourse, the subject $ goes to S1 and S2 (the signifiers that represent it). The master signifier S1 addresses knowledge S2 that produces the object of desire that returns in a circuit to the S1 in the agent position. The object produced by the discourse bypasses the subject and does not return to it. It is constitutive of discourse that it resists adequation because the circuit is not complete. This inadequacy corresponds to the constitutive incompleteness of the subject and the open-endedness of the signifier chain. The subject is an object of the signifier whose being is dependent upon signification and is subject to a desire that is not fulfillable.[23]

Capitalist discourse closes the circuit. It denies desire by giving the subject what it wants. The discourse of the capitalist is produced by a twist of the master's discourse so that the vector that runs through *objet a*/jouissance returns to the subject, and the subject is made whole by the attainment of the object. Vanheule calls this a 'mutant' or 'corrupted' form of the structure of discourse and is Lacan's attempt to understand how capitalism has changed social relations. The capitalist discourse is sketched by Lacan in 'Television' (1973)[24] and a number of minor texts and is developed by exegesis of his readers, principle among them Bruno, Tomšič, and Vanheule. In the discourse of the capitalist, the consumer (the subject) is in the place of the agent, driving the discourse, addressing the market (the market, not knowledge, is the other) producing enjoyment aimed directly at the subject. The master signifier, hidden under the consumer (as indeed it is hidden in the discourse of the university) is a variant of *spend spend spend* or *the more you shop the more you save* or *credit rules OK*, or simply, the capitalist himself pulling the strings from below.[25]

Every discourse is supported by a fantasy. The fantasy of the master's discourse is that you can master discourse, that mastery of a body of knowledge is possible, that you can tell the whole truth. The fantasy of the capitalist is that the incompleteness of the subject is accidental and the subject can be made whole again by the acquisition of an object. The structural cause of desire, which is the delay of the object, is no longer operative and desire is 'treated as if it is a demand' for consumption.[26] The constitutive incompleteness of the subject is not the human condition but a problem that can be solved by capitalism, whether the proffered commodity is an ice cream now, a Mondeo in the New Zealand outback, or green technology tomorrow. The circuit that is unique to the capitalist's discourse clarifies the difference between our relation to commodities and to objects of desire, which we introduced in an intuitive way in the last chapter as the difference between want and desire, and it explains why capitalist discourse approximates the death drive in the way that it replaces the delay of the object with its proliferation (*20 different Mondeos that are all the same Mondeo, all of them acquired with urgency*). It also explains why the shopping mall is not the microcosm of the city, even though it is often designed to be a simulacrum of the city. There is an alliance between capitalism and the ego. The capitalist fantasy that you can fill your desire with an object is another version of the denial by the ego of the moral duty of the subject to be true to its desire (Lacan's reading of Freud's *wo es war soll ich werden*). Desire constitutes 'an articulation of signifiers', all the Columbia's and other places where the subject encounters its desire.

The precise ways in which Lacan structures discourse opens the possibility that we may be able to find architectural forms or structures for discourse and the togetherness of people. This is, in any case, the architectural problem posed by discourse. These forms will need to remain open in critical ways. We could restage the Vitruvian campfire so that its constructors face outwards - this suggests a form of concourse that does not bring with it the implication of enclosure. Lacan's discourse apparatus makes it possible to think that if there is a collective agent for change, in particular environmental change, it will be a change of society, not technology. It will be written by many individuals speaking together for whom the city is the common field of signifiers. The form of this togetherness may be a form of incremental and open-ended construction that stages conflicts of interest between individuals and makes them material and spatial, and that does not simply contain them as parliamentary debate or abandon them to war. We do not yet have these forms and techniques for environmental consciousness because we do not yet have the common materials on which we write our individual desires. A survey of debating chambers confirms that politics is dominated by typologies of enclosure, which satisfy the ego by reflecting its fantasies of wholeness and completion.

Ethics for architecture

It is architecture's ethical duty to ensure that cities continue to be forms that bring people together in civil ways, rather than minimally to house and service them or protect them from nature, although it needs to do that too. If it is not bringing people together, it is failing them. In the present context, it is to bring people together to raise environmental consciousness in the only way possible to raise consciousness: to do it collectively. We began with Arendt's idea of the togetherness of people as the basis for their political power, which is the fundamental role of the city. We end with discourse. With the arts and humanities, architecture has the capacity to write new narratives about what it is to be human. The site for these narratives is the city because cities give form to social life. This is an ethical issue not because it is about saving blue whales and white rhinos, and certainly not because they are natural, all of which I want to save too, but they have no part in an ethics. We have traversed this argument long enough to know that nothing is natural except our capacity to construct this individual whose nature is to be destructive. It is an ethical issue because by damaging the environment, we are damaging ourselves. Our lifestyles, and the planning policies that support them, which may be loosely defined as a policy of dispersion, divide-mollify-conquer, constitute an epidemic of self-harm.

What is at stake is how architecture articulates the relation between the subject bound by language and the city. The one and the many. The multitude of linguistic ones versus the many that resist a single name, a single leader, a single form, but are collected by a grammar, a position and direction, desire and urgency. Architecture articulates this relation spatially. We need to develop typologies for concourse, collective self-reflection, and connectedness other than the ones we know from politics. These studies may begin by hybridising the ones we already know. We could cross piazza with website, the old and new sites for congregation. We could cross the boulevard with the confessional, or the analytic setting and the internet café, hybrids that cross public and private, that put individuals together with multitudes without renouncing the status of the subject as individual. We mention the analytic setting again because it is the space of appearance of the unconscious. This is where we would expect the discourse of the analyst to be brought to bear on cities. Architectural thinking on cities has the potential to bring analysis out of the analytic setting, which is a relation between two subjects and treat it as a collective relation between the multitude of subjects in discourses. Architecture usually takes the form of a container, its preoccupations with the envelope, with cladding (*thank you Semper, thank you Loos*) is an allusion to the internal resistance necessary to support civilisation. But the metaphor for our hybrids is less cladding not more. We need typologies that allow for self-reflection but do not isolate the individual in their individualness. We will also need to find new ways of mapping densities of interconnectedness. The city centre is an obvious site for connectedness, where densities are sufficient to support services – libraries, supermarkets, furniture and appliances stores, doctors' surgeries, public transport – within walking distances. The upper west side of Manhattan is a good model. So are the courtyard blocks of the Kreuzberg and Mitte districts of Berlin.

The challenge for architecture is to explore environmental consciousness in an age of commodity capitalism. Commodity capitalism is capitalism's most virulent form because capitalist discourse reduces us to individuals in a condition of greed, which is as close to the death drive as we are likely to get. This individual is not primitive but hollowed out. Desire is replaced by repetition. It is imagined in its contemporary form in zombie movies (*why is it always entertainment that speaks the truth when policy can't?*). A multitude of hollowed out individuals, each a solitary unto-itself, lurching forward, consuming everything in its path, without enjoyment or discrimination.

We divert ourselves from these critical ethical tasks when we treat cities as technological objects. Contemporary planning policy focuses on the technological aspects of sustainability as if cities were technological objects and not social ones. We castigated Foster because Masdar is the object of the technology industries and not a city. The smart city movement and the renewables industries – if we make cities turn themselves off, we can save energy, if we derive our energy more directly from the sun, we produce less carbon – miss the most pressing question, that cities are the forms by which people come together and it is by exploring forms of togetherness that we have the possibilities for raising environmental consciousness. We use the sustainable technological project to avoid the more painful task of addressing our greed and agency. Technology is the easy option, and it relieves our guilt without confronting the difficult truths of collective self-reflection. Technology is complicit in the pathology of environmental damage in the way that we all are. The renewables industry has become just another industry that exploits the earth's resources in its race for market share. Smart cities are putting busted circuitry and rare earth minerals into landfill. Smart and renewable technologies are subjected to the same speculative and competitive market conditions that contribute to environmental damage. It is beyond the scope of our expertise to address the economic problems of environmental damage, but until technology is financed, produced, and procured outside current capitalist market models, it is unlikely that technology will reduce rather than exacerbate environmental damage. Most technological solutions are developed within capitalist market conditions. In what appears to most people as an example of Orwellian newspeak, the aim of the EU carbon trading scheme is to reduce carbon production by creating a market for it.[27]

Regrettably, professional ethics such as it is inscribed in professional codes of conduct remain largely silent on this duty and are largely concerned with equitable office management and the treatment of staff. They are not about promoting what – for Aristotle – is the good life, where good life is defined as a life of togetherness. Ethics, the environment, and society appear in, e.g., the RIBA *Code of Professional Conduct*, but without the agency that architecture demands of them. We want to take ethics out of the office and conjoin it to environments and societies so that we can think about human settlement as a public good and machine for collective thinking about our agency in the environment. National planning policy documents are similarly silent on togetherness, and more critically, although they capture sustainability aims, they make no attempt to address the obvious and almost irreconcilable conflicts of interest between sustainability and the profit-motivated development of the markets.[28]

If there is a response that is not more regulation and management, not the management of a problem but the alleviation of suffering, architects may need to work closely with psychoanalysts on the form of the city. This may be a speculative design research project before it becomes integrated into first planning policy and secondly into the planning approvals process. Let us assume that the drive will always be in a dialectic relation with civilisation. There is no cure. There is only repositioning *objet a* in discourse, that hard kernel of the individual attached to the body. This is a symbolic object even as it resists symbolisation, and repositioning it is a symbolic act. There is no uncladding or recladding of the object and dissipation of the drive.

We need to build new spaces. Let us call them discursive spaces, spaces that construct environmental consciousness – involving individuals reflecting together on how their individual actions have cumulative effects. This is not yet a practical solution. It may not be any kind of solution, as there remains an amount of intellectual labour before we will be in a position to construct them. We suggested thinking about it as a kind of knotting. But it is where the ethical responsibility of self to other, and through others, of self to self, will appear. It may require renunciation, it may require forgiveness, and it will certainly require a form of civic life that creates safe places for concourse. It will become necessary in order to break the cycle of self-destructive behaviour and to face down the market power that encourages it; it will become necessary to break the cycle of consumption and technology – consumption whose drivers we don't understand and technology we let clean the mess afterwards. These spaces are necessary because if architecture cannot find ways back to this space of the Other, this hand that shadows us with our desire, and we really do what it looks like we are doing, destroying ourselves by destroying our environment, then we need to write new narratives of death and forgiveness, a kind of *Civilisation* … update. We will need to find a way to tell our children that we knew what we were doing, but we could not help it because it is our nature. We will need to be able to tell them with knowledge and dignity, the kind of grace and dignity that comes with self-knowledge. The space of appearance of environmental consciousness becomes the public staging of tragedy.

Notes

1 Saul Bass, director, *Phase IV* (Paramount Pictures, 1974). The quote is by Lesko, the 'good' scientist in the team. There is also a *Phase IV* (2002), which appears to be an unrelated movie set within a rogue AIDS drug testing program.

2 Cf. https://www.fosterandpartners.com/projects/masdar-city/ accessed 05 August 2020. Masdar hopes to attract a global nucleus of what Wikipedia calls 'clean tech' companies. Masdar is developed by Masdar a wholly owned subsidiary of the Mubadala Investment Company, which is a state-owned sovereign wealth fund formed by merging the Mubadala Development Company with the International Petroleum Investment Company which is an investment vehicle wholly owned by the government of Abu Dhabi. The original design is for 50,000 residents and 1500 businesses, over 6 square kilometres. https://en.wikipedia.org/wiki/Masdar_City, accessed 23 June 2019.

3 Here is an incomplete list: Darren Woods, CEO of ExxonMobil 2017; Rex Tillerson 2006–2017; Lee Raymond CEO of ExxonMobil 1999–2005; CEO of Exxon 1993–1999; Clifton C. Garvin Jr. 1975–1986. Rex Tillerson was the 69th United States Secretary of State in 2017–2018 for the Trump Administration.

4 *The Guardian* reported ('38 million pieces of plastic waste found on uninhabited South Pacific island', Monday 15 May 2017, accessed 01 October 2017) that when Dr. Jennifer Lavers (University of Tasmania) surveyed Henderson Island with a team of marine scientists in 2015, they were surprised to find the beaches covered in plastic debris. An estimated 17.6 tonnes; 38 million pieces. Henderson Island is a tiny atoll in the Pitcairn Group, one of the most remote places on earth. This image taken from the Guardian article, is from Lavers' report, published by the RSPB (UK). See Figure 33 'Enormous quantities of plastic debris on North-East Beach, Henderson Island' in Lavers, J.L., McClelland, G.T.W., MacKinnon, L., Bond, A.L., Oppel, S., Donaldson, A.H., Duffield, N.D., Forrest, A.K., Havery, S.J, O'Keefe, S., Skinner, A., Torr, N., and Warren, P., *Henderson Island Expedition Report: May–November 2015. RSPB Research Report 57* (RSPB Centre for Conservation Science, RSPB, The Lodge, Sandy, Bedfordshire, SG19 2DL. 2016). Rachel Carson, *Silent Spring* (Boston, MA: Houghton Mifflin, 1962) documented the adverse environmental effects of pesticides at a time when DDT was being used indiscriminately. It was widely read as a Book of the Month Club with a print run of 150,000. It was fiercely opposed by the chemical industry. Cf. https://en.wikipedia.org/wiki/Silent_Spring accessed 08 09 2020. Sir Darling (1903–1979) was a Scottish ecologist and conservationist. The Reith Lectures are available on the BBC1 website at https://www.bbc.co.uk/programmes/p00h6647 (lecture 1 of 6) accessed 08 September 2020. John Lennon, 'Gimme some truth' (1971) https://en.wikipedia.org/wiki/Gimme_Some_Truth accessed 08 September 2020. For Laugh-In, see https://en.wikipedia.org/wiki/Rowan_%26_Martin%27s_Laugh-In accessed 08 September 2020. It ran from 1968 to 1973 and was for a while the most popular TV show in America. Davis Guggenheim, dir., *An Inconvenient Truth* (2006) is a documentary about former Vice President Al Gore's campaign, based on his slide show, educating people about global warming. Cf. https://en.wikipedia.org/wiki/An_Inconvenient_Truth accessed 08 September 2020.

5 Francis Ford Coppola, director, *Apocalypse Now* (1979).

6 For WHO figures, see https://www.who.int/gho/ncd/risk_factors/overweight/en/ (accessed 04 August 2020).

7 See Melanie Klein, *Love, Guilt, and Reparation: And Other Works 1921–1945*, edited by Hanna Segal (London: Virago Press, 1988). Michael Rustin, 'How Is Climate Change an Issue for Psychoanalysis', in *Engaging with Climate Change: Psychoanalytic and Interdisciplinary Perspectives*, edited by Sally Weintrobe (Hove and New York: Routledge, 2013). Rustin and his respondents in this collection of papers also make the link between consumer capitalism and climate change. Michael Rustin is a Professor of Sociology at University of East London.

8 Donna M. Orange, *Climate Crisis, Psychoanalysis, and Radical Ethics* (Routledge, 2017), quote p. 84.
9 Georg Lukacs introduced renunciation with respect to capitalism in *History and Class Consciousness* (1923) in his critique of capitalism and his project for the self-conscious transformation of society. I quote Jodi Dean on Lukacs: 'Lukacs notes that the "freedom" of those of us brought up under capitalism is "the freedom of the individual isolated by the fact of property", a freedom over and against other, isolated individuals, "a freedom of the egoist, of the man who cuts himself off from others, a freedom for which solidarity and community exist at best only as ineffectual regulative ideas." He writes "The *conscious* desire for the realm of freedom can only mean taking the steps that will really lead to it. … because it is a case of unilateral privilege based on the unfreedom of others, this desire must entail the renunciation of individual freedom"'. Lukacs quote taken from *History and Class Consciousness: Studies in Marxist Dialectics*, trans. Rodney Livingstone (London: Merlin Press, 1971), p. 315. Cf. Dean, *The Communist Horizon* (London: Verso, 2012), p. 196.
10 In *Seminar 17*, he coins the terms *alethosphere* and *lathouse* to define the media ecology environment within which our subjectivity emerges and what is, in effect, the internet of things. Jacques Lacan, *The Seminar of Jacques Lacan, Book XVII: The Other Side of Analysis 1969–1970*, translated by Russell Grigg and edited by Jacques-Alain Miller (New York: W. W. Norton & Company, 2007) the chapter 'Furrows in the alethosphere' pp. 150–163. See also an excellent reading of this chapter in relation to climate change in a lecture by Dutch analyst Geert Hoornaert to the London Society of the New Lacanian School at https://www.youtube.com/watch?v=BVMxovCWdXw (accessed July 2021). There is another chapter to write, to take up Hoornaert's argument. He assimilates the alethosphere to the anthropocene.
11 Jacques Lacan, *The Seminar of Jacques Lacan, Book XVII: The Other Side of Analysis 1969–1970*, translated by Russell Grigg and Edited by Jacques-Alain Miller (New York: W. W. Norton & Company, 2007), quote p. 22; know-how and *episteme* reprised pp. 148–149. Knowledge and discourse are introduced together beginning p. 13ff. 'S1 … intervenes in a signifying battery that we have no right, ever, to take as … not already forming a network of what is called knowledge. Knowledge initially arises at the moment at which S1 comes to represent something, …'. We know from the immediately preceding context, this something is a subject.
12 Lacan, *Seminar XVII, op. cit.*, p. 170.
13 Lacan linked the master signifier to the *name of the father*, the name of the person in the subject's life (it is usually a man) who imposes the law. At a certain point in the Oedipal development of the child, the law of the father replaces the love of the mother. Lacan calls this the paternal metaphor. Not the real father, but the *name*, i.e. the signifier of the father, as in 'I arrest you in the name of the law'. Imagine father Brunelleschi imposing the law of space, i.e. the law of seeing in perspective, upon the child viewer of the Baptistery. To see in perspective is to see in the name of Brunelleschi. The *name of the father* is the guarantor of the symbolic order and symbolic mastery, and its loss or foreclosure is the key structure of psychosis. Lacan developed the concept of the *name-of-the-father* in connection with his understanding of psychosis in *The Seminar of Jacques Lacan, Book III: The Psychoses 1955–1956.* trans. Russell Grigg, ed. Jacques-Alain Miller (New York: W. W. Norton, 1993); and in 'On a Question Prior to Any Possible Treatment of Psychosis (1958)' in *Ecrits: The First Complete Edition in English*. Translated by Bruce Fink, Heloise Fink, and Russell Grigg (New York: W. W. Norton, 2006), pp. 445–488. I discuss psychosis in relation to perspective and space in 'Psychosis and the Ineffable Space of Modernism', *Journal of Architecture* 18 (2013), pp. 402–424.
14 Lacan, *Seminar XVII, op. cit.*, p. 13.
15 Lacan, *Seminar XX, op. cit.*, quotes p. 97. Lacan seems also to say that knowledge has use value but not exchange value, a departure from Marx for whom exchange value is primary. He also associates knowledge, its use, and acquisition with jouissance.

16 Patrick Geddes, *Cities in Evolution: An Introduction to the Town Planning Movement and to the Study of Civics* (London: William & Norgate, 1949). See also Lorens Holm, ed., *The City Is a Thinking Machine: Patrick Geddes and Cities in Evolution*, 4 vols (Dundee: Geddes Institute for Urban Research and the University of Dundee, 2016), and in particular vols 1 'The exhibition' and 2 'The Geddes archives' (download at https://www.dundee.ac.uk/geddesinstitute/projects/citythink/catalogue/). Nothing makes sense about Geddes' extensive output of plans, diagrams, and thinking machines, held in the archives of the Universities of Dundee, Edinburgh, and Strathclyde, until you realise that what Geddes was trying – and failing – to do his entire life was to understand ways of organising people and cities into a spatial and temporal discourse in which information emerges as knowledge. It is a discourse between a subject of the city, the city, and a tower which is a reading machine. The subject is always in motion, what appears as knowledge is always in flux. The temporality is interesting. The knowledge appears retroactively in the walls, windows, doorways, stone walls, and field furrows; it was always already there, but it needed the tower for it to appear as knowledge.

17 Lacan, *Seminar II, op. cit.*, p. 89, repeated p. 137.

18 Lacan, *ibid.*, pp. 89–90.

19 Lacan, *Seminar XVII, op. cit.*, pp. 12–14.

20 Lacan, *Seminar XX, op. cit.*, p. 17. In this text, Lacan labels the *a* as surplus jouissance. In *Seminar XVII, op.cit.*, p. 93, the four places are shown as 'desire/truth' and 'Other/loss'. '[H]ere ... we have desire, and on the other side the site of the Other. This represents ... man's desire is the desire of the Other. ... The place underneath desire represents the place of truth. Under the Other is the place where loss is produced, the loss of *jouissance* from whence we extract the function of surplus *jouissance*'. On the preceding page, Lacan diagrams the master's discourse as 'master signifier/subject' and 'knowledge/jouissance'. 'This putting into operation of discourse is defined by a split, precisely by differentiating out the master signifier with respect to knowledge.'

21 Lacan, *Seminar XVII, op. cit.*, p. 13 for the quotes on emerging subjects and knowledge. For Descartes see for instance *Seminar XVII, op. cit.*, pp. 153, 155.

22 In his reading of Lacan with Marx, Samo Tomšič describes each discourse as the parallax between a representative axis and a productive one. The signifier represents a subject and produces an object. It is parallax because there are two points of view in any discourse: the point of view of the subject; the point of view of the object. Cf. Tomšič, *op. cit.*, pp. 203–204.

23 In Lacan's discussion of discourse, this *a* is also referred to as surplus jouissance or enjoyment. The discourse produces jouissance that is surplus, an analogue of Marx's surplus value; it is surplus because it does not have a use value that returns it to the system. In either case, as *objet a* or as surplus jouissance, it is a negative value, a form of enjoyment that the subject never attains.

24 Jacques Lacan, 'Television' broadcast on French TV (1973), published (1974), translated in *October 40* (1987).

25 There is a number of great texts on Lacan's discourses which explore their relation to economics politics and climate change. My references for this synopsis of the capitalist's discourse include Stijn Vanheule 'Capitalist Discourse, Subjectivity and Lacanian Psychoanalysis' in *Frontiers in Psychology* 7 (2016); Samo Tomšič, *The Capitalist Unconscious: Marx and Lacan* (New York and London: Verso Books, 2015); and Pierre Bruno, *Lacan and Marx: The Invention of the Symptom*, translated by John Holland, *Cfar Library* (London: Routledge, 2020). In 'On Not Being Able to Build', Voela argues that the capitalist subject has lost the mobility necessary for building (it is glued up and stuffed). Cf. Angie Voela, 'On Not Being Able to Build' in *Architecture and Culture* 8:3+3 (November 2020). A subject *not* split by language, whose objects are not delayed, would suffocate on its own solidity, and approximates the limit to subjectivity where capitalism and the death drive converge.

26 Vanheule, *op. cit.*, pp. 6–7.

27 See the EU reports on carbon trading at https://ec.europa.eu/clima/eu-action/eu-emissions-trading-system-eu-ets_en.

28 In the *RIBA Code of Professional Conduct* (2019), care of the environment and care of society appear as competencies, not ethics, and devolve to the impact of projects upon their natural and social contexts; and ethics appears under relationships, where it is primarily concerned with equitable office management. In the *Ethics and Sustainable Development Commission Key Findings and Recommendations* (2018) which the RIBA published in response to the UN Sustainable Development Goals (SDGs), ethics remains synonymous with professional ethics, and environment and society are categories separate from it. The objectives of the NCARB *Model Rules of Conduct* (2018) are 'protection of the public health, safety, and welfare', but these are defined as compliance with laws and other statutory instruments, and these are qualified as US law, not the laws of other countries although American architects accept commissions all over the world. One of its core values is 'working together', but again, this is defined in an office context of cooperation with other professionals and sharing of expertise and does not extend into an existential context. *National Planning Policy Framework*, (Ministry of Housing, Communities, & Local Government, February 2019) leaves open critical questions about interpretation of its terms of compliance with them. See, for instance, 'Section 12. Achieving well-designed places' says that 'Planning policies and decisions should ensure that developments: ... create places ... which promote health and well-being, ...' (Para 127) and that 'Applicants should work closely with those affected by their proposals to evolve designs that take account of the views of the community' (Para 128), which 'include workshops to engage the local community, design advice and review arrangements, and assessment frameworks such as *Building for Life*'. These documents are available online.

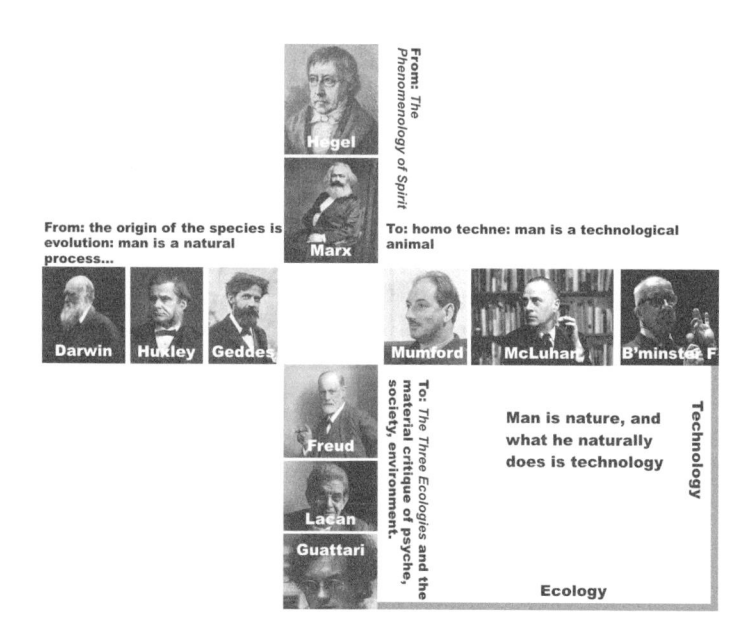

FIGURE P.1 The mostly male lineage of western thought.

POSTSCRIPT

Subjective theory and practice [rooms+cities]

The projective vision of architecture is to always place the individual within the infrastructural field of social, political and economic, ideological and historical, and technological and scientific forces that define the age (Mies called it *zeitgeist*). Architectural design is a speculative and theoretically informed practice for investigating the relation of the individual to the built environment and the social groups that inhabit it. It will only be activated when it comes out of the schools and into the planning process. In a world where our two most precious human resources – green land and the public realm – are everywhere under threat by squanderous development practices that favour junk space typologies and an overly instrumentalised reason that rarely recognises any other value in the public realm than monetary value, architecture has the capacity to imagine new models for dense city-making, new models for inhabitation, new models for private and public life, and relations of cities to the land. There is a continuous line of architectural thinking from the constructivists in the 1920s to the social housing of post-war European reconstruction that recognised the power of architecture to imagine new forms of social life (*UK and US experiments in post-war social housing are not dead, they are simply not maintained*).[1] The big questions facing architecture have to do with the different but related problems of defining ecological forms of settlement in an overheating earth and defining the social forms of public life through new forms of city design in a time when digital media is replacing urban space as the platform for congregation.

Against instrumental market thinking that is dispersing our collective environments and distracting our collective consciousness, we can use architecture to develop formal intelligence, historical consciousness, and architectural knowledge and practice at the regional scale. Hence the preoccupation with cities that links Brunelleschi, Giedion, Rossi, and Scott Brown/Venturi. Perspective had to be demonstrated in the centre of Florence, Giedion had to insist on the symbolic status of architecture at a time when modernism still had a social agenda; Rossi was obsessed with the construction of the city, with its architectural forms and the urban artefacts about which it grows; Scott Brown/Venturi were obsessed with the city of information. We believe in the ethical imperative of Architecture; sometimes, the right thing is to set a course that not everyone will want to follow. Against typologies of density comes the resistance that everyone wants to live in isolation, with off-street parking and big lawns. Americans don't need piazzas because they have televisions. We regard this as a cynical oversimplification of what *want* is, coupled with a wilful blindness to the manipulation of *want* by the instrumental reason of markets and politics. But we also accept that if this *is* what people want, then it is equally our task to visualise the death drive.

This text puts architecture and psychoanalysis together to forge new intellectual futures by reworking our intellectual pasts. This is what the humanities do. The humanities use close reading as an act of resistance to the power of entrenched and hegemonic thinking. Reading architecture with Freud and Lacan is subversive of the economic and political orders that manage and oppress communities. We propose a psychoanalytically informed architecture as a way to move sideways from the market-oriented thinking that has colonised architecture and planning. Although psychoanalysis is now also being displaced by market-oriented discourses, Giedion and Rossi were writing at a time when psychoanalytic thinking was central to intellectual discourse. We cannot go about procuring buildings and planning cities according to the profit motive and within evaluative frameworks based on the measurement of quantities. If this project is carried into practice, as it is intended to be, everything must change.

It is often best to begin from first principles. If this text has had a central concern, it has been to trace the consequences for architecture and for cities of the existence of the unconscious. The subject of architectural space is also the subject of the unconscious. The unconscious did not have to exist, but for better or worse it does. It is an effect of language in so far as language is activated by speaking subjects; we are all – whether we speak or not – speaking beings. To this end, we began this text by articulating what we argued to be the central concepts of each discipline, the unconscious and space, and attempted to demonstrate their affinities. If the unconscious is an effect of language, space is an effect of walls, windows, doorways, and ground planes and the geometries that we use to arrange them, principle amongst them the perspective geometry that is the template for realism in architecture. The ego has an attachment to reality at the expense of the unconscious, and consequently, the unconscious exists to the subject in the particular form of a denial.

We began this text with these two central principles, the unconscious and space, and they have formed the route we have followed throughout it. That it is possible to articulate the central principles of a discipline is perhaps necessary for its integrity; and it is necessary for any attempt to put two disciplines together in a discourse that has ambitions to be more than an accidental or anecdotal encounter and that has claims to be systematic. We argued for the affinity of these principles. We noted, by way of initial plausibility, that the unconscious and space share the descriptive qualities of being nowhere and – because nowhere – everywhere. More importantly, they share a certain form of conceptual and syntactical absence that positions subjects.

We looked at a number of problems in architecture and cities. For instance, we drew on Giedion's text to look at a problem with the key categories of architectural space, inside and outside; we were able to argue – without abandoning its essentially binary logic – that there are at least three horizons or outsides with respect to the subjective experience of space, which disrupts what otherwise appears to be the spatial logic of architecture. We drew on Rossi's text, his extraordinary preoccupation with history, forgetting, and the unconscious, to demonstrate how we might think about the unconscious attachment of people to places. This chapter came with a challenge to the planning profession, but without a practical solution: how to represent a form of attachment to places which is unacknowledged fleeting and labyrinthine, and which has nothing to do with community identity or wellbeing as a service delivery benchmark. We left it hanging, how to represent unconscious attachment in the planning application procedure.

We concluded with what I regard to be the single most pressing problem confronting people today, the problem of our continual damage to the environment. If we spend so long on this topic, it is because it raises the question of architecture's complicity with our nature. The question of our damage to nature appears to hinge on the question of whether it is our nature to be destructive. If it is, we may have to embrace it with dignity and prepare our children for a dirty death. Except that the question of nature is problematised in political, ethical, and psychoanalytic discourses, and it is probably tautological. Aristotle argues that it is our nature to be political and to pursue the good. When Freud argues that it is our nature to destroy the political, the nature he constructs is the mortal substrate of subjectivity, which is so reductive an object of thought, equally intractable and universal, that you can do nothing with it.

If environmental damage is a pathology, the 'cure' is analysis not regulation or management. If the drive to environmental damage resides in the individual, the ethical response for architecture is to think of new spatial forms for the togetherness of people and hence new forms for the appearance of environmental consciousness. These places may need to be hybrids with digital platforms. In any case, forms predicated upon typologies of enclosure like the debating chamber and piazza no longer seem adequate. They are part of the problem. They are where Freud's destructive individual appears. If our appetite for destruction is our nature, this individual is a construct of the producer-advertising-commodity complex that Lacan called capitalist discourse, which appeals to the ego at the expense of its own subjectivity, at the expense, in other words, of the inter-subject space of desire that we share.

The ethical call for spaces of togetherness is not about renouncing objects – this is not the call for cultural revolutionary style acts of public self-denunciation – nor is it about renouncing our nature, still less about repression, but about working through the discourses that are always operative by directing the attention of the subject to other subjects. We work through discourse of/by/for individuals so as to access our common nature. In the context of *Civilisation and Its Discontents*, a context where the destructive nature of the individual appears unrestrained, against which are posed injunctions to love, injunction to not covet, in this climate of ethics as regulation, Lacan says that the ethical imperative of the subject is to take care of yourself by being mindful that when you speak, you speak to others.

An intellectual lineage

The study of Lacan begins with the intellectual lineage within which he inserts himself. If there is one lesson to learn from Lacan's text, it is about how a discourse is enmeshed with other discourses to make a net that defines the known world.

We highlight two intellectual lineages, which treat the human subject: a symbolic lineage in which Lacan finds a place and a material one inaugurated by Darwin.

Lineage 1 – the development of the human subject whose attribute is a symbolic cluster called the unconscious:

- Hegel's concept of Spirit split and inhabited by absence; in *The Aesthetics: lectures on fine art*, Hegel argues that the history of civilisation is the history of Spirit reflecting upon itself in three stages, each stage sublimating the stage before it.[2]

- Marx's class consciousness, the general intellect, the social formation in which a material conscious finds its *classness* in labour and the collective means of production and exchange.
- Unconscious desire was developed by Freud as the central psychical agency of the individual.
- It was overwritten in terms of structural linguistics by Lacan as the field of signifier chains which, we argue, is a form of common.
- In *Capitalism and Schizophrenia* (1993), Deleuze & Guattari (a student of Lacan's) critique the unconscious as a 19th-century bourgeois exercise from which they retain Freud's hydraulic model of desire to link the components of human-machine assemblages and from which they elaborate the idea of the incompleteness of the dividual.[3]

Lineage 2 – the development of the human subject as a natural animal whose nature is technology:

- Charles Darwin's theory of evolution places man in the natural order of animals.
- T.H. Huxley, Darwin's champion, developed the theory of the type-form (extended to symbolic form by Ernst Cassirer and Erwin Panofsky).
- Patrick Geddes (a student of Huxley) brings the natural process of evolution to bear on the social organisation of the city.
- Lewis Mumford (student of Geddes), Giedion, and Marshall McLuhan rewrite evolution in terms of technology, from natural environments to mechanisation, to media environments.
- Technology is taken up in a line of architectural thinking that extends from Buckminster Fuller to Zaha Hadid and Patrik Schumacher.

There is an extended essay to write on how Lacan addresses technology, in particular in *Seminar XVII*. These lineages project psycho-architectural research into the 21st-century digital world. The inter-subjectivity of humankind is worked out in technology, in particular communication technology and architecture. We include the speech apparatus as technology. To the speech apparatus, we add the space apparatus. The digital environment is in a dialectic relation with the spatial environment. The key architectural questions are: how does the subject speak? from where does the subject speak? and in what medium?

Subjective theory and practice

Psychoanalysis is the most sustained and systematic reflection upon the subject in Western thought. Psychoanalysis should be the disciplinary partner for any discipline that wants to give a complete accounting of itself. Whether you think you need psychoanalysis depends on whether you think you can write a comprehensive science of cities and civilisations (*are they not the same?*) without taking into account the individual: the individual who writes that science, the individual who produces, curates, and narrates knowledge; the individual who encounters and responds to every entity bigger than itself, whether it is the scientific method, data collection, the institution, planning law, or the city; the individual in its fundamental syntactical incompleteness; the individual as constituent of a network that is both the multitude of individuals and the social group with its armoured carapace; in short the individual who brings with it an extended ethnography.

This subjective approach may lead to new objective accounts of the human subject that are more appropriate to the digital age. We exhale data the way we exhale CO_2. We are now immersed in digital data forms and automatic processes. We are constituents of social-spatial assemblages, we are signifier machines arranged in assemblages with non-human subjects, and it is our duty to ourselves to continue the process of humanising ourselves by rethinking ourselves within the environments we have created. I believe in social change, in the only way I know possible, by changing ourselves. We must not take our humanity for granted. We are all complicit in the project to humanise ourselves, which is a project without end. These theoretical writings that are poised between architecture and psychoanalysis, that have made the way for architecture to host psychoanalysis the way a house hosts a ghost, are a prolegomena to any architecture that may come forth as a tool for rethinking ourselves so that we can continue to be human.

rooms+cities

We propose to introduce a form of subjective urban practice that is articulated as a dialectic of two architectural terms, a practice which we provisionally name *rooms+cities*. They form a single lowercase couple whose form is thus autonomous of its position in a sentence. The room is the place where I appear in the city to myself and to others as a subject of desire, wherever and however that place is configured, understanding desire as a collective social formation organised around absence. It may be indoors or out, large or small, public or private, enclosed or open. These places constitute a commons not because they are in public ownership but because my desire is articulated in concourse with others. They may only be recognised in urban analyses that are equipped to recognise absences in the way that the analytic setting is equipped to recognise the unconscious. The city is the infrastructure, conventional or otherwise, that organises rooms, wherever and however that infrastructure is configured; it brings people together by organising rooms into intelligible formations. In urban analysis, it may appear as lines of togetherness between subjects. We include the network of roads, rails, services, utilities, and other fibres, public services and public pronouncements, rythmanalysis (Lefebvre) even, within which the room is situated. We include the material connectedness of party walls on streets, streets framing into boulevards, boulevards organising districts, districts distinguishing themselves between medieval and modern, centre and periphery. But also we note the 'tribal' form of the British Parliament; the particularly 'English' form of the speaker's corner; the public arrogance taught at Eton that covertly influences politics that leads to planning policy that defines development plans; the particularly French use of the boulevard for politics, a tradition that precedes *les soixante-huitards* – it goes back to the Paris commune of 1848 (cobbles make great barricades) and the blood spectacles of the Terror. A full accounting of infrastructure would make infrastructure synonymous with the discursive relations that bind subject to others and to their environments. It would include an infrastructure of predispositions and ideas, including politics, money, law: anything that can be said to flow. Architecture is tasked with working with media, including digital media, hence these rooms and infrastructures are not wholly spatial. One of the lessons of Vitruvius is that they never have been. With the rapid growth of media in politics and public life, these connections are increasingly digital. rooms+cities aims to make explicit the togetherness of people that is implicit in inter-subjectivity. It should be clear by now that the togetherness of people is both a precondition of politics and ethics and a function of unconscious desire. rooms+cities constitute the space of appearance of desire. *Wherever you go you will be a polis.*

rooms+cities structures architectural thinking in a way that reflects the formula for the split subject: ego-unconscious. This approach will not lead to one formal response or one sort of subject. This text notwithstanding, we don't have to develop a subjective practice; but if we don't, we have to abandon space as the core conceptual commitment and symbolic medium of architecture and abandon a lineage of spatial thinking that has infiltrated other disciplines. To continue to practice architecture as if space did not form an essential couple with the subject is a falsification of architecture. We recognise in this intransigence the *méconnaissance* of the ego, the ego whose stake in the world is directly proportional to its attempts to *not* acknowledge the unconscious desire of the subject.

Lefebvre says that urbanisation and urban society are virtual objects. They are conceptual, always forming, never here. To which we add that urbanisation and urban society, in our terms, the architecture of the city and its field of the Other, rooms+cities, are only possible in relation to each other. rooms+cities aims to develop a language for the social order of desire, which resists the realpolitik of development, finance, and policy, even as it has to work with them. The problem is not about function and only partially formal. It is a problem of analysis, imagination, and understanding.

We need a graphic notation that will allow us to reconfigure the city and its communities around absence. This space of appearance is as yet un-named and unrecognised, but it is as necessary for the appearance of the subject as the shopping mall is for the appearance of the consumer. We don't yet know what rooms look like or how to talk about them. They will be spatial, temporal, and digital hybrids. The city is not smart, but the collective is partially telecommunicational. The room may look like a knot – a knotting together of connectivities – and not an enclosure. Desire is never fully articulated. Our model for infrastructure – and it is a long way from an architectural typology, more an analytic tool – is the field of the Other. In the chapter on Rossi, we introduced the field of the Other as the open-ended network of signifier chains that attach people to places and things. As a subject of the city, I am distributed across the city by the relation of my bedroom to my flat, and my flat to my neighbour's, and the relation our flats to the façade they share, the façade to street, and our street to our library, tram lines, supermarket, parks, views, sunrises, darkness of winter nights on the Columbia Campus, …. These are my signifiers, and rooms+cities begins by unpacking them to build a new form of site and urban analysis. If rooms+cities is a research project, it is with the proviso that all architecture should be research.[4]

We may need new myths or we may need to reread old ones in new ways. We have seen that Vitruvius' myth of the primitive hut was about the emergence of a new social spatial grammar, from which has issued every form of concourse from Aldo van Eyck's studies of Dogon culture to the debating chamber. We only note here that in this reading of Vitruvius, everyone faces each other around the campfire, which presupposes a certain form of imaginary enclosure, and that we would derive an entirely different spatial typology for concourse if everyone sat around the campfire faced outwards. As a paradigm togetherness, this new model might function like the analytic setting.

We know that our social relations are inscribed in cities, but we need better tools for reading them. The industrial cities – New York, Paris, London, Barcelona, Berlin – that emerged in their current form in the 19th century in response to evolving relations of labour and capital have achieved canonic status in western thought, such that Kevin Lynch could diagram them in the *Theory of Good City Form*. But we need to read them with greater acuity. For example, although it is often noted that the rectangular grid of Manhattan codes for residential and commercial zones (the long sides of the block form the residential streets; the short sides form the commercial boulevards), what has remained unreported is the distinguishing feature of the grid. The threshold that mediates commercial and residential is the turning of the corner. Not the corner but the turning of the corner. The threshold is a performance. That this dynamic is an extension of the language and scale of the facades of the buildings that form the street wall does not detract from its essentially subjective-spatial nature.

It may seem blinkered to focus on western cities as paradigms for togetherness at a time when millions of refugees are excluded from them and we are locked down in a pandemic. Refugee camps are part of the rooms+cities project. Lacan said that creativity was about creating something from nothing. In the refugee camps, the living together of people is a life and death struggle for existence, within which something human emerges. The pandemic is either a temporary disturbance, in which case existing architectural studies of social space remain relevant, or else it is the beginning of the next stage in the 100,000-year old evolution of human suffering and we are participating in our greatest challenge to date, the challenge of going wholly digital; if this is the case, we need architectural reason more than ever, to evolve the new social platforms that have the capacity to replace the architecture of the city. We simply begin with what we know, the here and now, and whether we face forwards or backwards, we expand our practice and our cities tremulously outwards.[5]

Notes

1 Jane Rendell, *The Architecture of Psychoanalysis: Spaces of Transition* (London: I.B. Tauris, 2017).
2 Georg Wilhelm Friedrich Hegel, *Hegel's Aesthetics: Lectures on Fine Art* (Oxford: Clarendon Press, 1975). Hegel's three stages of civilisation are the symbolic, the classic, and the romantic.
3 Gilles Deleuze and Felix Guattari, *A Thousand Plateaux: Capitalism and Schizophrenia* (Minneapolis, MN: University of Minnesota Press, 1993).
4 A rooms+cities design research group resides in the Universities of Dundee and Central Lancashire, focusing on the political and ethical role for architecture with respect to cities. We use the architectural design of cities to project new forms of collective life. It has been published in Lorens Holm and Cameron McEwan, 'The City Is a Critical Project – A Poetics of Collective Life', *arq: Architectural Research Quarterly* 23:2 (2019) and Holm and McEwan, 'Narrating an Analogical Urbanism: rooms+cities', *MONU # 29: Narrative Urbanism* (October 2018).
5 Moria refugee camp on Lesbos, Greece, which was one of the largest European camps, burnt to the ground in early September 2020, for which see https://www.bbc.co.uk/news/world-europe-54082201. See Camillo Boano, 'Forms of (Collective) Life: The Ontoethics of Inhabitation', *Architecture and Culture* 8:3+4 (2020). There are currently 26 million refugees living under the UN mandate. https://www.unhcr.org/uk/figures-at-a-glance.html. Both sites accessed 27 September 2020. For creating something from nothing, see Lacan, *Ethics, op.* cit. pp. 121–122, 212–213.

BIBLIOGRAPHY

Reference works

Craig Calhoun, *Dictionary of the Social Sciences* (Oxford: Oxford University Press, 2002).
Dylan Evans, *An Introductory Dictionary of Lacanian Psychoanalysis* (London and New York: Routledge, 1996).
Jean Laplanche and Jean-Bertrand Pontalis, *The Language of Psycho-Analysis* (London: Hogarth Press and the Institute of Psycho-Analysis, 1973).

Jacques Lacan authoritative collections

Jacques Lacan, *Écrits* (Paris: Editions du Seuil, 1966).
Jacques Lacan, *Écrits: A Selection*, translated by Alan Sheridan (New York: W. W. Norton, 1977).
Jacques Lacan, *Écrits: The First Complete Edition in English*, translated by Bruce Fink (New York: W. W. Norton, 2006).
The first complete edition is more authoritative because it translates all the essays in *Écrits*. It does not contain all Lacan's essays. I reference Sheridan in cases where I prefer his translation. Sheridan also translated a number of the *Seminars*.

The *Écrits* and other publications by Jacques Lacan

Jacques Lacan, 'The Purloined Letter' (1955) in *Écrits: Complete, op. cit.* pp. 6–48.
Jacques Lacan, 'The Mirror Stage as Formative of the Function of the *I* as Revealed in Psychoanalytic Experience' (1937/1949) in *Écrits: Selection, op. cit.* pp. 1–7 and *Écrits: Complete, op. cit.* pp. 75–81.
Jacques Lacan, 'The Function and Field of Speech and Language in Psychoanalysis' (1953) in *Écrits: Selection, op. cit.* pp. 30–113 and *Écrits: Complete, op. cit.* pp. 197–268.
Jacques Lacan, 'The Freudian Thing or the Meaning of the Return to Freud in Psychoanalysis' (1955) in *Écrits: Selection, op. cit.* pp. 114–145 and *Écrits: Complete, op. cit.* pp. 334–363.

Jacques Lacan, 'The Agency of the Letter in the Unconscious or Reason since Freud' (1957) in *Écrits: Selection, op. cit.* pp. 146–178 and *Écrits: Complete, op. cit.* pp. 412–441.

Jacques Lacan, 'On a Question Prior to Any Possible Treatment of Psychosis (1958)' in *Écrits: Selection, op. cit.* pp. 179–225 and *Écrits: Complete, op. cit.* pp. 445–488.

Jacques Lacan, 'The Direction of the Treatment and the Principles of Its Power' (1958) in *Écrits: Selection, op. cit.* pp. 226–280 and *Écrits: Complete, op. cit.* pp. 489–542.

Jacques Lacan, 'Kant with Sade' (1963) *October 51* (1989) pp. 55–104. Translated and with notes by James B. Swenson, Jr. Also in *Écrits: Complete, op. cit.*, pp. 645–668.

Jacques Lacan, 'Of Structure as an In-Mixing of an Otherness Prerequisite to Any Subject Whatever' in *The Structuralist Controversy: The Languages of Criticism and the Sciences of Man*, edited by R. Macksey and E. Donato (Baltimore and London: The Johns Hopkins University Press, 1970/1972) pp. 186–200.

Jacques Lacan, 'Television: A Challenge to the Psychoanalytic Establishment' (1974) in *October 40* (1987) pp. 5–50. Translated by Denis Hollier, Rosalind Krauss, and Annette Michelson.

Jacques Lacan, 'Desire and the Interpretation of Desire in Hamlet', *Yale French Studies*, Vol. 55/56, 1977, pp. 11–52. Translated by James Hulbert.

Jacques Lacan, *The Four Fundamental Concepts of Psychoanalysis* (1978), translated by Alan Sheridan, edited by Jacques-Alain Miller (New York: Norton Press, 1981). This is the text of Seminar 11, 1963–1964, published outside the Seminar series.

Lacan websites

'Jacques Lacan in Ireland' at http://www.lacaninireland.com for the Cormac Gallagher editions in pdf format.

'Lacan' at http://www.lacan.com

'Lacanian Ink' at http://www.lacan.com/lacink/archive.html

'NO SUBJECT', based on the Evans dictionary, at http://nosubject.com

The seminars

Jacques Lacan, *The Seminar of Jacques Lacan*, in 27 Books running from *The Seminar Book 1: Freud's Papers on Technique 1953–54* (Cambridge: Cambridge University Press, 1988) ending in *The Seminar Book XXVII: Dissolution* in *Ornicar?: Bulletin Périodique du Champ Freudien* no. 20–23 (Paris: 1980).

Jacques Lacan, *The Seminar of Jacques Lacan, Book I: Freud's Papers on Technique 1953–1954*, translated by John Forrester (Cambridge: Cambridge University Press, 1988).

Jacques Lacan, *The Seminar of Jacques Lacan, Book II: The Ego in Freud's Theory and in the Technique of Psychoanalysis 1954–1955*, translated by Sylvana Tomaselli (Cambridge: Cambridge University Press, 1988).

Jacques Lacan, *The Seminar of Jacques Lacan, Book III: The Psychoses 1955–1956*, translated by Russell Grigg (New York: W. W. Norton, 1993).

Jacques Lacan, *The Seminar of Jacques Lacan, Book VII: The Ethics of Psychoanalysis 1959–1960*, translated by Dennis Potter (New York: W. W. Norton, 1992).

Jacques Lacan, *The Seminar of Jacques Lacan, Book XIII: The Object of Psychoanalysis 1965–1966*, translated by Cormac Gallagher (London: Karnac, n.d. 2002).

Jacques Lacan, *The Seminar of Jacques Lacan, Book XVII: The Other Side of Psychoanalysis*, translated by Russell Grigg (New York: W. W. Norton, 2007).

Jacques Lacan, *The Seminar of Jacques Lacan, Book XX: Encore, On Feminine Sexuality, The Limits of Love and Knowledge 1972–1973*, translated by Bruce Fink (New York: W. W. Norton, 1998).

Sigmund Freud authoritative collections

James Strachey, ed., *The Standard Edition of the Complete Psychological Works of Sigmund Freud* in 24 volumes (London: The Hogarth Press and the Institute of Psycho-Analysis, 1956–1974).

Angela Richards and Albert Dickson, eds., *The Penguin Freud Library* in 15 paperback volumes (London: Penguin, 1990–1991). Based on the *Standard Edition*.

Sigmund Freud

Sigmund Freud, *Project for a Scientific Psychology* (1895) in *The Standard Edition, op. cit., Volume 1* (1886–1899), pp. 283–397.

Sigmund Freud, *The Interpretation of Dreams* (1900) in *The Standard Edition, op. cit., Volume IV* (1900) and *Volume V* (1900–1901).

Sigmund Freud, *The Psychopathology of Everyday Life: Forgetting, Slips of the Tongue, Bungled Actions, Superstitions and Errors* (1901), translated by Alan Tyson (New York: W. W. Norton, 1960).

Sigmund Freud, *Jokes and Their Relation to the Unconscious* (1905) in *The Standard Edition, op. cit., Volume VIII* (1905).

Sigmund Freud, 'The Psycho-Analytic View of Psychogenic Disturbances of Vision' (1910) in *The Standard Edition, op. cit., Volume X1* (1910), pp. 209–218.

Sigmund Freud, 'Psychoanalytic Notes on an Autobiographical Account of a Case of Paranoia (Dementia Paranoides) 1911 (1910)' in *The Penguin Freud Library Volume 9: Case Histories II: 'Rat Man', Schreber, 'Wolf Man', Female Homosexuality*, edited by A. Richards (London: Penguin Books, 1981).

Sigmund Freud, 'Papers on Technique (1911–1915)' in *The Standard Edition, op. cit., Volume 12* (1911–1913), pp. 85–171.

Sigmund Freud, 'Remembering, Repeating, Working-Through' (1914) in *The Standard Edition, op. cit., Volume 12* (1911–1913), pp. 145–156.

Sigmund Freud, 'Instincts and Their Vicissitudes' (1915) in *Sigmund Freud 11: On Metapsychology: The Theory of Psychoanalysis*, translated by James Strachey, edited by Angela Richards and James Strachey (London: Penguin, 1991) pp. 113–138.

Sigmund Freud, 'Repression' (1915) in *On Metapsychology, op. cit.*, pp. 139–158.

Sigmund Freud, 'The Unconscious' (1915) in *On Metapsychology, op. cit.*, pp. 167–222.

Sigmund Freud, 'A Metapsychological Supplement to the Theory of Dreams (1917/1915)' in *On Metapsychology, op. cit.*, pp. 223–243.

Sigmund Freud, *Beyond the Pleasure Principle* (1920) in *On Metapsychology, op. cit.*, pp. 269–338.

Sigmund Freud, 'The Ego and the Id' (1923) in *On Metapsychology, op. cit.*, pp. 339–407.

Sigmund Freud, 'Neurosis and Psychosis' (1924/1923) in *The Standard Edition, op. cit., Volume XIX* (1923–1925), pp. 147–154.

Sigmund Freud, 'The Loss of Reality in Neurosis and Psychosis' (1924) in *The Standard Edition, op. cit., Volume XIX* (1923–1925), pp. 181–188.

Sigmund Freud, *Inhibitions Symptoms and Anxiety (1926)*, translated by Alix Strachey (London: Hogarth Press and Institute of Psycho-Analysis, 1971).

Sigmund Freud, *Civilization and Its Discontents (1930)*, translated by Joan Riviere (London: Hogarth Press and Institute of Psycho-Analysis, 1975).

Sigmund Freud, *New Introductory Lectures on Psycho-Analysis* (1933), translated by James Strachey (London: Hogarth Press and Institute of Psycho-Analysis, 1974).

Sigmund Freud, 'A Disturbance of Memory on the Acropolis (1936)', in On *Metapsychology, op. cit.*, pp. 443–456.

Sigmund Freud, 'Splitting of the Ego in the Process of Defense (1940/1938/1937)' in *On Metapsychology, op. cit.*, pp. 457–464.

Select topic in Lacanian psychoanalysis

Didier Anzieu, *The Skin Ego* (New Haven, CT: Yale University Press, 1989).

Bice Benvenuto and Roger Kennedy, *The Works of Jacques Lacan: An Introduction* (London: Free Association Press, 1986) in particular, 'The Mirror Stage' (1936), 'The Rome Discourse' (1953), and 'The Instance of the Letter' (1956).

Malcolm Bowie, *Lacan* (London: Fontana, 1991).

Roger Caillois, 'Mimicry and Legendary Psychasthenia' (1935) in *October* 31 (1984) pp. 17–32. Translated by John Shepley.

Richard Feldstein, Bruce Fink and Maire Jaanus, eds., *Reading Seminar XI: Lacan's Four Fundamental Concepts of Psycho-Analysis* (Albany, NY: State University of New York Press, 1995).

Richard Feldstein, Bruce Fink and Maire Jaanus, eds., *Reading Seminars I and II: Lacan's Return to Freud* (Albany, NY: State University of New York Press, 1996).

Bruce Fink, *The Lacanian Subject: Between Language and Jouissance* (Princeton, NJ: Princeton University Press, 1995).

Bruce Fink, *A Clinical Introduction to Lacanian Psychoanalysis: Theory and Technique* (Cambridge, MA: Harvard University Press, 1997).

Philippe Julien, *Jacques Lacan's Return to Freud: The Real, the Symbolic, the Imaginary* (New York: New York University Press, 1994).

John P. Muller and William J. Richardson, *Lacan and Language: A Readers Guide to Écrits* (New York: International Universities Press, 1982).

Dany Nobus, ed., *Key Concepts in Lacanian Psychoanalysis* (London: Rebus, 1998).

Madan Sarup, *Jacques Lacan* (New York: Harvester Wheatsheaf, 1992).

Stuart Schneiderman, ed., *Returning to Freud: Clinical Psychoanalysis in the School of Lacan* (New Haven, CT and London: Yale University Press, 1980).

Daniel Paul Schreber, *Memoirs of My Nervous Illness* (1903) translated and edited by Ida Macalpine and Richard A. Hunter (London: Dawson, 1955).

Samo Tomšič, 'Homology: Marx and Lacan', *S: Journal of the Jan Van Eyck Circle for Lacanian Critique Vol. 5* (2012) pp. 98–113.

Samo Tomšič, *The Capitalist Unconscious: Marx and Lacan* (New York and London: Verso Books, 2015).

Stijn Vanheule, 'Capitalist Discourse, Subjectivity and Lacanian Psychoanalysis', *Frontiers in Psychology*, Vol. 7:1948 (2016) pp. 1–14.

Anthony Wilden and Jacques Lacan, *Speech and Language in Psychoanalysis* (Baltimore, MD: Johns Hopkins University Press, 1968) includes Wilden, 'Lacan and the Discourse of the Other' (1968) and Lacan, 'The Function and Field of Speech and Language in Psychoanalysis', translated by Wilden with introduction and notes.

Slavoj Zizek, *Looking Awry: An Introduction to Jacques Lacan through Popular Culture* (Cambridge, MA: MIT Press, 1991).

Slavoj Zizek, *Enjoy Your Symptom: Jacques Lacan in Hollywood and Out* (Abingdon, UK: Routledge, 2001).

Slavoj Zizek, 'The Eclipse of Meaning: On Lacan and Deconstruction' in *Interrogating the Real*, edited by R. Butler and S. Stephens (London: Continuum, 2005).

Movies

Saul Bass, *Phase IV* (Alced Productions, 1974).

Francis Ford Coppola, *Apocalypse Now* (Omni Zoetrope, 1979).

Jean-Luc Godard, *Le Mepris [Contempt]* (Rome Paris Films, 1963).

Peter Greenaway, *The Cook the Thief His Wife and Her Lover* (Allarts, 1989).

Martin Scorsese, *Taxi Driver* (Columbia Pictures, 1976).

Ridley Scott, *Alien* (20th Century Fox, 1979).

Literature

Aeschylus, *Agamemnon*, edited by David Greene and translated by Richard Lattimore (New York: Modern Library, 1942).

Al Alvarez, 'The New Poetry, or beyond the Gentility Principle', the introduction to *The New Poetry: An Anthology Selected and Introduced by A. Alvarez* (Harmondsworth: Penguin, 1962) pp. 21–32.

Samuel Beckett, *The Unnamable* (1952) in *The Beckett Trilogy: Molloy; Malone Dies; The Unnamable* (London: Picador, 1966).

Samuel Beckett, '*Not I*' (1973) performed by Billie Whitelaw, the Royal Court Theatre, London, available at [https://www.youtube.com/watch?v=M4LDwfKxr-M].

Homer, *The Odyssey* (8th Century BCE), translated by Robert Fitzgerald, drawings by Hans Erni (New York: Doubleday Anchor, 1963).

Adrienne Janus, 'In One Ear and Out the Others: Beckett ... Mahon ... Muldoon', *Journal of Modern Literature*, Vol. 30, no. 2 (2007) pp. 180–196.

William Shakespeare, *King Lear*, The Arden Shakespeare, edited by R A Foakes (London: Thomas Learning, 1997).

Leo Tolstoy, *War and Peace* (1869) no translator cited (London: Penguin Popular Classics, 1997).

Texts on the human subject in philosophy the humanities and the social sciences

Hannah Arendt, *The Human Condition* (Chicago: University of Chicago Press, 1958).

Ferdinand de Saussure, *Course in General Linguistics (1916)*, translated by Wade Baskin (New York: The Philosophical Library, 1959).

Gilles Deleuze and Felix Guattari, *Anti-Oedipus: Capitalism and Schizophrenia*, translated by Robert Hurley, Mark Seem, and Helen R. Lane (London: Penguin, 1977).

Deleuze Gilles and Guattari Felix, *A Thousand Plateaus: Capitalism and Schizophrenia*, translated by Brian Massumi (Minneapolis, MN: University of Minnesota Press, 1993).

Jacques Derrida, 'Freud and the Scene of Writing' in Derrida, *Writing and Difference*, translated by Alan Bass (Chicago: University of Chicago Press, 1978).

Jacques Derrida, 'Différance' in Derrida, *The Margins of Philosophy*, translated by Alan Bass (Chicago: University of Chicago Press,1982) pp. 1–27.

Rene Descartes, *The Optics* in *Discourse on Method: Optics, Geometry, Meteorology*, translation of *La Dioptrique* (1637) by Paul J. Olscamp (Indianapolis: Bobbs-Merrill, 1965).

Rene Descartes, *Meditations on First Philosophy – With selections from the Objections and Replies* (1641), translated by John Cottingham (Cambridge: Cambridge University Press, 1986).

Emile Durkheim, *The Rules of Sociological Method*, translated by W.D. Halls (Basingstoke: Macmillan, 1982). See esp. Chapter 1, 'What is a Social Fact?'

Roberto Esposito, *Communitas: The Origin and Destiny of Community*, translated by Timothy Campbell (Stanford, CA: Stanford University Press, 2010).

Michel Foucault, *The Order of Things: An Archaeology of the Human Sciences* (New York: Vintage, 1970).

Felix Guattari, *The Three Ecologies* (1989), translated by Ian Pindar and Paul Sutton (London: Athlone, 2000).

Maurice Halbwachs, *The Collective Memory* (1950) introduction by Mary Douglas (New York: Harper & Row Colophon Books, 1980).

Maurice Halbwachs, *On Collective Memory* (1952), translated by Lewis A. Coser (Chicago and London: University of Chicago Press, 1992).

Georg Wilhelm Friedrich Hegel, *Hegel's Aesthetics: Lectures on Fine Art*, translated by T.M. Knox (Oxford: Clarendon Press, 1975).

Denis Hollier, ed., *The College of Sociology 1937–1939*, translated by Betsy Wing (Minnesota: University of Minnesota Press, 1988).

Fredric Jameson, *The Political Unconscious: Narrative as a Socially Symbolic Act* (Ithaca, NY: Cornell University, 1981).

Alexandre Kojeve, *Introduction to the Reading of Hegel: Lectures on the Phenomenology of Spirit*, translated by James H. Nichols (New York: Basic Books, 1969).

Henri Lefebvre, 'The Right to the City', in *Writings on Cities*, edited by Eleonore Kofman and Elizabeth Lebas (Malden, MA: Blackwell Publishers, 1968), pp. 147–159.

Henri Lefebvre, *The Urban Revolution*, translated by Robert Bononno (2003) (Minneapolis, MN: University of Minnesota Press, 1970/2003).

Claude Levi-Strauss, *Introduction to the Work of Marcel Mauss*, translated by Felicity Baker (London: Routledge and Kegan Paul, 1987).

Karl Marx, *Capital: A Critical Analysis of Capitalist Production (1887)* translated by Samuel Moore and Edward Aveling, edited by Frederick Engels (Moscow and London: Foreign Languages Publishing House and Lawrence and Wishart Ltd., 1961).

Plato, *Timaeus* in *Timaeus and Critias*, translated by Desmond Lee (London: Penguin Classics, 1971).

Mark C. Taylor, ed., *Deconstruction in Context: Literature and Philosophy* (Chicago: University of Chicago Press, 1986).

Paolo Virno, A Grammar of the Multitude: For an Analysis of Contemporary Forms of Life, in *Semiotext(E) Foreign Agents Series*, edited by Isabella Bertoletti, James Cascaito and Andrea Casson (New York: Semiotext(e), 2004).

Paolo Virno, 'Three Remarks Regarding the Multitude's Subjectivity and Its Aesthetic Component' in *Under Pressure: Pictures, Subjects, and the New Spirit of Capitalism*, edited by Daniel Birnbaum and Isabelle Graw (Frankfurt: Sternberg Press, 2008).

Texts on the human subject in art theory and history

Leon Battista Alberti, *On Painting* (New Haven, CT: Yale University Press, 1966). Translation of *Della Pittura* (1433) by John Spencer.

Nicolas Bourriaud, *Relational Aesthetics*, translated by Simon Pleasance, Fronza Woods, and Mathieu Copeland (Dijon: les presses du reel, 2002).

Bettina Brand-Claussen, Inge Jadi and Caroline Douglas, *Beyond Reason: Art and Psychosis: Works from the Prinzhorn Collection* (London: Hayward Gallery: The South Bank Centre, 1996).

Hubert Damisch, *The Origin of Perspective*, translated by John Goodman (Cambridge, MA: MIT Press, 1994).

James Elkins, *The Object Stares Back: On the Nature of Seeing* (New York: Harvest, 1996).

Hal Foster, *The Return of the Real: The Avant-Garde at the End of the Century* (Cambridge, MA: MIT Press, 1996).

Rosalind Krauss, *The Optical Unconscious* (Cambridge, MA: MIT Press, 1993).

Christian Metz, 'The Imaginary Signifier', *Screen*, Vol. 16, no. 2 (1975) pp. 14–76.

Erwin Panofsky, *Perspective as Symbolic Form* (1927), translated by Christopher S. Wood (New York: Zone Books, 1991).

Rudolf Wittkower, 'Brunelleschi and "Proportion in Perspective"' in Wittkower, *Idea and Image: Studies in the Italian Renaissance* (London: Thames and Hudson, 1953) pp. 125–135.

Heinrich Wölfflin, *Renaissance and Baroque*, translated by Kathrin Simon (Ithaca, NY: Cornell University Press, 1964).

Texts on architecture and cities and the critique of architecture and cities

Diana Agrest, 'Architecture of Mirror/Mirror of Architecture', *Oppositions*, Vol. 26 (Spring 1984), pp. 118–133.

Diana Agrest and Mario Gandelsonas, 'Semiotics and Architecture: Ideological Consumption or Theoretical Work', *Oppositions*, Vol. 1 (September 1973), pp. 93–100.

Walter Benjamin, *Arcades Project*, translated by Howard Eiland and Kevin McLaughlin (Cambridge, MA and London: Belknap Press of Harvard University Press, 1999).

Peter Brooks, 'The Text of the City', *Oppositions*, Vol. 1 (Spring 1977), pp. 7–11.

Jakob Burckhardt, *Civilisation of the Renaissance in Italy* (1860), translated by S.G.C. Middlemore (London: Penguin Classics, 1990).

Emma Cheatle, *Part-Architecture: The Maison de Verre, Duchamp, Domesticity, and Desire in 1930's Paris* (London: Routledge, 2017).

Auguste Choisy, *Histoire de l'Architecture* (Paris: Gauthier-Villars, 1899).

Maxine Collignon, *Le Parthenon: L'Histoire, L'Architecture, Et La Sculpture* (Paris: Librairie Hachette, 1914).

Beatriz Colomina, 'Le Corbusier and Photography', *Assemblage* no. 4 (Cambridge, MA: MIT Press, 1987) pp. 7–23.

Beatriz Colomina, *Privacy and Publicity: Modern Architecture as Mass Media* (Cambridge, MA: MIT Press, 1994).

William Curtis, *Modern Architecture since 1900* (Englewood Cliffs, NJ: Prentice-Hall, 1982).

Philippe Duboy, *Lequeu: An Architectural Enigma* (London: Thames and Hudson, 1986).

Peter Eisenman, 'Aspects of Modernism: Maison Dom-ino and the Self-Referential Sign', *Oppositions*, Vol. 15/16 (Winter/Spring 1979) pp. 118–128.

Adrian Forty, *Words and Buildings: A Vocabulary of Modern Architecture* (London: Thames and Hudson, 2000).

Kenneth Frampton, 'A Synoptic View of the Architecture of the Third Reich', *Oppositions*, Vol. 12 (Spring 1978) pp. 54–87.

Kenneth Frampton, 'Towards a Critical Regionalism: 6 Points for an Architecture of Resistance' in *The Anti-Aesthetic: Essays on Postmodern Culture*, edited by Hal Foster (Seattle: Bay Press, 1983) pp. 16–30.

Mario Gandelsonas, 'From Structure to Subject: The Formation of an Architectural Language', *Oppositions*, Vol. 17 (1978) pp. 6–29.

Patrick Geddes, *Cities in Evolution: An Introduction to the Town Planning Movement and to the Study of Civics* (1915) (London: Ernest Benn/Williams & Norgate, 1968).

Sigfried Giedion, *The Eternal Present: The Beginnings of Architecture: A Contribution on Constancy and Change* (London: Oxford University Press, 1964).

Sigfried Giedion, *Space Time and Architecture: The Growth of a New Tradition* (Cambridge, MA: Harvard University Press, 1967).

Peter Green, *The Parthenon* (New York and London: Newsweek and Readers Digest, 1973).

Giuliano Gresleri, *Le Corbusier: Viaggio in Oriente* (Venice: Marsilio, 1984).

Jacques Guillerme, 'The Idea of Architectural Language: A Critical Inquiry', *Oppositions*, Vol. 10 (Fall 1977), pp. 21–26.

K. Michael Hays, *Sanctuaries: The Last Works of John Hejduk* (New York: The Whitney Museum of American Art with Harry Abrams, Inc., 2002).

John Shannon Hendrix, *Architecture and Psychoanalysis: Peter Eisenman and Jacques Lacan* (New York: Peter Lang, 2006).

John Shannon Hendrix, *Unconscious Thought in Philosophy and Psychoanalysis* (New York and Basingstoke: Palgrave MacMillan, 2015).

John Shannon Hendrix, 'Architecture and the Kantian Unconscious' in John Shannon Hendrix and Lorens Holm, eds., *Architecture and the Unconscious* (Abingdon, UK: Ashgate/Routledge, 2016).

John Shannon Hendrix and Lorens Holm, eds., *Architecture and the Unconscious* (Abingdon, UK: Ashgate/Routledge, 2016).

Lorens Holm, 'What Lacan Said, Re: Architecture', *Critical Quarterly* 42, no. 2 Summer (2000) pp. 29–64.

Lorens Holm, *Brunelleschi, Lacan, Le Corbusier: Architecture Space and the Construction of Subjectivity* (Abingdon: Routledge, 2010).

Lorens Holm, 'Psychosis and the Ineffable Space of Modernism', *Journal of Architecture*, Vol. 18, (2013) pp. 402–424.

Lorens Holm, 'Space and Its Assembled Subjects: The Neurotic the Psychotic and the Pervert' in *Transgression: Towards an Expanded Field of Architecture*, edited by L. Rice and D. Littlefield (Abingdon: Routledge, 2015).

Lorens Holm, 'Aldo Rossi and the Field of the Other', in *Architecture and the Unconscious op. cit.*

Lorens Holm and Cameron McEwan, 'The City Is a Critical Project – A Poetics of Collective Life', *arq: Architectural Research Quarterly* Vol. 23, no. 2, (2019).

Lorens Holm and Cameron McEwan, 'Introduction: We Construct Collective Life by Constructing Our Environment', *Architecture and Culture* 8, no. 3+4 (2021) pp. 529–48.

Lorens Holm and Cameron McEwan, eds., *Architecture and Culture: Architecture & Collective Life A Special Issue*, Vol. 8, no. 3+4 (2020).

Rem Koolhaas, 'Dali and Le Corbusier: The Paranoid Critical Method', *Architectural Design*, Vol. 2–3, 1978. This paper also appears in *Delirious New York*.

Rem Koolhaas, *Delirious New York: A Retroactive Manifesto for Manhattan* (New York: The Monacelli Press, 1978/1994).

Rem Koolhaas and Bruce Mau, *S,M,L,XL: OMA* (Rotterdam: 010 Publishers, 1995).

Rem Koolhaas, 'Junkspace', *October: Obsolescence A Special Issue*, no. 100 (2002) pp. 175–190.

Bruno Latour, *Paris: Invisible City* at http://www.bruno-latour.fr/virtual/EN/index.html.

Le Corbusier, *New World of Space* (New York and Boston: Reynal & Hitchcock and the Institute for Contemporary Art, 1948).

Le Corbusier, *The Final Testament of Père Corbu: A Translation and Interpretation of Mise au point* (New Haven: Yale University Press, 1997), edited and translated by Ivan Zaknic from the original French edition (Paris: Forces Vives, 1966).

Le Corbusier, *Journey to the East* (Cambridge: MIT Press, 1987), translated by Ivan Zaknic of *Le Voyage d'Orient* (Paris: Forces Vives, 1966).

Le Corbusier, 'Nothing Is Transmissible but Thought', *Le Corbusier Oeuvre Complete Vol 8 Les Dernieres Oeuvres* (Zurich: Les Editions d'Architecture Artemis, 1965) pp. 173–177. Also appears in *Mise au Point*.

Le Corbusier, *Towards a New Architecture* (1923), translated by Frederick Etchells (New York: Holt Rinehart, and Winston, 1960).

Le Corbusier, *Vers Une Architecture*, edited by Jean-Louis Cohen (Paris: Flammarion, 2005). Facsimile of the 1923 French edition.

Le Corbusier, *Towards an Architecture* (1923), translated by John Goodman (Los Angeles: Getty Research Institute, 2007).

Henri Lefebvre, *The Production of Space*, translated by Donald Nicholson-Smith (Oxford: Blackwell, 1991).

Kevin Lynch, *The Image of the City* (Cambridge, MA: MIT Press, 1960).

Greg Lynn, ed., *Folding in Architecture* (London: Wiley-Academy, 2004).

Antonio di Tuccio Manetti, *The Life of Brunelleschi* (University Park, PA: Pennsylvania State University Press, 1970).

Timothy Martin, 'Psychoanalytic Diagnosis in Architecture and Urban Design' in *Architecture and the Unconscious*, edited by J. Hendrix and L. Holm (Abingdon: Routledge, 2016).

Marshall McLuhan, *Understanding Media – The Extensions of Man* (London: Routledge ARK Paperbacks, 1987).

Rafael Moneo, 'On Typology', *Oppositions*, Vol. 13 (Summer 1978) pp. 22–45.

Lewis Mumford, *Technics and Civilization* (New York: Harcourt Brace, 1934).

Lewis Mumford, *The Myth of the Machine: Technics and Human Development* (New York: Harcourt Brace, 1967).

Christian Norberg-Schultz, *Meaning in Western Architecture* (New York: Rizzoli, 1980).

Andrew Payne, 'Architecture Lacan Deleuze', *Harvard Design Magazine*, Vol. 35 (2013) pp. 1–36.

Andrea Pozzo, *Perspective in Architecture and Painting* (New York: Dover, 1989). Reprint of the 1707 English edition of *Perspectiva Architectorum et Pictorum*.

Quatremere de Quincy, 'Type: Introduction by Anthony Vidler', *Oppositions*, Vol. 8 (Spring 1977) pp. 146–150.

Jane Rendell, *The Architecture of Psychoanalysis: Spaces of Transition* (London: I.B. Tauris, 2017).

Aldo Rossi, *A Scientific Autobiography* (Cambridge, MA: MIT Press, 1981).

Aldo Rossi, *Architecture of the City* (Cambridge, MA: MIT Press, 1982/1966).

Aldo Rossi, *Three Cities: Perugia, Milano, Mantova* (Milan and New York: Electra/Rizzoli, 1984).

Colin Rowe and Robert Slutzky, 'Transparency: Literal and Phenomenal', *Perspecta*, Vol. 8 (1963) pp. 45–54, reprinted in Colin Rowe, *Mathematics of the Ideal Villa and Other Essays* (Cambridge, MA: MIT Press, 1976).

Colin Rowe, *The Mathematics of the Ideal Villa and Other Essays* (Cambridge, MA: MIT Press, 1978).

Joachim Schlandt, O.M. Ungers, and Sima Ingberman, 'The Vienna Superblocks', *Oppositions*, Vol. 13 (Summer 1978) pp. 76–111.

Georg Simmel, 'The Metropolis and Mental Life' (1903) in *Georg Simmel: On Individuality and Social Forms*, edited by Donald N. Levine (Chicago: University of Chicago Press, 1971).

Sir John Newenham Summerson, *The Classical Language of Architecture* (Cambridge, MA: MIT Press, 1966).

Georges Teyssot, 'Emil Kaufmann and the Architecture of Reason: Klassizismus and "Revolutionary Architecture"', *Oppositions*, Vol. 13 (Summer 1978), translated by Christian Hubert, pp. 46–75.

Bernard Tschumi, 'Architecture and Transgression', *Oppositions*, Vol. 7 (Spring 1977) pp. 55–63.

Bernard Tschumi, 'Architecture and Transgression', in Tschumi, *Architecture and Disjunction* (Cambridge, MA: MIT Press, 1994) pp. 65–78.

Anthony Vidler, 'Framing Infinity: Le Corbusier, Ayn Rand, and the Idea of "Ineffable Space"' in Vidler, *Warped Space: Art, Architecture, and Anxiety in Modern Culture* (Cambridge, MA: MIT Press, 2000) pp. 51–64.

Anthony Vidler, 'The Third Typology', *Oppositions*, Vol. 7 (Winter 1976) pp. 1–4.

Anthony Vidler, *Warped Space: Art, Architecture, and Anxiety in Modern Culture* (Cambridge, MA: MIT Press, 2000).

Bruno Zevi, *Architecture as Space: How to Look at Architecture: 186 Photographs Drawings Plans* (New York: Horizon Press, 1957).

FIGURE CREDITS

0.1 Preface Frontispiece: The possibility of a tympanic subject [Montage by Lorens Holm]

1.1 Frontispiece: The possibility of a linguistic formation [Andrea Branzi and Archizoom Associati, *No Stop City* (1969)]

1.2 Two drawings of the self: Freud's first topography (the psychical apparatus) and Freud's second topology (the ego and the id) [both images © Institute of Psychoanalysis. Published under a Creative Commons Non-Commercial Licence] with additional text by Holm

2.1 Frontispiece: The speaking subject [Montage by Holm incorporating a still from the BBC production of *Not I*, courtesy of the BBC]

2.2 Giedion's three space conceptions: archaic, classic, modern [table by Holm incorporating thumbnail images in the public domain or in fair use]

2.3 Giedion's three space conceptions, three subjects [table by Holm incorporating thumbnail images, *op. cit.*]

2.4 Giedion's three space conceptions, three horizons [table by Holm incorporating thumbnail images, *op. cit.*]

2.5 Diagramming the arguments [table by Holm]

3.1 Frontispiece: Object-Subject [Montage by Lorens Holm incorporating thumbnail images, *op. cit.*] with additional text by Holm

3.2 Descartes' Cogito from *The Dioptrics* (1637) + Durer's method for drawing a perspective, from *The Painters Manual* (1527) [both images in the public domain]

3.3 Object image Point, Point screen Picture [Diagrams from Lacan, *The Four Fundamental Concepts of Psychoanalysis* redrawn by Holm]

3.4 The drive and the visual field [Diagrams from Lacan, *The Four Fundamental Concepts of Psychoanalysis* redrawn by Holm]

3.5 Pozzo and Brunelleschi incorporating Plate 1 from Andrea Pozzo, *Perspective in Architecture and Painting* in the public domain and a photo of San Lorenzo Copyright Alinari

4.1 Frontispiece: Aldo Rossi, Drawing with theatre, hand of the saint and shadows (1978) © Eredi Aldo Rossi, Courtesy: Aldo Rossi Foundation, Milan

4.2 Lacan's Schema L + Freud forgetting Signorelli [Diagrams redrawn by Holm] with additional text by Holm

4.3 The visual field is a mobius strip [drawing by Holm on photograph, attribution not found]

4.4 Holbein Alberti Lacan [incorporating *The Ambassadors* in the public domain, Lacan's *Schema L* redrawn by Holm, and other diagrams by Holm]

4.5 Rossi's elements [diagram by Holm]

5.1 Frontispiece: Venturi and Nolli [Montage by Holm] with additional text by Holm

5.2 Lacan and Vitruvius [Lacan's diagram of the drive redrawn by Holm + woodcut of from Vitruvius, in the public domain]

6.1 Frontispiece: Headlines [Text by Holm]

6.2 Death driving towards paradise. Montage by Holm incorporating film stills from Saul Bass, dir., *Phase IV* (1974) [Courtesy Paramount Pictures & Alced Productions] with additional text by Holm.

6.3 A genealogy of not-knowing [Photo of Henderson Island courtesy of Jennifer Lavers | Adrift Lab with text by Holm]

6.4 I love the smell of napalm …. Film still from Francis Ford Coppola, dir., *Apocalypse Now* (1979) [Courtesy of American Zoetrope & Zoetrope Studios] with text by Holm

6.5 The four discourses + the discourse of the capitalist [Table by Holm]

P.1 Postscript Frontispiece: The mostly male lineage of western thought [Montage by Holm incorporating thumbnail images in the public domain or in fair use] with additional text by Holm

FIGURE NOTES

0.1 Montage by Lorens Holm incorporating elements of the cover art of *Waiting for Godot* (Grove Press/Evergreen, 1954) and a section of the Sanborn Fire Insurance Map for the City of St. Louis (n.d.), for which see https://www.loc.gov/collections/sanborn-maps/articles-and-essays/introduction-to-the-collection/

1.1 No Stop City 'typewriter' plan, 1969, image courtesy of Andrea Branzi and Archizoom Associati, downloaded from https://www.pinterest.at/pin/469429961133986724/

1.2 Two diagrams with additional text by Lorens Holm, including …

Diagram reproduced from *The Standard Edition of the Complete Psychological Works of Sigmund Freud vol. V: The Interpretation of Dreams (second part) (1900)*, trans. James Strachey (London: Hogarth Press and Institute of Psychoanalysis, 1953), p. 541.

'Usage terms Sigmund Freud: This material is in the Public Domain. James Strachey's translation: © Institute of Psychoanalysis. Published under a Creative Commons Non-Commercial Licence'.

https://www.bl.uk/20th-century-literature/articles/the-hogarth-press

Diagram reproduced from *The Standard Edition … op. cit.*, vol. XIX: *The Ego and the Id (1923)* (London: Hogarth Press and Institute of Psychoanalysis, 1961), p. 24.

'Usage terms Sigmund Freud: This material is in the Public Domain. James Strachey's translation: © Institute of Psychoanalysis. Published under a Creative Commons Non-Commercial Licence'.

https://www.bl.uk/20th-century-literature/articles/the-hogarth-press

2.1 Montage and image manipulation by Lorens Holm incorporating a still from the BBC production of *Not I* by Billie Whitelaw as found at https://www.youtube.com/watch?v=M4LDwfKxr-M montaged against a black background.

2.2 Table by Lorens Holm incorporating 13 thumbnail images from internet sources:
   1 'Ictinus, Callicrates & Phidias: The Parthenon, Athens (447–432 BC)'
      Bruno Zevi, *Architecture as Space: How to Look at Architecture: 186 Photographs Drawings Plans*, trans. Milton Gendel (New York: Horizon Press, 1957), p. 69

Pyramid of Cheops, 'Volumes in Space: The cosmic unity between pyramid, sky, and the limitless desert. From Lipsius, 1849–59, I (Abt. I) Pl 17'.

Sigfried Giedion, *The Eternal Present: The Beginnings of Architecture: A Contribution on Constancy and Change* (London: Oxford University Press, 1964), pl. 317, p. 505.

'Temple of Luxor, Inner Court of Amenhotep III: 144 × 168 feet, with excellently preserved papyrus-bundle columns of granite. p: G.E. Kidder-Smith'.

Sigfried Giedion, *The Eternal Present, op. cit.*, pl. 255, p. 394.

'Plan of the Citadel of Mycenae, "Mycenae" in *Encyclopaedia Britannica*, 11th ed. v. 19, 1911, p. 104, fig.1. Based on the plan in Schuchhardt, *Schleimann's Excavations'*. https://commons.wikimedia.org/wiki/File:EB1911_Mycenae_-_plan_of_the_citadel.jpg

2 Photograph of the interior of Brunelleschi's San Lorenzo, Florence, reproduced from Rudolf Wittkower, 'Brunelleschi and "proportion in perspective"' in Wittkower, ed., *Idea and Image: Studies in the Italian Renaissance* (New York and London: Thames & Hudson, 1978), pl. 166, p. 133. Copyright Alinari.

Engraving by Bernardo Prevedari after a drawing by Donato Bramante of a church interior, 1481 reproduced from https://commons.wikimedia.org/wiki/File:Gravureprevedari.png

Piranesi, *Le Antichita Romane, Opere di Giovanni Battista Piranesi tomo II, tav. LX* (1756) reproduced from https://commons.wikimedia.org/wiki/File:Piranesi-2061.jpg

Giovanni Paolo Panini, Interior of the Pantheon, Rome, c.1734, National Gallery of Art, Washington, DC, accession number 1939.1.24, https://www.nga.gov/collection/art-object-page.165.html

Nolli Plan of Rome, 'Nuova Pianta di Roma (1748)' 5th of 12 panels, reproduced from https://commons.wikimedia.org/wiki/File:Giovanni_Battista_Nolli-Nuova_Pianta_di_Roma_(1748)_05-12.JPG

3 Interior of Le Corbusier's Villa Church, Ville D'Avray, copyright FLC/ADAGP photograph 8/13 reproduced from https://commons.wikimedia.org/wiki/Category:Works_by_Le_Corbusier#/media/File:Villa_church.jpg CC BY-SA 3.0

Façade of Villa Stein at Garches, 1927, from Le Corbusier, *Oeuvre Complete*, ed. Willy Boesiger (Zurich: Les Editions d'Architecture (Artemis), 1965), vol. 1, 1910–1929, p. 147.

Concrete detail of 'Le Palais de l'Assemblée vu depuis le Palais de Justice' in Le Corbusier, *Oeuvre Complete*, ed. Willy Boesiger (Zurich: Les Editions d'Architecture (Artemis), 1965), vol. 7 1957–1965, p. 107., Photograph by L. Stynen, Bruxelles.

'Plan ... de Capitol' in Le Corbusier, *Oeuvre Complete*, ed. Willy Boesiger (Zurich: Les Editions d'Architecture (Artemis), 1965), vol. 7, 1957–1965, p. 72.

2.3 Table by Lorens Holm incorporating six thumbnail images from internet sources

1 Photograph of the Parthenon, Zevi, *op. cit.*

Interior of Brunelleschi's San Lorenzo, Florence, Wittkower, *op. cit.*

Interior of Villa Church at Ville d'Avray, FLC/ADAGP photograph 8/13, *op. cit.*

2 Greek vase, depicting Odysseus assisted by Athena encountering Nausicaa, ca.450 BC, in the Staatliche Antikensammlungen, Munich

Photograph by ArchaiOptix reproduced from https://commons.wikimedia.org/
wiki/File:Nausicaa_Painter_ARV_1107_2_Odysseus_and_Nausicaa_(03).jpg
CC Attribution-Share Alike 4.0 International licence

Descartes' diagram of the seeing *Cogito*, in *La Dioptriques*, in *Discours de la Methode*
(1637), Reproduced from https://1000wordphilosophy.com/2018/08/04/
descartes-meditations-1-3/

'Paul Klee: "Die Scene mit der Laufenden' (Scene with Running Woman) Drawing,
1925. Klee Stiftung, Basel; © S.P.A.D.E.M., 1961, by French Reproduction Rights
Inc." in Sigfried Giedion, *The Eternal Present, op. cit.*, p. 497, pl. 316.

2.4   Table by Lorens Holm incorporating nine thumbnail images from internet sources
1 Photograph of the Parthenon, Zevi, *op. cit.*

Greek vase, depicting Odysseus assisted by Athena encountering Nausicaa,
ca.450 BC, in the Staatliche Antikensammlungen, Munich, Photograph by
ArchaiOptix, *op. cit.*

Star-Forming region LH95 in The Large Magellanic Cloud

Photograph reproduced from NASA/Hubblesite, https://hubblesite.org/
contents/media/images/2006/55/2024-Image.html?news=true

Image credit: NASA, ESA, and the Hubble Heritage Team (STScI/AURA)-
ESA/Hubble Collaboration; Acknowledgement: D. Gouliermis (Max Planck
Institute for Astronomy, Heidelberg).

2 Interior of Brunelleschi's San Lorenzo, Florence, Wittkower, *op. cit.*

Descartes' diagram of the seeing *Cogito*, in *La Dioptriques*, in *Discours de la Methode*
(1637), Reproduced from https://1000wordphilosophy.com/2018/08/04/
descartes-meditations-1-3/

https://commons.wikimedia.org/wiki/File:White-noise-mv255-240x180.png

White noise generated greyscale image produced by Jorge Stolfi and licenced by
use under a Creative Commons Attribution-Share Alike 3.0 Unported licence.

3 Interior of Villa Church at Ville d'Avray, FLC/ADAGP photograph 8/13, *op. cit.*

Paul Klee, 'Scene with Running Woman, Sigfried Giedion, *op. cit.*, p. 497.

'Heads of a Horse and Three Cows. Ceiling of Axial Gallery' in Georges
Bataille, *Prehistoric Painting: Lascaux or the Birth of Art*, trans. Austryn Wainhouse,
in series ed. Albert Skira, *The Great Centuries of Painting* (New York: Skira, Inc.
Publishers, n.d.), p. 76.

2.5   Three diagrams by Lorens Holm

3.1   Montage by Lorens Holm incorporating text with thumbnail and partial images
from various sources:

1 Portrait of Brunelleschi painted by Paolo Uccello, ca.1450, as found in Pierre
Granveaud, Monique Mosser, Jacques Barda, Vincent Follea, eds., *Filippo
Brunelleschi 1377–1446: La Naissance De L'architecture Moderne* (Fontenay-sous-
Bois: L'Equerre – Direction de l'architecture, 1978), p. 61.

Image by Sailko reproduced from https://en.wikipedia.org/wiki/Filippo_
Brunelleschi [CC BY 2.5]. The image was flipped about its vertical axis to face
right instead of left and incorporated into montage.

Diagram of Brunelleschi's perspective apparatus by Alessandro Parronchi, *Studi
su la dolce Prospettiva* (Milan: Aldo Martello Editore, 1964), found in Pierre
Granveaud, *op. cit.*, p. 70 and in Eugenio Battisti, *Filippo Brunelleschi* (Milano:
Electa, 1976), p. 109.

Reproduced from https://www.raphysarkissian.com/sean-scully-eleuthera-albertina

2 Lacan's diagram of the visual field in Jacques Lacan, *The Four Fundamental Concepts of Psycho-Analysis*, trans. Alan Sheridan, ed. Jacques-Alain Miller (New York: W. W. Norton Press, 1981). Redrawn by Lorens Holm.

Portrait of Manetti painted by Paolo Uccello, ca.1450, as found in Pierre Granveaud, *op. cit.*, p. 61.

Image by Sailko reproduced from https://en.wikipedia.org/wiki/Antonio_Manetti and incorporated into montage.

3 *The Ideal City*, attributed to Luciano Laurana, ca.1460, National Gallery, Urbino, as found in Pierre Granveaud, *op. cit.*, p. 69.

Central portion of the painting reproduced from https://en.wikipedia.org/wiki/The_Ideal_City_(painting)

Photo of the Florence Baptistery, similar to central portion of Illustration X-2 in Samuel Y. Edgerton, *The Renaissance Rediscovery of Linear Perspective* (New York: Basic Books, 1975), p. 146. Image source unknown.

Site plan of Florence Cathedral in Bernardo Sansone Sgrilli, *Descrizione e studi dell' insigne fabbrica di Santa Maria del Fiore*, Florence 1733, as found in Edgerton, *op. cit.*, p. 141.

Reproduced from https://www.rijksmuseum.nl/en/collection/RP-P-OB-39.190

3.2 Descartes' diagram of the seeing *Cogito* from *La Dioptriques*, in *Discours de la Methode* (1637) reproduced from https://1000wordphilosophy.com/2018/08/04/descartes-meditations-1-3/

Durer's perspective from *The Painter's Manual (Underweysung Der Messung,* 1527) (New York: Abaris Books Inc., 1977) reproduced from https://commons.wikimedia.org/wiki/File:Albrecht_D%C3%BCrer_-_Draughtsman_Drawing_a_Recumbent_Woman_-_WGA7261.jpg

3.3 Diagram from Lacan, *Four Fundamental Concepts* …, *op. cit.*, p. 91, redrawn by Lorens Holm, and reproduced with adjacent text.

3.4 Diagram of the drive from Lacan, *Four Fundamental Concepts* …, *op. cit.*, p. 178, redrawn by Lorens Holm, and reproduced with adjacent text.

Diagram of the visual field from Lacan, *Four Fundamental Concepts* …, *op. cit.*, p. 106, redrawn by Lorens Holm, and reproduced with adjacent text.

3.5 Montage by Lorens Holm incorporating:

Photograph of the interior of Brunelleschi's San Lorenzo, Florence, reproduced from Rudolf Wittkower, 'Brunelleschi and "proportion in perspective"', *op. cit.* Copyright Alinari.

Plate 1, p. 15, from Andrea Pozzo, *Perspective in Architecture and Painting (Perspectiva Architectorum Et Pictorum)* (New York: Dover, 1989). Image scanned from Dover.

4.1 Aldo Rossi, Drawing with theatre, hand of the saint and shadows, 1978,

Pen on paper, 24 × 41 cm. © Eredi Aldo Rossi, Courtesy: Aldo Rossi Foundation, Milan, https://www.fondazionealdorossi.org/crediti/

Courtesy: Francesco Moschini and Gabriel Vaduva Collection AAM Architettura Arte Moderna, http://ffmaam.it/collezione/aldo-rossi#aldo-rossi

4.2 Diagram from Lacan, *Seminar: Book II The Ego in Freud's Theory and in the Technique of Psychoanalysis 1954–1955* (Cambridge: Cambridge University Press, 1988), p. 243, redrawn by Lorens Holm.

Diagram from Sigmund Freud, 'The Forgetting of Proper Names', in *The Psychopathology of Everyday Life*, translated by Alan Tyson, edited by James Strachey (New York: W. W. Norton, 1960) p. 5, redrawn by Lorens Holm.

4.3   Perspective diagram by Lorens Holm, drawn on top of photograph of *tromp l'oeil fresco* by Baldassare Peruzzi in Villa Farnesina Rome. Photograph reproduced from https://www.pinterest.co.uk/pin/150026231306776194/

4.4   Table by Lorens Holm incorporating thumbnails of

Holbein's The Ambassadors reproduced from https://en.wikipedia.org/wiki/The_Ambassadors_(Holbein)#/media/File:Hans_Holbein_the_Younger_-_The_Ambassadors_-_Google_Art_Project.jpg

The Ambassadors put into perspective (in photoshop) by Lorens Holm

A diagram of perspective from Leon Battista Alberti, *On Painting (Della Pittura)*, trans. John Spencer (New Haven, CT: Yale University Press, 1966), p.111, redrawn by Lorens Holm

Lacan's Schema L diagram from Lacan, *Seminar: Book II The Ego in Freud's Theory ...*, *op. cit.*, redrawn by Lorens Holm.

4.5   Table by Lorens Holm

5.1   Montage incorporating text by Lorens Holm and the iconic image reproduced from Brown and Venturi, *Learning from Las Vegas: The Forgotten Symbolism of Architectural Form* (Cambridge, MA: MIT Press, 1986) p. 21, superimposed upon the 5th of 12 panels of the Nolli Plan of Rome, reproduced from Wikipedia *op. cit.*

5.2   Campfire in *Vitruvius, Ten Books on Architecture* (Como, 1521) trans. and illustrated by Cesariano, reproduced from http://architectura.cesr.univ-tours.fr/traite/Notice/BPNME276.asp

Diagram of the drive from Lacan, *Four Fundamental Concepts ...*, *op. cit.*, p. 178, redrawn by Lorens Holm, and reproduced with adjacent text.

6.1   Montage by Lorens Holm

6.2   Montage incorporating text by Lorens Holm and two stills from the film *Phase IV* (1974). Paramount Pictures & Alced Productions.

6.3   Montage by Lorens Holm incorporating the photo '**East Beach on Henderson Island in 2015**'. Image courtesy of Jennifer Lavers | Adrift Lab. Similar images downloadable from University of Tasmania Institute of Marine and Antarctic Studies, https://www.imas.utas.edu.au/news/news-items/clean-up-mission-for-remote-island-polluted-by-38-million-bits-of-plastic

6.4   Montage of text and image incorporating a still from the film *Apocalypse Now* (1979) Courtesy of American Zoetrope & Zoetrope Studios.

6.5   Text and diagrams by Lorens Holm.

P.1   Montage by Lorens Holm incorporating text and 12 thumbnail images from readily available internet sources

1   Charles Darwin, 1809–1882, https://en.wikipedia.org/wiki/Charles_Darwin

Thomas Henry Huxley, 1825–1895, https://en.wikipedia.org/wiki/Thomas_Henry_Huxley

Patrick Geddes, 1854–1932, The Patrick Geddes Centre, https://www.patrickgeddescentre.org.uk/

Lewis Mumford, 1895–1990, https://en.wikipedia.org/wiki/Lewis_Mumford

Marshall McLuhan, 1911–1980, https://www.abc.net.au/rn/legacy/features/mcluhan/ The McLuhan Project

Buckminster Fuller, 1895–1983, https://miamirail.org/performing-arts/the-love-song-of-r-buckminster-fuller-review-interviews-with-sam-green-and-ira-kaplan/ The Miami Rail (arts politics culture) 'Buckminster Fuller in 1978. Photo: Fred Blocher'.

2 Georg W.F. Hegel, 1770–1831, https://en.wikipedia.org/wiki/Georg_Wilhelm_Friedrich_Hegel. Portrait by Jakob Schlesinger, 1831.

Karl Marx, 1818–1883, https://en.wikipedia.org/wiki/Karl_Marx. Photography by John Mayall, 1875.

Sigmund Freud, 1856–1939, https://en.wikipedia.org/wiki/Sigmund_Freud. Photo by Max Halberstadt.

Jacques Lacan, 1901–1981, https://en.wikipedia.org/wiki/Jacques_Lacan

Deleuze & Guattari, 1925–1995 & 1930–1992, https://criticalposthumanism.net/deleuze-gilles/. Photograph of Gilles Deleuze by Uferaf/Network.

INDEX

Note: Page references in *italics* denote figures, in **bold** tables and with "n" endnotes.

The Aesthetics: Lectures on Fine Art (Hegel) 131
Agamben, Giorgio 84, 91
alethosphere 116, 125n10
Althusser, Louis 7
The Ambassadors (Holbein) 48, 52, 53
analogical cities 75–76
analytic setting 5–6, 18n30
Apocalypse Now 110
Arcades Project (Benjamin) 77, 119
the Archaic space 19, 31, 37–38; and Archaic subject 32; and cosmos 27–29, 30; of Egypt 20; of Greece 20; of Sumer 20
Archaic subject 32, 39
architectural space 39; conception 19–20
architecture 40, 55–57; ethics for 121–123; primitive 57; and psychoanalysis 12–13; and space 4
Architecture and Psychoanalysis (Hendrix) 3
The Architecture of Psychoanalysis (Rendell) 15
The Architecture of the City (Rossi) 12, 63, 70, 75
Arendt, Hannah 4, 74, 83–85
Aristotle 8, 82, 83–85, 116
Augustine, Saint 8
Aureli, Vittorio 85

Badiou, Alain 8
Baird, George 84

Baptistery, Florence 44–45
Bataille, Georges 8
Beckett, Samuel 32–33, 34
Bell, David 105n37
Benjamin, Walter 77, 119
Berman, Marshall 88
Beyond the Pleasure Principle (Freud) 85, 88, 114
Big Brother 17n12, 47
Borromean knot 26–27
Breton, André 8
Brunelleschi, Filippo 50, *56*, 116–117, 125n13, 129; architecture 55; demonstration of perspective 50–51; effect of reality 57; perspective 44, 45–46
Brunelleschi Lacan Le Corbusier (Holm) 50, 52, 90
Bruno, Pierre 120, 126n25

Caillois, Roger 8
Cancun Agreements 113
capitalism 98; commodity 94, 107, *109*, 110, 122; consumer 55, 124n7; and ego 120; Marx on 11, 88, 98
Capitalism and Schizophrenia (Deleuze & Guattari) 132
capitalist discourse 119–120
Carson, Rachel 109
Certeau, Michel de 77, 86, 119

cities: analogical 75–76; construction of 70–71

city of the Other 76–78, 100

Civilization and Its Discontents (Freud) 11, 82, 85–87, 94, 113, 115, 131

class consciousness 96, 132

Classical episteme 40n2

the Classical space 19, 22, 31, 37; empty screen 30; of Rome 20; *see also* space

Classic subject 32–33, 39

climate change: discourse 116–121; environment and damage 108–114; ethics for architecture 121–123; psychoanalytic approaches to environment 114–115

Climate Crisis, Psychoanalysis, and Radical Ethics (Orange) 114

Cogito 32, 34, *48*, 49

collective memory 36, 63, 72–74, 76–77, 78–79n4, 96, 97

collective place of the subject 73–74

commodity capitalism 94, 107, *109*, 110, 122

common sense 59n14

construction: of the city 70–71; of histories 71–73

consumer capitalism 55, 124n7

consumers 98–99

The Cook the Thief His Wife and Her Lover 10

Copernicus 2

Coppola, Francis Ford 111

cosmos 27–29, 30

The Critique of Pure Reason (Kant) 42n17

Dali, Salvador 8

Damisch, Hubert 45

Darling, Sir Frank Fraser 109

Darwin, Charles 131–132

death 52–53

Della Pittura 28

De Niro, Robert 10

Derrida, Jacques 79n7

Descartes, René 8, 32, 48–49, 118

desire 54–58; of the subject 47–52; subject's object of 33; unconscious 2, 5, 9–10, 46–47, 58, 64, 69, 95–96, 98, 100, 115, 132, 134; *vs.* want 3

dialectic of individual and collective 82–83

Dictionary of Lacanian Psychoanalysis (Evans) 25

discourse 125n11; capitalist 119–120; climate change 116–121

dreams 7; Freud on 3

drive 87–88

Duchamp, Marcel 91

Durkheim, Emile 25

Earth Summit (Rio de Janiero) 113

Écrits (Lacan) 8

Écrits: a selection (Lacan) 8

Écrits: the first complete edition in English (Lacan) 8

ego 9, *64*; and capitalism 120; identity of 46–47; *vs.* subjects 18n23; *vs.* unconscious 9–10

ego-unconscious 9–10, 36, 39, 65, 95, 115, 134

Eisenman, Peter 12

Emerson, Ralph Waldo 91

emptiness 57–58

environment: and damage 108–114; psychoanalytic approaches to 114–115

episteme 40n2; Classical 40n2; Modern 40n2

The Eternal Present: the beginnings of architecture (Giedion) 19, 36

Ethics and Sustainable Development Commission Key Findings and Recommendations 127n28

ethics for architecture 121–123

The Ethics of Psychoanalysis (Lacan) 57, 82, 86, 94, 115

Evans, Dylan 8, 25

field of the Other 2, 4, 11–13, 25, 33, 58

Fink, Bruce 4, 8

forgetting 64–65, 73, 75–77, 130

Foster + Partners Architects 108

Foucault, Michel 7; episteme 40n2; on subject 10

The Four Fundamental Concepts of Psychoanalysis (Lacan) 8, 47, 52, 54, 57, 89–90, 94

Frampton, Kenneth 81–101

free-floating attention 5

Freud, Anna 7

Freud, Sigmund *64*, 85–87; description of ego 46; on dreams 3; first and second topographies *9*; Lacan reading 89–91; talking cure 5; texts 6–7; on unconscious 2–3, 4; *wo es war, soll ich werden* 115

'From Structure to Subject' (Gandelsonas) 70

Fuller, Buckminster 132

Gallagher, Cormac 8

Gandelsonas, Mario 10, 70

Gay, Peter 96
gaze/look 52–53
Geddes, Patrick 72, 78, 117, 132
geometral optics 48
ghost writing 78
Giedion, Sigfried 2, 23, 28, 72, 75, 129, 132; architectural space conception 19–20, 26–27, 30; *innenwelt-umwelt* 54; and Lacan 27–40; Modern history *30*; and Modern subject 36–39; prehistoric space 22–23, 30–31; and subjects 31
Graham, Dan 94
Greenpeace 109
The Guardian 124n4
Guattari, Felix 93

Hadid, Zaha 132
Halbwachs, Maurice 63
Hans Holbein the Younger 48, 53, 57, *69*
Harvey, David 103n22
Hegel, Georg Wilhelm Friedrich 8, 22, 116, 131, 136n2
Hendrix, John 3
History and Class Consciousness (Lukacs) 125n9
Hogarth Press 7
'Homes for America' (Graham) 94
'How Is Climate Change an Issue for Psychoanalysis' (Rustin) 114
The Human Condition (Arendt) 82, 84
Huxley, T.H. 132

id 9, 46, 95–96
identity: defined 46; of ego 46–47
imaginary register 24
An Inconvenient Truth 109
ineffable space 33
Inhibitions Symptoms and Anxiety (Freud) 62
'Instincts and their Vicissitudes' (Freud) 85, 88, 91, 94
International Psychoanalytic Association (IPA) 17n18
International Renewable Energy Agency (IRENA) 108
The Interpretation of Dreams (Freud) 1, 3, 6–7, 9
Introduction to the Work of Marcel Mauss (Lévi-Strauss) 25
An Introductory Dictionary of Lacanian Psychoanalysis (Evans) 8

Jakobson, Roman 4, 7
Jarzombek, Mark 22
Jefferson, Thomas 103n22

Jokes and their Relation to the Unconscious (Freud) 1
Jung, Carl 73

Kant, Immanuel 8, 26, 42n17
Klee, Paul 31
Klein, Melanie 114
Klein Square 29–31, 37, 42n24
knowledge 6, 40n2, 73, 116–120, 123, 125n11
Kojève, Alexandre 7
Kunze, Donald 67
Kyoto Protocol 113

Lacan, Jacques 2, *64*; on emptiness 58; on formation of ego 46; and Giedion 27–40; intellectual lineage 131–132; introduction of the term *subject* 10; mirror stage 8, 10; operational montage 49; Other space 67–68; reading Freud 89–91; registers of subjective experience 23–26; *Schema L* 65; texts 7–8; topography 9–10; on unconscious 3–4, 5; visual field 55–56
language 65–66
The Language of Psycho-Analysis (Laplanche and Pontalis) 7
Laplanche, Jean 7
Las Meninas (Velasquez) 48
lathouse 125n10
Laugh-In (Rowan and Martin) 109
Lavers, Jennifer 124n4
Learning from Las Vegas (Venturi, Scott Brown and Izenour) 61
Le Corbusier 20, 22, 26, 29, 33, 81, 90
Lefebvre, Henri 98
Le Mepris 28
Lévi-Strauss, Claude 7, 25
Lukacs, Georg 125n9
Lynch, Kevin 135

Manetti, Antonio 44
Marx, Karl 88; on capitalism 11, 98
Masdar 124n2
Masdar Institute of Science and Technology 108
master signifier 116, 118–120, 125n13
McLuhan, Marshall 132
meconnaissance 10, 24
Meditations on First Philosophy (Descartes) 32
memory 12; collective 36, 63, 72–74, 76–77, 78–79n4, 96, 97
Merleau-Ponty, Maurice 8
Miller, Jacques-Alain 8

mirror stage 8, 10, 24, 46, 53–55
mobius strip *68*, 68–69
Modern episteme 40n2
Modern space 19, 20–22, 29, 37–38; *see also* space
Modern subject 32–33; and Giedion 36–39; *see also* subjects
Mumford, Lewis 72, 132

National Planning Policy Framework 127n28
NCARB *Model Rules of Conduct* 127n28
The New Introductory Lectures on Psychoanalysis (Freud) 96
Not I (Beckett) 33, 34

objet petit a 48
'Of The Gaze as *objet petit a*' (Lacan) 48
operational montage 49
Orange, Donna 114
The Order of Things (Foucault) 40n2
The Origin of Perspective (Damisch) 45
Other: city of 76–78; space 67–68
Outlook Tower 117

Paine, Thomas 103n22
parallax 119
Paris Agreement 113
Paris commune of 1848 134
perception 50–51
perspective 44, 45–46, 68–70; and architects 55; *vs.* vision 48
perspective geometry 48
Phase IV 107, *109*, 124n1
phenomenology 51
Plato 8, 91
The Politics (Aristotle) 82, 84, 116
Pontalis, Jean-Bertrand 7
Pozzo, Andrea 55, *56*
prehistoric space 22–23, 30–31
primitive architecture 57
Project for a Scientific Psychology (Freud) 7
psyche 9–11, 12; in Lacan's topography 9
psychoanalysis: and architecture 12–13; overview 13–14
The Psychologizing of Modernity (Jarzombek) 22
The Psychopathology of Everyday Life (Freud) 1, 64

real register 24, 26
reflector 24
Reigl, Alois 28
relativity theory 43n32
Rendell, Jane 15

RIBA Code of Professional Conduct 123, 127n28
Richards, Angela 7
Rights of Man (Paine) 103n22
The Right to the City (Lefebvre) 98
rooms+cities design research group 133–136, 136n4
Rossi, Aldo 12, 60–78, 129; analogical city 75–76; perspective 68–70; and *Schema L* 65; on signification 74–75
Rustin, Michael 114, 115, 124n7

Saussure, Ferdinand 25
Scene with running woman (Klee) 31
Schema L 65, 79n6
Schrumpeter, Joseph 88
Schumacher, Patrik 132
Scott Brown, Denise 81–101, 129
self-image 24
The Seminar Book I: Freud's Papers on Technique (Lacan) 8
The Seminar Book II: The Ego in Freud's Theory and in the Technique of Psychoanalysis (Lacan) 11, 118
The Seminar Book VII: The Ethics of Psychoanalysis (Lacan) 11, 33
The Seminar Book XXVII: Dissolution (Lacan) 8
The Seminars (Lacan) 8
The Seminar Book XI. See *The Four Fundamental Concepts of Psychoanalysis (Lacan)*
The Seminar Book XIII The Object of Psychoanalysis (Lacan) 48
The Seminar Book XVII The Other Side of Psychoanalysis (Lacan) 116–117, 118, 125n10, 132
The Seminar Book XX Encore (Lacan) 117
sense 4, 38; common sense 59n14; and symbols 25
Shell Oil 113
Sheridan, Alan 8
signification 74–75
Signorelli (painter) 61, 64–65, 67, 75, 77
Silent Spring (Carson) 109
Slutzky, Robert 22
smart cities 122
Socrates 8
space 40; and architecture 4; as conceptual category 20; as conceptual or symbolic entity 2; ineffable 33; inside and outside 30; types of 19
Space Time and Architecture (Giedion) 22, 37

spatial subject 15
speaking subject: architectural model of
    34–36, *35*; lacks being 33–34; *see also*
    subjects
*The Standard Edition of the Complete
    Psychological Works of Sigmund Freud*
    (Freud) 7
statesmen 98–99
Strachey, Alix 7
Strachey, James 7
subjective theory and practice 132–136
subjectivity 11, 14
subjects 11, 14–16, 40; collective place of
    73–74; defined 10; desire of 47–52; *vs.*
    ego 18n23; forms of 15; Foucault on
    10; and Giedion 31; Lacan introduction
    of term 10
superego 9
symbolic register 24, 25

talking cure 5
Taxi Driver 10
'Television' (Lacan) 120
The Ten Books on Architecture (Vitruvius)
    82–83
Theory of Good City Form (Lynch) 135
things-in-themselves 26
Thoreau, Henry David 91
three space conceptions 2, *21*, 27
Thurber, Shellburne 16n11
Tomšič, Samo 119, 120, 126n22
topographies 9–11; Freud's first 9; Lacan's
    9–10; Freud's second 9
Tyson, Alan 7

unconscious 2–5, 16n9; and the city
    11–12; as concept of psychoanalysis

2; *vs.* ego 9–10; Freud on 2–3, 4, 7;
    Lacan on 3–4, 5; short course on
    65–66; as symbolic entity 4; urban 12
unconscious desire 2, 5, 9–10, 46–47, 58,
    64, 69, 95–96, 98, 100, 115, 132, 134
United Nations Framework Convention
    on Climate Change (UNFCCC) 113
United States Declaration of Independence
    (Jefferson) 103n22
The Unnameable (Beckett) 32–33
UN Sustainable Development Goals
    (SDGs) 127n28
The Urban Revolution (Lefebvre) 98
"urban society" 104n36
urban unconscious 12

van Eyck, Aldo 135
Vanheule, Stijn 119–120
Velasquez, Diego 48
Venturi, Robert 81–101, 129
Vietnam War 111
Virno, Paolo 70, 74
vision 49–50; *vs.* perspective 48
visual field 47, 55–56
Vitruvius 82–83; concourse of 91–94
Vittorio Aureli, Pier 84–85

Wilderness and Plenty 109
Wittkower, Rudolf 55
Wo es war soll ich werden (desire is an
    ethical position) 94–97
Woolf, Leonard 7
Woolf, Virginia 7

Zevi, Bruno 20
Žižek, Slavoj 8, 91